THE Good Breakfast BOOK

by Nikki and David Goldbeck
The Supermarket Handbook: Access to Whole Foods
The Dieter's Companion

by Nikki Goldbeck
*Cooking What Comes Naturally: A Natural Foods Cookbook
  Featuring a Month's Worth of Natural-Vegetarian Menus*

Good Morning

THE Good Breakfast BOOK
BY NIKKI AND DAVID GOLDBECK

A PERIGEE BOOK

Perigee Books
are published by
G. P. Putnam's Sons
200 Madison Avenue
New York, New York 10016

Copyright © 1976 by Nikki and David Goldbeck
All rights reserved. This book, or parts thereof,
may not be reproduced in any form without permission.
Published simultaneously in Canada by General Publishing
Co. Limited, Toronto.

Library of Congress Catalog Card Number: 74-21211
ISBN 0-399-50705-1

Book design by Douglas Parker
Cover design by Betty Binns

First Perigee printing, 1982
Printed in the United States of America

To all of our families

CONTENTS

Foreword by Beatrice Trum Hunter ix
The Good Breakfast xi
We Need a Good Breakfast xv
Good Beginnings 1
Hot and Cold Cereal 16
Cheese and Other Dairy Dishes 38
The Eggery 54
Meat, Fish, and Even Poultry for Breakfast 67
The Bread in Your Breakfast 85
Griddlecakes and Waffles 103
Soup for Breakfast 115
Milk and Main-Dish Beverages 119
High-Protein Morning Snacks 129
Your Own Breakfast Breads 139
Potatoes and Other Breakfast Side Dishes 161
Coffee Cakes 168
Hot Drinks 177

Appendix
Breakfast Recommendations From Infancy to Infinity 185
The Selection of Ingredients and Cooking Utensils 188
Out to Breakfast 197
Index 200

FOREWORD

"Breakfast" literally means "to break the fast," and a good breakfast is recognized to be of utmost importance for a feeling of well-being. Yet many Americans begin the day without breakfast, or solely with coffee, or with coffee and a sweet roll. Such faulty food habits are deplored by nutritionists who repeatedly have stressed the importance of a good breakfast. For example, it has been demonstrated that the feeling of well-being that we experience by mid-afternoon may *not* result from the recently consumed lunch, but rather from the breakfast that we consumed much earlier in the day.

Even for those who do recognize the value of a good breakfast, all too often the meal is less challenging in its variety than other meals. Too many people are in a narrow rut with breakfast menus, limiting choices to the fruit juice–eggs–toast–and–coffee routine.

In *The Good Breakfast Book*, Nikki and David Goldbeck provide a wealth of offerings to entice the non-breakfast eater to reform his or her poor habits; to guide the skimpy-breakfast eater toward better choices; and to lift the unimaginative-breakfast eater out of his or her rut with tempting dishes ranging from orange juice to eat, egg-free french toast, cream corn porridge, to kippers on pumpernickel. And why not? There should be no hard-and-fast rules concerning breakfast fare. Indeed, menus from earlier years show that Americans ate lamb chops, fish, chowder, and other hearty fare for breakfast.

By all means, let's restore breakfast to its rightful role, make it nutritionally sound, balanced, varied, tempting to the palate, and prepared with a minimum of effort. The Goldbecks demonstrate how this can be achieved, in their useful guide, *The Good Breakfast Book*.

Beatrice Trum Hunter, author of *Consumer Beware!*

THE GOOD BREAKFAST

Let's bring back breakfast!

Years ago, when family life centered on the home, the farm, and the family business, it was common to prepare a large breakfast of which the whole family would partake. But in those days the activities and needs of all members of the family were somewhat similar. Today much of this has changed. The older members of the household may leave at different hours to get to their jobs; the younger ones set out to school at yet another time; still others in the family may spend much of their day close to home—all of which requires varying amounts of physical and mental energy. Thus, the common morning meal becomes pretty fragmented, and, although doctors and nutritionists advise us of the importance of a nourishing breakfast and the consequences of going without, what could be a pleasant way to start the day is all too often a hastily gulped meal or no meal at all.

To complicate matters further, the American movement toward "convenience" foods has taken a large toll at breakfast time. In the morning, when most of us are pressed for time, not quite awake enough to be concerned, and maybe not hungry enough to take notice, the attraction of foods that are "instantly" prepared and *claim* to be good for us is hard to resist. Unfortunately, the food value provided by most of these breakfast items is not what it could be; their labels reveal an abundance of refined carbohydrates (white flour and sugar), synthetic vitamins, artificial coloring and flavoring, preservatives and child-alluring give-aways. Though the high starch and sugar content of such a morning meal may satisfy us temporarily, it has no "staying power"; thus, we require periodic office breaks and ravenous lunches. Without the other essential nutrients, particularly those provided by unrefined carbohydrates and protein, the feeling of fullness soon subsides and the "poor-breakfast syndrome" sets in.

Because a good breakfast not only is a pleasurable experience in itself but can serve to make the whole day a lot nicer, it seems important to us that people start realizing the alternatives to their usual breakfast.

The Good Breakfast Book is a cookbook of alternatives—recipes and suggestions to help you find breakfast foods that can fit into your life, your table, and your spirits in the morning without setting back your time schedule or your pocketbook. The almost 400 recipes in this book are designed to suggest breakfasts that couple the highest nutritive values with low calorie ratings.

You will find the use of certain foods vigorously

promoted, while others are approached with caution or altogether ignored. Foods high in saturated fats are played down and sweets are designed to be nutritionally sound. Emphasis is taken away from meat as a source of protein in lieu of more economical and resourceful foodstuffs. In addition, wherever possible, each recipe is rated according to its protein-calorie content to help you obtain at least one third of your daily protein in the morning.

For the most part, the recipes that follow are geared toward quick breakfast service and require the shortest possible preparation and cooking time. To ease the morning rush, recipes are also given for breakfasts that can be prepared in advance. For days off, vacations, and leisurely weekend breakfasts, you'll find more elaborate suggestions too. Also scattered throughout these pages are tips for service, budgeting of time, and food storage, along with bits of historical facts and other trivia. Use them all, as needed, to embellish your meal and to bring back breakfast.

N. G.
D. G.
Woodstock, N.Y.
July 1974

We would like to thank all those who shared breakfast with us, and especially,
- Nikki's parents, Florence and Irwin Schulman
- Dick Goldman and Susan Goldman
- John Tancredi and Laurie Beecroft, all for helping us with the recipes,
- Ethel Shapiro for preparing the manuscript, and
- Merle Cosgrove for her fine illustrations.

WE NEED A GOOD BREAKFAST

No matter how much food you consumed yesterday, you still must eat today. Each day your body has certain food needs—calories (for energy), protein (for the building and maintenance of muscles, bones, blood, and all the bodily organs), minerals (which act along with the proteins), and vitamins (which serve as a catalyst to keep the work of the other food elements in progress). Once the daily requisite for calories and protein has been satisfied *any excess is stored as fat*; the body cannot put away protein from one day to fill a deficiency in the coming days. While you can store some of the minerals in small quantities, and the vitamins A, D, E and K, all other unassimilated vitamins and minerals are excreted.

Consequently, when you begin a new day it is important to give your body a fresh source of nutrients to run on. Those who become cranky, inattentive, nervous, and prone to headaches in the early part of the day, seemingly for no reason, may find that there is a reason after all—too little morning nourishment.

Poor breakfasts have also contributed to many of our national ills, both physical and economic. Low blood sugar, obesity, diabetes, heart conditions, hyperactivity, chronic constipation, and many other ailments could all be controlled more effectively with a nourishing breakfast.

With a good breakfast under your belt you can eat smaller, more evenly balanced meals. You no longer have to stuff yourself in the evening after starving yourself during the day. Thus you can eliminate the strain on your heart from overindulging and the nighttime stress on the digestive organs. By choosing less-processed breakfast foods—like fresh and dried fruits and whole-grain cereals and baked goods—you will receive more roughage in your meal. For many this means improved regularity without resorting to laxatives.

A good breakfast, one balanced with protein, fat, carbohydrates, vitamins, and minerals, also makes it easier to resist the pastry wagon at coffee-break time. You can enjoy a shorter, lighter meal at noon and spend the remainder of the hour in a stroll through the neighborhood rather than shuttling from the chair behind your desk to the chair behind the lunch counter. At the same time you are conserving calories and getting some good exercise, you will also be saving money—the expense of lunch being one of the biggest salary-eaters.

Many people who swear by a morning "meal" of a cigarette and a cup of coffee would not need the "coffee kick" if they would accustom their systems to some real *food energizing* instead.

Moreover, work efficiency and learning ability can be enhanced by a satisfied stomach. Your brain, like all your body organs, is dependent on food for nourishment. Unless the blood, which feeds all cells, is supplied with fresh fuel in the morning your mind will remain as empty as your stomach. As one UNESCO official succinctly phrased it, "If you want to have democracy in education, you have to feed the children first."

WHAT CONSTITUTES A GOOD BREAKFAST?

Everyone has his or her own opinion of what foods qualify as breakfast fare. While eggs, cereals and sweet rolls are popular in this country, in Egypt, Fuul Mudammas (a cooked bean dish) is the morning staple. In Japan, the traditional breakfast includes rice and miso (fermented soybean soup), while in Israel a huge buffet including yogurt, fish, radishes, turnips, other vegetables, eggs, and cheese is set out each morning.

The fact is, most foods that are good for you are good for you at any time of day. Thus, food selection at breakfast time is limited only by your imagination. Of course, for some, time may be a consideration, but this too can be easily surmounted with a little advance planning. Many families that are out all day still enjoy dinners of stews, casseroles, and roasts, which demand lengthy preparation or cooking time. They are able to do this because they prepare in advance. There is no reason why some of this time cannot be spent planning breakfast, for actually, if given a choice between a substantial morning meal or a substantial evening meal, you would be better off opting for the former.

Although there are no hard and fast rules about what to serve for breakfast, rich sauces, heavy spices, and the use of alcoholic beverages in cooking are generally avoided. These all tax the digestive system and serve to weigh you down rather than invigorate you. Though some fat is important to prolong digestion and keep you satisfied longer, too much fat also has a depressing effect on the body systems.

Here are several essential dietary factors that should be met at breakfast:

* A good supply of protein
* Foods besides protein to furnish energy
* The fat-soluble and water-soluble vitamins

* An abundance of minerals, including calcium, iron, and phosphorous
* Roughage or bulk-forming foods
* Appetizing foods, sometimes referred to as pan-peptogenic, to stimulate the appetite

All this constitutes a well-balanced menu.

To give you an idea of the actual nutritional value of foods, a table of Food Values for a Balanced Breakfast is provided in the Appendix. Also, whenever possible, energy value (calories) and protein content are given along with the recipes. These values can serve as a reference point in planning a menu and can help keep your food intake in perspective. Keep in mind that breakfast should make up *at least* 1/3 of your daily requirement for calories, protein, vitamins, and minerals. The Table of Recommended Daily Allowances, also in the Appendix, can guide you in determining what your needs are. These figures, prepared by the Food and Nutrition Board of the National Academy of Sciences—National Research Council, are the accepted standard for suggested nutrient intake for the average, healthy individual living in the United States. Though individual traits and circumstances may alter your personal nutrient requirements somewhat, this table will provide a general picture of how you should be eating.

The Appendix also contains two additional sections, Breakfast Recommendations from Infancy to Infinity and The Selection of Ingredients and Cooking Utensils, to round out your education in the good breakfast.

SERVE BREAKFAST TO SUIT YOUR SITUATION

How you present these essential foods at breakfast time will depend on your life style. If you are rushed in the morning it might speed things up if you lay out your breakfast in the evening, setting the table with nonperishables and placing other necessary ingredients in a prominent spot in the refrigerator. This is not an uncommon habit.

If there are several people to feed in your household, weekday breakfasts can be served buffet or cafeteria style, set up in the kitchen where food can be piled onto plates and taken to the table by each person as needed. The Kibbutz Breakfast and Breakfast Sundaes are good examples of meals that work well with large families, as are hot cooked cereals or soups that can be held warm until served.

When you have more time in the morning, or when the entire family sits down together, you can choose foods that have to be served immediately. For even more leisurely breakfasts, you can look forward to more elaborate dishes such as Baked Apple Pancake,

Cheese Pudding, French Toast Fondue, or even the "Gothic" Brunch.

One last note on our recipes: *The Good Breakfast Book* contains two distinct types of recipes. First, there are the recipes for creating foods that are nutritious in themselves and qualify as the basis for good breakfasts. In addition, there are recipes for spreads, sauces, and various toppings designed to boost the nutritional quality of both our own recipes and more conventional, commercial prepared foods—to minimize morning madness.

THE GOOD BREAKFAST AND INGREDIENT SELECTION

Those who know us know that we approach food and nutrition from two perspectives. Our ultimate goal is to create dishes that are interesting and tasty. But we are equally as concerned with the wholesomeness of food, and in our last book, *The Supermarket Handbook/Access to Whole Foods*, we explored the selection of ingredients by consumers. We believe in using foodstuffs that are as "unadulterated and unprocessed" as possible, ideally free even from pesticides and chemical fertilizers.

In *The Good Breakfast Book* we go one step further and demonstrate how to use some of these foods. Most of the ingredients for our recipes can be found right in your local supermarket; a few, such as soy flour, sesame seeds, pumpkin seeds, and raw cashews, for example, are rarities in most supermarkets but are stocked by natural-food stores. This, then, may be an opportunity for some of you to explore these less familiar foods and food outlets.

GOOD BEGINNINGS

A meal that begins with fresh fruit or fruit juice has an almost magical effect on the body. The potency of fruit first delights the mouth, where it stimulates taste buds, starting the flow of saliva and other digestive enzymes. Fruit continues to arouse your well-being by supplying:

* Valuable vitamins A, B, and C, depending on the kind
* Essential minerals, including phosphorous, potassium, calcium, and iron
* Cleansing acids
* Immediately assimilable fruit sugar
* Pure distilled water
* A mild laxative effect

Since vitamins and minerals are no less important to good health than protein, fats, and carbohydrates, fruit should be regarded as an essential part of breakfast.

Each season there is a constant supply of fruit juice and fresh fruit on the market. Though all fruits have something of importance to offer, the most noteworthy sources of certain essential nutrients appear on the accompanying Table of Fruit Values (p. 15), along with the best time to buy for freshness and economy.

FRUIT JUICES
O.J.

Universal short-order jargon, the expression "O.J." has firmly embedded itself in the English language. Fresh orange juice—its pleasures transcend race, sex and even class.

Orange juice, liquid sunshine.

We've found that the burden of squeezing oranges can easily be lightened by taking the trouble to find the right tool for the job. There are many types of juicers ranging from the traditional ceramic or glass hand squeezers to the electrified models. The traditional squeezer, readily available in hardware and variety stores, has the virtue of being the cheapest appliance. The downward turning motion that is required, however, is very uncomfortable, which is probably why so few people use it for drink-juicing. It is fine for squeezing a lemon or a child's portion, but will leave you numb by the second or third glass.

Hand Type Juicer

Gear Style Juicers

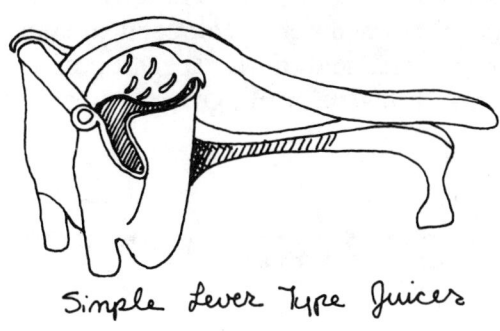

Simple Lever Type Juicer

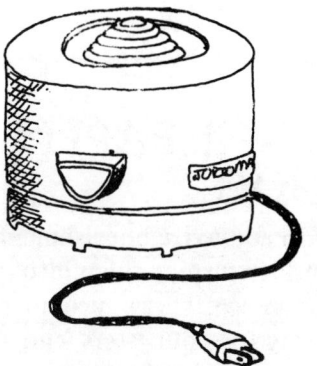

Electric Juicer

The only difference between the traditional juicer and the electric juicer is that the head of the electric model rotates. This, we feel, is a waste; you may not have to turn the orange, but you still have to press down hard at the same awkward angle. What's more, this machine tends to chew into the rind, imparting a bitter taste to the juice. And, they make too much noise.

Our favorite juicer is the simple lever type. We found one at a lawn sale for 25¢; new they are considerably more (if you can find them), probably $8 to $10. Their beauty is that they require only a downward push of the handle at a comfortable angle. They are small, easy to clean, indestructable and you can make glasses of fresh citrus juices smilingly and often.

Another highly recommended juicer is the gear style that you once saw in diners and luncheonettes. They need to be anchored to a counter but work very well. Best for mass squeezing.

FROZEN ORANGE JUICE

In many homes pre-squeezed orange juice has superseded fresh-squeezed juice, with frozen concentrates the leading replacement. While frozen orange juice concentrate is comparable to fresh juice in vitamins and minerals, it does lack the native fruit enzymes. And, if allowed to defrost before preparation, the vitamin C content dissipates.

If you are using frozen orange juice concentrate, make sure you are getting the real thing. Do not be persuaded by brands that profess to "taste more like the real thing" while they are actually adulterated with sugar and chemicals.

ORANGE JUICE TO EAT

Here is a real treat for children made with frozen orange juice concentrate.

1½ tablespoons unflavored gelatin
1 cup cold water
¼ cup honey
1 can (6 ounces) frozen
    orange juice concentrate
1½ cups ice water

Sprinkle gelatin over cold water in a saucepan and heat, stirring constantly, until dissolved, about 3 minutes. Remove from heat and add remaining ingredients, continuing to stir until honey and orange juice melt. Pour into 6 juice glasses and chill. Will set in about 1 hour.

ORANGE-POMEGRANATE JUICE

Pomegranates can be squeezed exactly like oranges. Their juice is tart and rich in color and vitamins.

Surprise yourself and squeeze a quarter of a pomegranate into each glass of fresh or even frozen orange juice.

ORANGE-APRICOT NECTAR

2 cups orange juice
2 tablespoons lemon juice
½ cup softened (soaked) dried apricots
½ cup ice

Process all ingredients in blender until smooth and frothy.
Makes 3 cups.

ORANGE-PINEAPPLE JUICE-NOG

If you want to add extra nourishment to fruit juices you might consider turning them into juice-nogs with the addition of an egg. These juice-nogs are recommended primarily for youngsters who are difficult eaters or for people who don't consume large quantities of eggs in other forms.

2 cups combined orange and pineapple
   juices in any proportion
1 tablespoon honey
1 tablespoon lemon juice
1 egg
¼ cup ice

Process all ingredients in blender or shaker until ice is melted and juice-nog is smooth and frothy.
Makes 3 cups.

STRAWBERRY DRINK

2½ cups strawberries
¼ cup honey
2 cups water
Juice of ½ lemon

Mash berries and honey together with a fork, add remaining ingredients, shake in a covered container, and chill. Or, puree all ingredients in blender.
Makes 1 quart.

UNIVERSAL LEMONADE

A world-renowned bowel conditioner, prepared both hot and cold.

Squeeze juice of ½ lemon into a cup of freshly boiled water or mineral water. Serve plain or, if desired, sweeten the hot lemonade with a touch of honey.

FRESH CRANBERRY JUICE

For 1 quart juice: combine 4 cups cranberries with 4 cups water and cook 15 minutes until quite soft. Mash berries with a fork or wooden spoon, strain juice into a jar, and add 1 tablespoon lemon juice and ¾ cup honey, stirring briskly until dissolved. Chill.
Reserve berries for baking or mash with honey and use in place of jam.

LIGHT FRUIT NECTAR

For 2 cups juice: cover 1 cup dried fruit with 3 cups water, bring to boil, reduce heat, and simmer gently 20 minutes. Strain, add 1 thin slice lemon, and chill. Reserve fruit for compotes, baking, cereals, and so forth.

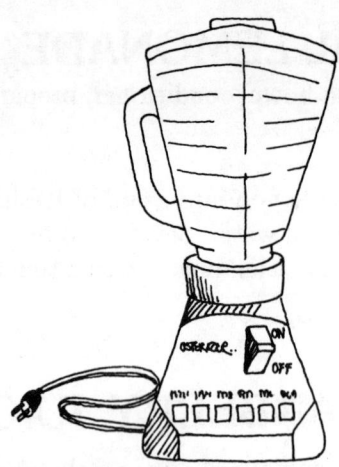

With the aid of the electric blender you can add these to your morning juice repertoire:

FRESH PINEAPPLE JUICE

Dice very ripe pineapple and puree in blender. Thin with ice if desired.

FRESH MELON JUICE

Dice cantaloupe, honeydew, or watermelon, remove pits, and puree in blender. Add a slice of fresh lemon or lime and thin with ice if desired.

PINEAPPLE-CARROT JUICE

2 cups pineapple juice
2 diced carrots
1 ¼-inch-thick slice peeled lemon
¼ cup ice

Process all ingredients in blender until juice is smooth and ice is melted.
Makes 3 cups.

DRIED-FRUIT NECTAR

Use any dried fruit alone or in combination. Cover each cup of dried fruit with 4 cups water, bring to boil, and simmer gently 20 minutes to extract flavor. Strain, then puree juice in blender, adding a few pieces of fruit for a rich consistency. Reserve remaining fruit for cereals, fruit salads, beverages, and so forth.

One cup (6½ ounces) dried fruit will make 24 ounces nectar.

SPROUTED JUICE

The addition of sprouts to any juice makes a highly nourishing drink. Add ¼ cup sprouts (alfalfa, wheat, millet, or sunflower seed) per cup of juice (pineapple, tomato, apple, prune, orange) and blend until smooth.

seasonal juice companions

By mixing fruits and fruit juices that have complementary nutrients you can create a wide selection of juices with multiple vitamin and mineral content. The fruits and juices in the following examples are grouped together by both nutritional compatability and seasonal availability.

SUMMER JUICE NUMBER 1

For every 8 ounces juice puree in blender:

1/3 cup diced peaches
1/3 cup fresh raspberries
1/3 cup orange juice

SUMMER JUICE NUMBER 2

For every 8 ounces juice puree in blender:

1/3 cup blackberries
1/3 cup diced cantaloupe
1/3 cup pineapple juice

FALL JUICE

For every 8 ounces juice puree in blender:

1/3 cup diced, pitted watermelon
1/3 cup diced pear
1/3 cup grape juice

WINTER JUICE NUMBER 1

For every 8 ounces juice puree in blender:

1/3 cup diced apples
1/3 cup pineapple chunks
1/3 cup orange juice

WINTER JUICE NUMBER 2

For every 8 ounces juice puree in blender:

1/3 cup diced carrot
1/3 cup avocado pulp
1/3 cup tomato juice

SPRING JUICE

For every 8 ounces juice puree in blender:

1/3 cup strawberries
1/3 cup sliced banana
1/3 cup apple juice

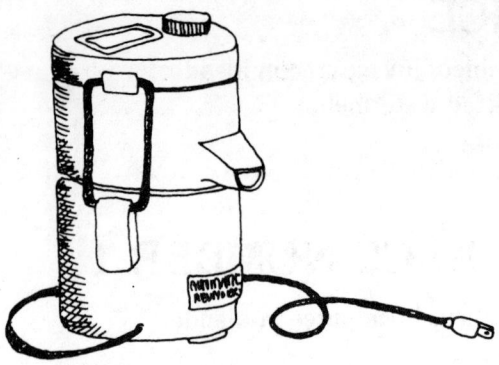

extracted juices

A juice extractor is an expensive but worthwhile investment for those who cherish rich fruit and vegetable juices and can be economically practical if you purchase damaged or bottom-of-the-box produce for juicing. If you own a juice extractor you can make best use of it in the morning with apples, pears, pineapples, grapes, cherries, peaches, plums, apricots, beets, celery, or carrots, alone or combined. While the precise yield is difficult to predict, in general, one pound of raw produce will provide about 8 ounces of fresh juice. Pears, apples, grapes, peaches and berries form a very rich nectar; if you find it too thick it can be thinned with water or thinner juices, or served over ice.

more about fruit juices

With few exceptions, fresh whole fruit is a better food than fruit juice. Though fresh fruit juices possess most of the natural fruit nutrients, they lack the bulk that assists digestion and peristalsis. Canned juices, though still rich in vitamins and minerals, are devoid of native fruit enzymes, which, being sensitive to heat, are destroyed during canning.

If fruit juice is preferred to fresh fruit at breakfast, however, there are many good choices you can make. And though drinking anything other than orange juice is likely to be considered unpatriotic (and with good reason, since orange juice is among the best sources of vitamin C), it also makes good sense to vary the morning fruit juice to incorporate some of the other valuable fruit assets into your diet.

In addition to the juice suggestions we have given there are many prepared juices you can buy. Among them, unsweetened orange and grapefruit juices, frozen (unsweetened) orange, tangerine, and grapefruit juice concentrates, apple juice, pineapple juice, tomato juice and canned carrot juice are the best breakfast choices. More variety will come from combining these to create, for example, pineapple-orange juice, apple-grape juice, orange-grapefruit juice or carrot-apple juice.

Powdered breakfast drinks, sweetened juices, fruit nectars, fruit cocktails, fruit juice drinks and fruit drinks on the market are all less acceptable, since they are highly sugared and watered down, so that you receive proportionately fewer vitamins and minerals and more calories.

FRUIT

Fruit that is just tender and bursting with juice is at its peak in flavor and food value. Whether fresh, cooked, or dried, it cannot be overemphasized at breakfast time.

If not completely ripe, fruit should be held at room temperature to ripen; once it has ripened to your liking, store it in the refrigerator. Be sure to wash all fruit before eating, to remove surface dirt and as much of the residual chemical spray as possible.

Service may be simple or sophisticated. The simplest way to begin a meal with fresh fruit is, of course, to eat it plain, out of hand. But, there are some other ideas that might not have crossed your mind which may make fruit dishes more appealing in the morning. Although raw fruit is a more reliable source of nutrients, cooked fruit is often more digestible and is valuable for the variety it gives.

apples
PICNIC BREAKFAST

Cut apples in wedges and serve with crackers and cheese.

Hold the wine for dinner.

APPLEWICH

Core apple and slice into rings. Dip slices into orange juice to inhibit browning, and form into sandwiches with a slice of cheddar cheese in the middle. If not served immediately wrap in foil and refrigerate. Applewiches will keep up to 24 hours.

APPLE SNACKS

Dice apples and combine with raisins and nuts. Serve as is or with milk.

APPLESAUCE

Dice apples (no need to peel or core), place in saucepan with ¼ cup water to prevent sticking, cook 10 minutes until barely tender, and puree in food mill. Return to heat to thicken if necessary. Sweeten to taste with honey and cinnamon and serve hot or cold, plain or with milk, or with chopped nuts and raisins.

HONEY APPLES

¾ cup honey
½ cup cider vinegar
3 cups peeled, sliced apples

Bring honey and vinegar to boil in small saucepan. Drop in apples a few at a time. Skim out when transparent, or after about 3 minutes. Serve warm or cold, plain or with yogurt.
Makes 6 servings.

BAKED APPLES

Remove apple core to within ½ inch of bottom, fill hollow with chopped nuts and dried fruit moistened with honey, place in a baking dish, and add water or fruit juice to a depth of ½ inch to prevent sticking and promote steaming. Cover and bake in a 375° oven about 40 minutes, until tender, but not mushy. Serve hot or chilled.

BAKED APPLES WITH ALMOND

1 cup almonds, ground in blender
¼ cup honey
2 egg whites
8 medium apples
2 tablespoons melted butter
½ cup wheat germ

Whip almonds, honey, and egg whites in blender to a smooth paste. Peel and core apples almost to bottom. Brush surface with butter, roll in wheat germ, and fill hollow center with almond paste. Spread remaining wheat germ, butter, or filling on top. Place apples, sides just touching, in a baking pan, add water to a depth of ¼ inch, cover, and bake in a 375° oven 40 minutes, until fork tender. Serve warm for late breakfasts or prepare in advance and serve chilled. Excellent with a topping of Golden Milk or Cream Sauce (see Index).

Makes 8 servings.

bananas

BANANA ROLL

Peel banana, cut on the diagonal to expose as much surface as possible, and spread with peanut butter or other nut butter. Roll in wheat germ. Serve immediately or chill before serving.

FROZEN BANANA POPS

Slice banana in half crosswise, insert an ice cream stick into flat end, coat as for Banana Roll, and freeze. Serve frozen banana appetizers in warm weather.

BAKED BANANA

Make a slit in banana skin from end to end. Bake in a 400° oven for 10 minutes. Serve in peel like a baked potato with jam and yogurt or Nut Butter Dressing (see Index).

dried fruit

DYNAMITE FRUIT COMPOTE

To prepare a dried-fruit compote, place any combination of dried fruits into a bowl or jar, add boiling water or hot apple juice to cover, and let stand in the refrigerator overnight. Some people simmer the fruit in water for 10 minutes to increase tenderness. Either version will keep for weeks in the refrigerator.

SPICED PRUNES

Cover 1 pound of dried prunes with cold water and let stand overnight. Add 2 slices of orange, with peel, and a 3-inch stick of cinnamon, and cook over gentle heat in a covered saucepan until tender, about 10 minutes.

REFRIGERATOR FRUITANAS

1 cup raisins
1 cup mixed dried fruit
½ cup almonds
2 tablespoons wheat germ
¼ cup sunflower seeds, ground in blender
¼ cup orange juice

Chop raisins, dried fruit, and almonds. Combine with wheat germ, ground sunflower seeds, and enough juice to moisten. Press into a waxed-paper-lined 8-inch baking pan, cover, and let harden in refrigerator several hours. To serve, cut into squares with a knife dipped in hot water. Keeps indefinitely in the refrigerator.

oranges

To peel an orange for easy eating, score peel from top to bottom with a sharp paring knife, repeating every inch (see diagram). Slip thumb under each scored segment, starting at the top, and lift toward the bottom.

Or, slice a thin piece from the top with a sharp paring knife. Slip knife under peel and go round and round the orange spiral fashion until the orange is bare (see diagram).

grapefruit
BROILED GRAPEFRUIT

Especially appealing in the winter.
Cut grapefruit in half crosswise. Remove core and cut around each section to loosen fruit from membrane. Cover surface with a thin layer of honey, place under broiler and let surface become brown and bubbly.

melon
MELON CUBES

Balls or cubes of watermelon, honeydew, cantaloupe, and avocado, sprinkled lightly with fresh lemon or lime, are a great way to wake up on a hot summer morning.

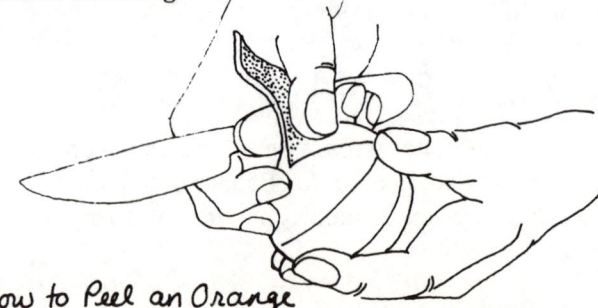

How to Peel an Orange

CANTALOUPE CUP

Cantaloupe halves can be scooped out and filled with any diced fruit for openers. A combination of oranges, grapes, and dates topped with orange-sweetened yogurt or buttermilk will awaken you to the potential of this fruit dish.

pears
POACHED PEARS

Bring 1½ cups grape juice to boil in small saucepan. Add 3 cups diced or sliced pears and simmer 5 to 8 minutes, until fruit is tender. Serve warm or cold with a spoonful of yogurt and some grated nuts.

Makes 4 to 6 servings. (Can be prepared with apples and peaches as well.)

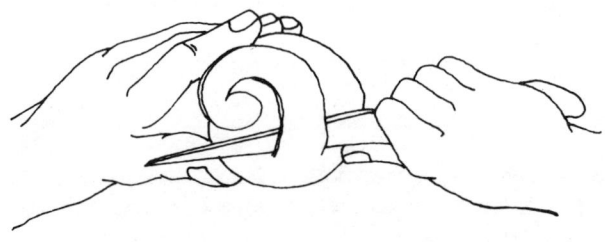

BAKED PEARS

Cut pears in half lengthwise, remove core, and fill hollow with chopped dried fruit and nuts. Drizzle surface with honey, arrange in baking dish, and add ¼ inch water to promote steaming. Cover and bake in a 375° oven 1 hour. Serve hot or cold.

peaches
BAKED OR POACHED

Peaches, too, are enjoyable baked, as in Baked Pears, and will be tender in about 40 minutes; or poach, as in Poached Pears.

PEACH SALADS

Fresh peaches in combination with fresh berries are essential to any summer breakfast fruit salad. They are exceptional with Nut Butter Dressing (see Index).

guavas, mangoes, and papayas

These three tropical favorites are wonderful cubed and served in a bowl with milk and honey.

fruit plus protein

Your fruit course and your main course can merge into one with the addition of a high protein dressing.

CREAM SAUCE

For each cup of sauce combine ½ cup cottage cheese, 1 tablespoon lemon juice, 2 tablespoons jam and ½ cup yogurt and process at low speed in blender until smooth.

¼ cup sauce furnishes 75 calories and 5 grams protein.

POT CHEESE TOPPING

Mash pot or cottage cheese with honey and chopped walnuts and spoon over fruit.

NUT BUTTER DRESSING

For each cup of sauce combine ½ cup nut butter, 2 tablespoons honey, 1 tablespoon lemon juice and ½ cup orange juice. Beat with a fork or wire whip until smooth. Add additional juice if necessary to achieve a creamy consistency.

1 tablespoon sauce furnishes 58 calories and 2 grams protein.

STRAWBERRY WHIP

For each cup of sauce combine 1 cup diced strawberries, ½ cup raw cashews and 1 tablespoon honey in blender and process until smooth and creamy. Use a rubber spatula to push mixture from the sides of the blender into the center periodically.

¼ cup sauce furnishes 100 calories and 3 grams protein.

table of fruit values

The Principal Fruits Contributing Vitamin C

Oranges (December — June)
Grapefruits (September — April)
Tangerines (November — January)
Lemons (Year round)
Limes (Year round; peak June, July)
Strawberries (April — July)
Cantaloupe (June — September)
Tomatoes (June — September)
Mango (May — August)
Guavas (Year round)
Papaya (May, June)

Principal Fruits Contributing Vitamin A

Apricots (June, July)
Yellow peaches (June — September)
Nectarines (July, August)
Cantaloupe (June — September)
Watermelon (May — August)
Avocado (Year round)
Dried prunes

Principal Fruits Contributing B Vitamins

Bananas (Year round)
Avocado (Year round)
Dried dates, figs, prunes, peaches, raisins
Guavas (Year round)

Principal Fruits Contributing Iron

Raisins
Dried apricots, dates, figs, prunes

Principal Fruits Contributing Calcium

Dried dates, figs, raisins

Principal Fruits Contributing Potassium

Bananas (Year round)
Avocado (Year round)
Dried fruit

HOT AND COLD CEREAL

No other food in human history has provided such an important source of nourishment as grains. Whether milled into flour for bread or coarsely ground as cereal, in every culture there is at least one grain food on which the majority of people depend for their daily supply of energy and nutrition.

The cultivation of grain, which proved to be easily grown, high yielding, and successfully stored, was an important event in the foundation of modern civilization, for only with such a dependable food supply could tribal wanderings in search of food come to an end. The goddess of grain, Ceres, honors the women who took charge of the agriculture; thus the name "cereal."

There are many reasons cereal has remained such an important dietary staple. In addition to being readily available, inexpensive to produce, and storable, cereals are one of the most valuable forms of food for nutrition. Though often categorized as "carbohydrate foods," cereal grains are actually a rich source of vitamins, minerals, and vegetable protein. Technically speaking, the cereal grain is a seed, capable of growing into a new crop of grain if planted under the right conditions. Like all seeds, cereal grains are composed of three elements: the germ, the endosperm, and the bran.

The germ is the heart of the seed, the portion that sprouts when the seed is planted. It is here that the highest-quality protein and the B vitamin thiamine are most plentiful. Iron, riboflavin, niacin, vitamin E, carbohydrates, and fat are also present in the germ.

The endosperm is the food reserve for the germinating plant. Though it contains some protein, it is composed mainly of carbohydrates, which supply energy for plant growth. It is the endosperm that remains when grains are milled into refined flour and processed cereals.

Finally, there is the bran, which is composed of several layers of protective coating around the seed. The outer layers of the bran are mainly cellulose—bulk-forming carbohydrates, well known as a natural bowel regulator. Iron and B vitamins are also found in this outer portion of bran, while the inner layers are rich in protein and phosphorous.

As you can see, not only is the grain seed the vital center of growth for a new plant, but it is endowed with many of our own dietary essentials: carbohydrates, protein, iron, phosphorus, thiamine, riboflavin, niacin, vitamin E, and some calcium. In addition, grains are extremely rich in trace minerals and native enzymes.

Cereals are, in fact, the original source of most of our dietary protein. Cattle, lamb, and poultry all feed on cereals or grasses, which they synthesize into the meat, milk and eggs we eat. But, as with money, cereal goes further without the middleman, or in this

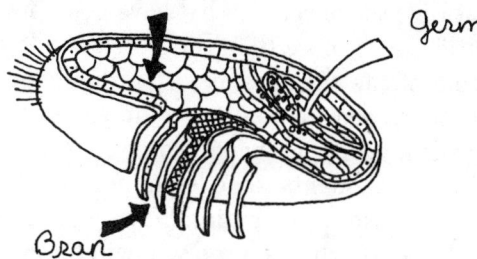

case the middle-animal, and so cereals for us, too, should comprise a large part of our daily protein.

Most of us have been taught that only animal proteins contain all the essential amino acids needed to build bodily protein. In the case of cereals, two of these amino acids, lysine and isoleucine, are indeed limited in quantity. But this need not matter, for as nature has fortunately provided, milk and cheese, eggs, dried beans, wheat germ, and brewer's yeast all contain an abundance of these missing amino acids.

Therefore, cereal, combined with these foods, offers protein of excellent quality.

One thing often ignored in selecting cereals is that once the grain is milled and the seed is no longer intact or whole, all the essential nutrients begin to depreciate. Thus, only whole ground cereals—those that are neither "debranned," "degerminated," or "bolted"—can be counted on for high-quality nutrition. In contrast (and this is where cereals get their bad reputation), those cereals that have been processed contain little more than the starch and low-grade protein of the endosperm. Often the manufacturer attempts to restore quality to these grains through enrichment, but since it is impossible to replace all those elements removed in milling, it is always better to use whole grains. When you see the word "enriched" on the package you will know that nutrients have been destroyed. Of the many vitamins and minerals that are lost, only iron, thiamine, niacin, and riboflavin are restored in the enriching process. By the way, the caliber of the protein that has been diminished by refining remains unimproved.

HOT CEREALS

Hot cereals are a convenient breakfast food whether you are cooking for one or for a crowd, and from the roster of whole-grain cereals there is remarkable variety to choose from. Oats, sold as either rolled oats or oatmeal, provide the best source of protein, followed by buckwheat, whole wheat, rye, corn, brown rice, and barley. Cracked wheat and couscous also provide good cereal nourishment.

Less valuable are the cereals made from farina and refined wheat and rice, including commercial cream of wheat and cream of rice. Cornmeal must be "unbolted" to be of good food value, and the term "degerminated" on the package label is notice that most of the essential nutrients have been removed. The purchase of other cereals, which have been pared down to carbohydrate plus added synthetic flavoring and nutrients, is unnecessary.

cooking hot cereal

Years ago it was thought that cereals had to cook for hours before they were edible. According to recent research, however, cereals are ready to be eaten as soon as the starch granules fully absorb the hot liquid they are cooked in. As a result, it is easy to serve up a steaming bowl of cereal within 5 to 15 minutes, although a few more options are available when you have a little more time to give to breakfast preparation.

For all hot cereals the cooking procedure is similar. The dry cereal is added slowly to rapidly boiling water and stirred quickly so that it is immediately surrounded by the hot liquid. Then the heat is lowered and the water is kept just at the boiling point so the grains remain well separated and the cereal does not become gummy.

When everyone does not breakfast together, cereal can be kept warm over a double boiler, low heat, or simply in the covered pot.

Though most packaged cereals come with cooking instructions, we have often found that they do not work out well. For best results consult the Foolproof Cereal Cookery instructions that follow. Keep in mind, however, that some people prefer their cereal thin, whereas others like it cooked to a heavy mass. You can adjust the cereal-liquid ratio according to your preference or, for a thicker gruel, increase the cooking time. Cereal that is too thick can, of course, be thinned at the table with milk.

foolproof cereal cookery

1 cup of cereal, before cooking, will yield four to six servings.

For Each Cup of Uncooked Cereal	Liquid (cups)	Cooking Time (minutes)
Oatmeal	2-4	5
Steel-cut oats	3	35-45
Cornmeal	4-6	10
Whole wheat (as Wheatena)	2-4	5
Cracked wheat (bulgur)	2	15
Wheat germ	2	2
Couscous	2	5
Rye, rolled	2	5
Rye flour	3	20
Buckwheat (kasha)	2	20
Millet	2	30
Brown rice	2	45
Cream of brown rice	4-6	15
Hominy	3	2 hours

Add ½ teaspoon salt (optional) to water and bring to boil. Slowly sprinkle in cereal so that water never stops boiling; stir so that the grain is completely moistened. Reduce heat to a gentle boil and cook, stirring only enough to keep cereal from sticking; too much stirring makes cereal gummy. When liquid is absorbed and grain is tender, remove from heat and cover until serving time.

For fine-grained cereals like cornmeal, rye flour, cream of brown rice, which have a tendency to stick together and form lumps, mix the grain to a smooth paste with part of the cold liquid before it is added to the remainder of the liquid which has already been brought to a boil.

To reduce cooking time by about half, grains can be soaked in water overnight.

For higher-quality protein use milk to replace half the water in cooking, or, better still, add ¼ to ½ cup nonfat dry milk powder along with each cup of uncooked grain. Or add 1 to 2 tablespoons wheat germ or 2 teaspoons brewer's yeast per serving during the last few minutes of cooking.

good breakfast porridges

CREAM OF WHOLE WHEAT

Takes only 10 minutes, even with half-opened eyes.

1 cup whole-wheat flour
¼ cup nonfat dry milk powder
2 cups cold water
3 cups boiling water
½ teaspoon salt

Combine flour, milk, and cold water and stir until smooth. Add salt to boiling water, then stir in cereal paste. Cook 10 minutes, stirring occasionally. Serve sweet or savory with milk and wheat germ.

Makes 6 servings, each furnishing 80 calories and 4 grams protein (before the addition of milk, wheat germ, and so forth).

CREAM OF BROWN RICE

To prepare cereal mix:

Wash 2 cups brown rice, drain well, and toast in an ungreased skillet until grain is completely dry, about 5 minutes. Grind to a powder at high speed in blender, return to skillet, and toast lightly.

To cook:

Follow directions in Foolproof Cereal Cookery, using the smaller amount of liquid for a thick porridge that can be thinned with milk at the table, or the larger amount of liquid along with nonfat dry milk powder.

Cracked Rice Cereal

CRACKED-RICE CEREAL

1 cup raw brown rice
4 cups milk, whole or skim
½ cup raisins

Grind rice to one half its size in blender. Combine all ingredients, bring to boil, cover, and simmer gently until rice is thick and tender, about 20 minutes.

Makes 4 generous servings, each furnishing 312 calories (382 calories with whole milk) and 13 grams protein; or 6 smaller servings, each furnishing 208 calories (255 calories with whole milk) and 8.5 grams protein.

INDIAN PUDDING

Cook cornmeal as outlined in Foolproof Cereal Cookery, using the greater amount of liquid and adding nonfat dry milk powder along with the grain. Spoon into serving bowls and sweeten to taste with molasses; stir in a fistful of raisins and serve with lots of cold milk.

MAMMALIGA

A traditional Rumanian dish.

Cook cornmeal as outlined in Foolproof Cereal Cookery, using the smaller amount of liquid. Serve the hot, thick cornmeal with butter, a scoop of cottage cheese, and salt or jam.

CHOCOLATE-PUDDING CEREAL

A small amount of cocoa makes this cornmeal cereal especially appealing.

1 quart skim milk
¼ cup nonfat dry milk powder
2 tablespoons cocoa
⅔ cup white cornmeal
¼ cup turbinado sugar
¼ teaspoon salt

Combine all ingredients, bring to boil, and cook, stirring occasionally, until thickened, about 5 minutes. Serve with additional milk, and chopped walnuts if desired.

Makes 4 generous servings, each furnishing 240 calories and 12 grams protein; or 6 smaller servings, each furnishing 160 calories and 8 grams protein.

WHIP AND CHILL CEREAL

Whip and Chill Cereal can be prepared in a variety of flavors—pineapple, apple, tangerine, orange—using frozen juice concentrate. The kids can help prepare this one before they go to bed and have it cold in the morning.

2½ cups water
1 can (6 ounces) frozen juice concentrate
½ cup nonfat dry milk powder
½ cup white cornmeal (or farina)

Combine water and juice concentrate in saucepan and bring to boil. Slowly sprinkle in milk powder and cereal and beat with a rotary beater until smooth. Cook over low heat until thick, about 7 minutes. Pour into a mixing bowl and beat with a rotary beater or electric mixer for about 1 minute at a time, at 3-minute intervals until cereal is creamy and cool. Chill. Serve cold with additional milk.

Makes 6 servings, each furnishing 102 calories and 4 grams protein.

SWEET COUSCOUS

A cereal variation based on the North African staple couscous.

3 cups skim milk
3 tablespoons peanut butter
½ cup raisins
¼ teaspoon salt
⅔ cup couscous (semolina)
½ cup chopped almonds

Bring milk, peanut butter, and raisins to boil. Add remaining ingredients and return to boil for 1 minute. Remove from heat, cover, and let stand 10 minutes.

This cereal is of grain consistency and should be served with additional milk.

Makes 6 servings, each furnishing 230 calories and 10 grams protein.

HOT RAISIN BRAN

3 cups water
½ teaspoon salt
⅓ cup wheat germ
⅔ cup bran
¼ cup nonfat dry milk powder
2 tablespoons raisins

Bring water to boil. Stir in remaining ingredients and cook gently 10 minutes. Serve with additional milk, and honey or molasses to taste.

Makes 4 servings, each furnishing 94 calories and 6 grams protein.

COUNTRY-STYLE KASHA

A coarser-grain cereal dependent on the traditional Russian buckwheat groats.

1 egg, lightly beaten
1 cup buckwheat groats (kasha)
½ teaspoon salt
2 cups boiling water
½ cup wheat germ
½ cup cottage cheese
½ cup yogurt

Combine egg, kasha, and salt and cook in dry saucepan until grains are separate and dry. Add water and cook, covered, over low heat until liquid is completely absorbed, about 20 minutes. Stir in wheat germ, spoon into bowls, and top with cottage cheese and yogurt.

Makes 6 servings, each furnishing 175 calories and 10 grams protein.

MILK-TOAST CEREAL

For every 2 to 3 servings, toast, lightly butter, and dice 4 slices whole-wheat bread. Divide into serving bowls. Lightly sweeten 2 cups milk, skim or whole, with 1 tablespoon honey or molasses and ¼ teaspoon vanilla. Heat, then pour over toast cubes.

BREAD CEREAL

For when you run out of cereal, or simply want a thick, soft, tasty porridge for breakfast.

3 cups diced whole-grain bread (about 8 slices or ½ pound)
4 cups milk, whole or skim
¼ cup wheat germ
½ teaspoon salt

Combine all ingredients and bring to boil over moderate heat. Reduce heat and cook gently, mashing bread with a fork, until thickened, or 3 to 5 minutes.

Serve with additional milk if desired, and raisins, chopped nuts, or other cereal garnish.

Makes 4 generous servings, each furnishing 298 calories (224 calories with skim milk) and 15 grams protein; or 6 servings, each furnishing 198 calories (149 calories with skim milk) and 10 grams protein.

souped-up cereal

Here are some other ways to increase the food power of both homemade and store-bought cereals:

* Little or no additional sweetening is needed if you cook raisins or chopped dates along with the cereal.
* Bananas, peaches, and berries are as welcome on hot cereal as they are on cold. Fresh figs, orange sections, and sliced pears offer more offbeat variations. Applesauce makes a good hot-cereal topping.
* Two tablespoons finely chopped sunflower seeds, pumpkin seeds, peanuts, walnuts, raw cashews, or almonds can be added for each person either before cooking or on top of the cereal bowl.
* To sweeten cereal use honey, pure maple syrup, molasses, the liquid from soaked dried fruits, or date sugar rather than refined white sugar.
* The addition of fat slows down the digestive process so that a bowl of cereal with a pat of butter or whole milk added will keep you satisfied longer.
* For savory cereals and calorie savers season with salt, sesame salt, soy sauce, or nut butter.
* *Always serve hot cereal with lots of milk.*

cereal the second (and third) day

We find it almost impossible to predict how much cereal will be consumed in a morning. Since cooked cereal can be stored in the refrigerator for about a week and has a wide range of uses, the wise cook makes at least double the amount needed and intentionally plans for leftovers.

To store cooked cereal, cover with a lid or thin layer of cold water and refrigerate. This covering will prevent a hard crust from forming on top.

To reheat, pour off the water, thin with a little milk, and place over gentle heat or in the top of a double boiler.

Leftovers can also be transformed into any of the following dishes which you might enjoy even more than the original version.

ONCE-WARMED GRAINS

Warm plain milk or Golden Milk and pour over any cooked grain. Sprinkle with cinnamon, sweeten with honey, and add chopped dried fruits, nuts, and wheat germ as desired.

MOLDED CEREAL

Best when milk has been used in cooking the grain.

Sweeten cooked cereal, using 1 teaspoon honey and ½ teaspoon vanilla per cup. Rub custard cups or small fruit dishes with oil, pack in cereal, and cover with paper to keep a crust from forming. Chill.
To serve, unmold and garnish with sliced fruit and plain or any Just-for-Cereal Milk (p. 36).

CREAM OF FRUIT CEREAL

For infants on up.

Combine any cooked grain (oatmeal, brown rice, barley, millet, kasha), milk, and softened dried or diced fresh fruit in blender. Allow ½ cup cereal, ½ cup fruit, and 1 cup milk for every two servings. If grain is unsalted add ¼ teaspoon salt. Puree at low speed until smooth, then heat gently. Serve with wheat germ, thin with milk to taste, and add additional sweetening if necessary.

RICE-PUDDING CEREAL

The combination of brown rice and nut milk forms a high-quality protein, but cow's milk can be used if preferred.

1 cup cooked brown rice
1½ cups nut milk
2 eggs, lightly beaten
2 tablespoons honey
1 cup fresh or frozen berries

Combine rice, milk, eggs, and honey, and cook over low heat, stirring until thick, about 10 minutes. Do not boil. Add berries and serve hot or cold.
Makes 3 servings, each furnishing 330 calories and 11 grams protein.

Variation: Omit berries and serve with applesauce.

OATMEAL PUDDING

2 cups cooked oatmeal
1 cup diced apple (1 large apple)
1 cup chopped peanuts
½ cup raisins
⅓ cup molasses
½ teaspoon cinnamon
¼ teaspoon salt

Combine all ingredients in a greased casserole and bake in a 400° oven 20 minutes. Serve warm or cold, with milk.

Makes 6 servings, each furnishing 305 calories and 10 grams protein.

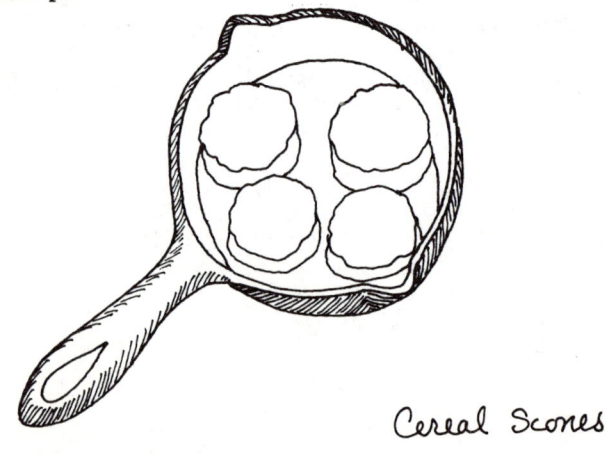

CEREAL SCONES

Crisp on the outside, soft on the inside. These scones can be served warm or stored in the refrigerator and split and toasted as needed.

¾ cup whole-wheat flour
1 teaspoon baking powder
1 cup cold cooked cereal
1 tablespoon oil
½ teaspoon salt (if cereal is unsalted)
¼ cup skim milk

Combine flour and baking powder. Add cereal, oil, salt, and milk to form a thick batter. Drop by soupspoons to form mounds on a hot, well-greased griddle. Brown on each side about 5 minutes, turning only once, or scones will be heavy. Cool on a wire rack and serve plain or with jam.

Makes 6 scones, each furnishing 105 calories and 3.5 grams protein.

Cereal Scones

FRIED MUSH AND VARIATIONS

Of Southern extraction.

Pour cooked cornmeal into a loaf pan that has been lightly oiled or rinsed in cold water to prevent sticking, cover, and chill. Allow 2 cups leftover cereal for every 2 to 3 servings. If you do not have enough cereal to fill a loaf pan use a baking pan that is 1 inch deep instead. To cook, unmold, cut into slices ½ inch thick, dip quickly into lightly beaten egg, then coat with a mixture of whole-wheat flour and wheat germ. Saute quickly in hot fat.

Variations:
1. Add chopped peanuts to leftover cornmeal before chilling.
2. Add ¼ cup grated Cheddar per cup of cornmeal before chilling. Omit egg and simply dust with flour to fry.
3. Substitute cooked kasha for cornmeal. Serve with maple syrup and yogurt.
4. Substitute cooked oatmeal or whole-wheat cereal (Wheatena) for cornmeal. Serve with honey.

POLENTA

Pour 4 cups cooked cornmeal into a shallow, greased 9-inch baking dish, cover, and chill. Cut into squares, sprinkle with 1 cup grated cheese (Cheddar, Monterey Jack, Bel Paese), dot with butter, and brown under broiler or in a 400° oven until cheese melts, about 10 minutes.

COLD CEREALS

Better than all the dry cereal you can buy is the dry cereal you make at home. Such cereal will always be free of added chemicals and rich enough in natural ingredients to eliminate the need for vitamin and mineral enrichment, and you can personally guarantee its freshness. By making your own dry cereal you will get excellent value and top flavor for very little money, since commercial dry cereals represent a fantastic markup on relatively inexpensive raw ingredients.

BRAN FLAKES

One hundred percent better than any commercial variety. Very moving.

2 cups bran
2 cups whole-wheat flour
½ cup nonfat dry milk powder
3 tablespoons brewer's yeast
1 teaspoon salt
¼ cup safflower oil
1 tablespoon molasses
1 cup water

Combine dry ingredients. Make a well in the center and add oil, molasses, and water. Mix well, then roll out between two sheets of waxed paper as thin as possible. It is easier to divide dough into 3 or 4 pieces to roll. Place rolled dough on oiled cookie sheets and bake in a 350° oven 15 to 20 minutes, until lightly browned and crisp. If dough is not completely dry turn the oven off and let dough rest in oven until it is easily crushed. Break into small pieces by placing in a plastic bag and pounding or rolling with a rolling pin. Store in airtight container.

Makes 1 pound of cereal; 1 ounce (¼ cup) furnishes 118 calories and 4.5 grams of protein.

CHOATE WHEAT FLAKES

1½ cups whole-wheat flour
¼ cup soy flour
¼ cup wheat germ
¾ teaspoon salt
¼ cup peanut butter
About ¾ cup water

Combine flours, wheat germ, and salt. Beat peanut butter with water until smooth, then add to dry ingredients to make a soft dough. Add another tablespoon or two of water, if necessary, so that dough can be rolled. Prepare as for Bran Flakes (above).

Makes 10 ounces cereal; 1 ounce (¼ cup) furnishes 115 calories and 5.5 grams protein.

granola

The ingredients for granola can be altered according to availability and your personal tastes to include any dried fruits, nuts, or seeds you might favor, or, of course, to exclude any you might not like.

DAVID'S FAVORITE GRANOLA

½ cup almonds
½ cup peanuts
4 cups rolled oats
½ cup wheat germ
¼ cup sesame seeds
¼ cup sunflower seeds
¼ cup pumpkin seeds
¼ cup millet
⅓ cup honey
⅓ cup safflower oil
½ teaspoon vanilla
1 cup raisins

Chop nuts into tiny pieces. A chopping jar makes this easy but a sharp chopping knife on a wooden surface will do. Combine oats, wheat germ, nuts, and seeds in a large mixing bowl. Heat together honey and oil, remove from heat, stir in vanilla, and pour over oat mixture, stirring to coat all ingredients. Spread cereal onto a large shallow baking dish and brown lightly in a 325° oven for 20 to 30 minutes, stirring occasionally. Cool and add raisins. Store in tightly covered jar or container. For a change serve with yogurt instead of milk.

Makes 2 pounds cereal; 1 ounce (¼ cup) furnishes 137 calories and 4 grams protein.

SUSAN'S GRANOLA

7½ cups rolled oats
1 cup raw wheat germ
1 cup unsweetened coconut
1 cup sesame seeds
1 cup chopped almonds
½ cup millet
½ cup chopped dates
½ cup chopped nuts, your choice
½ cup sunflower seeds

Sauce: ½ to ¾ cup honey
¼ cup oil (preferably corn-germ oil)
⅓ cup water
½ cup peanut butter
½ teaspoon vanilla
½ teaspoon cinnamon

Combine nuts, grains, and dried fruit in large mixing bowl. Heat together sauce ingredients, spoon over dry ingredients, then spread onto shallow baking dishes and bake in a 375° oven about 15 minutes, until dry and lightly browned.

Makes 4 pounds cereal; 1 ounce (¼ cup) furnishes 120 calories and 3.8 grams protein.

SESAME DELIGHT

This cereal offers a concentrated source of nutrients and can be used to fortify other cereals in addition to being a cereal itself.

1 cup sesame seeds
¼ cup sunflower seeds
¼ cup almonds
½ cup coconut
½ cup wheat germ
⅓ cup nonfat dry milk powder
¼ cup raisins
¾ teaspoon cinnamon

Grind sesame seeds and sunflower seeds in blender to a fine meal. Chop almonds. Combine all ingredients and store in airtight container in a cool place.

Makes 1 pound of cereal; 1 ounce (¼ cup) furnishes 102 calories and 4 grams protein.

APPLE GRIST

½ cup bran
½ cup wheat germ
1 cup unsweetened applesauce
1 cup milk, skim or whole
cinnamon, raisins, nuts, coconut

Combine bran, wheat germ, applesauce, and milk. Let mixture soften a few minutes and, when liquid is absorbed, spoon into individual bowls. Garnish to taste with cinnamon, raisins, nuts, grated unsweetened coconut, and milk as desired.

Makes 4 servings, each furnishing 132 calories (149 calories with whole milk) and 8 grams protein before the accouterments are added.

MUESLI

Muesli is a Swiss movement. Unlike other cold cereals, it cannot be prepared in quantity and stored but must be made fresh each time. Since the oats must be soaked from ½ hour to overnight it is best to plan for this cereal the night before, but it is worth it, since muesli is very rich in essential vitamins, minerals, and enzymes.

For every two servings: soak 6 tablespoons rolled oats in ½ cup water or orange juice from 30 minutes to overnight. Before serving grate in 1 apple and add ½ teaspoon lemon juice and 3 tablespoons chopped almonds. Spoon into serving bowls and vary as follows:

Traditional Muesli: Add 2 tablespoons yogurt sweetened with 1 teaspoon honey, per serving.
One bowlful furnishes 232 calories (259 calories if soaked in orange juice) and 6.6 grams protein.

Muesli with Milk: Add ½ cup whole or skim milk per serving.
One bowlful with skim milk furnishes 222 calories (250 calories if soaked in orange juice) and 9 grams protein.

One bowlful with whole milk furnishes 260 calories (287 calories if soaked in orange juice) and 9 grams protein.

Muesli with Condensed Milk: Add 2 tablespoons sweetened condensed milk per serving.
One bowlful furnishes 306 calories (334 calories if soaked in orange juice) and 7.8 grams protein.

Strictly Vegetarian Muesli: Add 1 tablespoon nut butter whipped smooth with 1 tablespoon water and 1 teaspoon honey, per serving.
One bowlful furnishes about 286 calories (313 calories if soaked in orange juice) and 8.5 grams protein, although this will vary with the choice of nut butter.

Mixed-Fruit Muesli: Add ½ cup fresh berries, cherries, peaches, apricots, banana, tangerines, oranges, or softened dried fruit along with or in place of the apple.
Top with chopped pumpkin or sunflower seeds.

COLD RICE CEREAL

Cold cooked brown rice is the basis of this cereal; one of the tastiest ways we know of to use up leftovers. Extremely high in mineral content.

2 cups cold cooked brown rice
2 cups blueberries, or chopped apples, or a combination of both
¼ cup unsweetened, shredded coconut
¼ cup sunflower seeds
2 tablespoons honey
1 cup yogurt

Combine all ingredients and serve.
Makes 4 servings, each furnishing 235 calories and 6 grams protein.

simple cereals

If these recipes seem too involved you can always rely on one of the really simple homemade cereals coming up instead of resorting to the supermarket shelf. Though the food value of these cereals will vary with the original breadstuffs, any of the baked goods in this book will make a nutritious cereal.

CRUNCHY CRUMB CEREAL

Use any leftover baked goods, combined, for this one.

4 cups stale bread or muffin crumbs
4 tablespoons pure maple syrup

Mix crumbs with syrup, spread onto a shallow baking pan and place in a 350° oven for about 20 minutes, until lightly browned. Allow cereal to remain in oven as it cools to dry completely. Store in airtight container.
Makes 10 ounces cereal.

SIMON BREAD CEREAL

Save crusts from stale or trimmed bread and chop coarsely. Let stand, uncovered, overnight to dry. Store in airtight container. Serve as cereal with diced figs, raisins, or dates.

MUFFIN CEREAL

For the "dunkers" in the house.

Split any day-old muffins in half, spread lightly with jam, and break into small pieces in cereal bowl. Pour in ½ cup milk, hot or cold, and sprinkle with 1 teaspoon wheat germ. Highly recommended with Blueberry, Choco Bran, and Corn Muffins (see Index). Be sure to drink any milk left in the bowl.

CRACKERS 'N MILK

Break up whole-grain crackers into a bowlful of plain or Golden Milk (see Index). Add fresh berries or diced fruit.

MINDY'S NUTS AND BERRIES

A very simple cereal can be made right at the table letting everyone fill his or her cereal bowl with pieces of walnuts, raw cashews, peanuts, sunflower seeds, pine nuts, raisins, grated unsweetened coconut . . . Bathe liberally in milk and sprinkle with a spoonful of wheat germ. Add fresh fruit in season if you like.

store-bought varieties

There are two sets of clues which can help you select the best packaged dry cereals when you go shopping. The first is the list of ingredients; the second is the nutritional information on the label. Any boxed cereal that contains artificial flavoring, coloring, or preservatives is unsuited to the good breakfast. Artificial coloring is particularly important to watch for, since it is thought to contribute to hyperactivity in sensitive children and is often an unsuspected cause of allergies.

Whole grains, such as whole wheat, undegerminated corn, and oats should provide the basis of any dry cereal you buy. Salt, and especially sugar, if present at all, should appear at the bottom of the list of ingredients.

A fairly extensive rundown of calories and vitamin and mineral content appears on most boxes of dry cereal. For a cereal to qualify as a good breakfast, 1 ounce should contain *at least* 2 grams of protein; thus when ½ cup of milk is added, a serving of the cereal will provide a minimal 6.5 grams of protein.

Most processed dry cereals boast an impressive list of vitamins and minerals—primarily from synthetic enrichment. Anyone who incorporates whole grains, wheat germ, nuts, and seeds into his or her diet will have an ample supply of these nutrients and more, *naturally*.

Though the majority of commercial breakfast cereals do not meet the above criteria, there is still quite a variety you can choose from. The acceptable list excludes all the "gimmicky" cereals, which, like candy, not only are chock full of synthetics and sugar but also average less than 1.3 grams protein (and 112 calories) per 1-ounce serving.

Among the better choices are puffed wheat, shredded whole wheat, grapenut flakes, bran cereals, muesli, and some of the newer granola and "natural" cereals. Try to buy a brand without preservatives and, again, if sugar is added, it should be at the end, not the beginning, of the list of ingredients. Don't be deceived by the promotion—many of the so-called "natural" and "country" cereals are too highly sweetened.

For an idea of how some of the most widely distributed dry cereal products compare in terms of calories and protein, take a look at the table that follows. This chart is based on 1 ounce of cereal. If you're counting calories or protein, you might want to remember while you're pouring that, in actual volume, 1 ounce may vary from ¼ to 2 cups.

a comparison of packaged dry cereals[1]

Compare these values to the calorie-protein contribution of the cold cereals you can make at home.

Cereal (1 ounce)	Volume (cups)	Calories	Protein (grams)
Special K	1¼	100	6
Uncle Sam	¾	111	4.3
Puffed Wheat	2	102	3.8
Cheerios	1¼	112	3.8
All Bran	½	60	3
Heartland	¼	125	3
Country Morning	⅓	130	3
Quaker 100% Natural	¼	130	3
40% Bran	¾	100	2.8
Post Grape Nuts	¼	104	2.5
Wheaties	1¼	101	2.5
Shredded Wheat	about 1 biscuit	102	2.4
Raisin Bran	½	92	2.4
Rice Crispies	1	110	2
Corn Flakes	1⅓	110	2
Product 19	1	110	2
Puffed Rice	2	112	1.8
Cocoapuffs	1	109	1.5
Cap 'n Crunch	¾	123	1.3
King Vitamin	¾	118	1.1
Sugar Frosted Flakes	¾	110	1
Sugar Pops	1	110	1

[1] Based on information provided by the manufacturer.

storing dry cereal

To maintain freshness, dry cereal should be stored in a well-sealed container. If moisture does get in and the cereal becomes stale or soggy it can be recrisped in a 350° oven for 5 to 10 minutes.

serving dry cereal

All dry cereals, store-bought or homemade, will benefit from the addition of a tablespoon of wheat germ at serving time. (For a really high-powered topping make up a blend of equal parts of wheat germ, ground sesame seeds, and ground sunflower seeds.)

Try to use at least ½ cup milk per bowl, whole or skim, nut, seed, or soy according to preference. Those who prefer the vegetable "milks" despite their amino acid deficiencies will be heartened to know that they complement the whole grains contained in cereals to give you excellent protein quality. (For more information on vegetable milks see "Milk and Main Dish Beverages," p. 119.)

When you feel the need for extra nourishment try one of the Just-for-Cereal Milks instead of plain milk. Drink any milk that is left in the bowl after the cereal is eaten.

Other taste enhancers, both old and new, include:

* Fresh berries, apple chunks, bananas, pears, peaches, nectarines, or diced melon
* Stewed or softened dried fruit
* Raisins, dates, or chopped figs
* Chopped nuts or seeds
* Applesauce
* Fresh alfalfa, wheat, or millet sprouts
* Cantaloupe bowls, made by cutting the melon in half, scooping out the seeds and putting the cereal right in the cavity.

table of cereal toppings

Food	Amount	Calories	Protein (grams)
Sugar	1 teaspoon	17	0
Molasses	1 teaspoon	18	0
Honey	1 teaspoon	21	0
Raisins	1 tablespoon	29	.3
Sunflower seeds	1 tablespoon	40	1.7
Peanuts	1 tablespoon	86	4.0
Almonds	1 tablespoon	50	1.7
Walnuts	1 tablespoon	49	1.1
Sesame seeds	1 tablespoon	42	1.3
Unsweetened coconut	2 tablespoons	83	.5
Wheat germ	1 tablespoon	27	2.0
Whole milk	¼ cup	40	2.2
Skim milk	¼ cup	22	2.2
Half and half	¼ cup	80	1.9
Nonfat dry milk powder	1 tablespoon	20	2.0

JUST-FOR-CEREAL MILKS

As a change from plain milk, and to add additional protein, vitamins, minerals, and flavor to hot and cold cereals, use these special Cereal Milks.

GOLDEN MILK

1 egg yolk
1 cup milk, skim or whole
2 tablespoons honey
½ teaspoon vanilla

Combine all ingredients in top of double boiler, place over boiling water, and beat with egg beater or wire whisk until foamy. Serve hot or cold.

Makes 1¼ cups and furnishes 275 calories (346 with whole milk) and 11 grams protein.

FRUIT CREAM

½ cup yogurt
¼ cup diced fruit (melon, berries, peaches, pineapple, banana, or soaked dried fruit)

Puree until smooth at low speed in blender.

Makes ¾ cup and furnishes about 90 calories and 4 grams protein, plus the vitamins of the chosen fruit.

WHIPPED FRUIT CREAM

½ cup sliced banana, peaches, or strawberries, alone
  or in combination
6 tablespoons nonfat dry milk powder
¼ cup ice water
squirt of fresh lemon juice

Whip on high speed in blender.
Makes ¾ cup and furnishes about 170 calories and 13 grams protein, plus the vitamins of the chosen fruit.

NUT CREAM

½ cup peanut butter
¾ to 1 cup skim milk

Gradually beat milk into peanut butter, using a rotary beater or wire whisk, until smooth and creamy.
Makes 1¼ cups and furnishes 810 calories and 40 grams protein.

NONDAIRY NUT CREAM

A good way for those who do not take milk to enjoy cereal.

½ cup raw cashews
1 cup water
1 teaspoon honey
dash of vanilla

Grind nuts to a powder in blender. Add water gradually and blend at high speed until smooth. Add remaining ingredients and blend once more to distribute.
Makes 1 cup and furnishes 300 calories and 9 grams protein, plus a rich supply of thiamine and niacin.

CALORIE-CUTTING MILK

To reduce the amount of sweetening needed on any cereal, add ½ teaspoon vanilla extract to each cup of milk.

CHEESE AND OTHER DAIRY DISHES

Cheese, like the milk it is made from, is a powerhouse of nutrients, notably protein, riboflavin, and calcium. Its calorie and fat contents vary with the richness of the original milk; skim-milk cheeses like pot cheese and yogurt are low in fat and proportionately higher in protein, whereas cheeses derived from cream, like sour cream and cream cheese, are primarily fat with little body-building capacity.

Cheese is highly acclaimed as a breakfast food: it can be mild to piquant in flavor, is soothing in texture, requires no special preparation, and at the same time is so versatile that it can be transformed into a myriad of dishes.

MAIN DISHES

While the simplest way to enjoy cheese, including yogurt, cottage cheese, and ripened varieties like Cheddar, Gouda, Muenster, and Swiss, is plain on crackers or bread, cheese can also provide the basis for more entertaining breakfasts. Within moments several variations are possible, but because cheese is such a valuable food, even the more time-consuming recipes are worthy of attention.

quick cheese main dishes

BREAKFAST SUNDAE

A great breakfast that lets everyone be creative and select the foods he or she likes best; requires no cooking, just getting it together. All you have to do is assemble yogurt, nuts, and fresh and dried fruits on the table and let everyone make his or her own combination. Elders can concoct sundaes for those too young to handle food themselves. You can even simulate a soda fountain frappe to tantalize troublesome eaters.

* Place your storage containers or bowls full of peanuts, walnuts, raw cashews, almonds, and sunflower and pumpkin seeds on the table (protein and minerals).
* Do the same with dried fruits, including raisins, dates, apricots, and figs (vitamins and minerals).

Breakfast Sundae

* Give each person a container or bowl of unflavored yogurt (protein).
* Provide a platter of fresh fruits in season, offering bananas, pears, oranges, and apples in the winter and adding strawberries, melons, peaches, apricots, cherries, and so forth, in the summer (vitamins).
* Have honey or pure maple syrup and wheat germ in easy reach (more vitamins and minerals).

Now let everyone mix and match to create a breakfast sundae to his or her own taste. Or even a banana split.

KIBBUTZ BREAKFAST

The Kibbutz Breakfast is another breakfast where everyone can pick and choose what they like. A meal such as this is served each morning (and each evening as well) on every Israeli kibbutz.

Place any or all of the following foods on the table:

sliced tomatoes
sliced cucumbers
strips of green pepper
radishes
scallions
kohlrabi
olives
carrot sticks
shredded cabbage
sprigs of parsley and dill
oil, lemon, and vinegar
sour cream
yogurt
cottage cheese
hard-cooked eggs
herring
sardines
sliced cheeses
butter, nut butters
honey
assorted breads and crackers
a pot of coffee, tea, and a pitcher of milk

Give each person a plate and let everyone pile it on according to taste. Forget the formalities like peeling the eggs or trimming the vegetables; let everyone prepare their own. Just place a large bowl on the table to hold the egg shells, vegetable peelings, and the like.

CONTINENTAL YOGURT

Break rusks or whole-grain crackers into a bowl or container of plain, unflavored yogurt. Spoon a thin layer of honey over the surface and eat without mixing. As you eat through the honey coating you can spoon on some more, but be sparing or you'll be getting far too much sugar and calories.

Whole-grain crackers are also delicious crumbled into flavored yogurt. If you select preflavored yogurt choose a brand that contains only yogurt, honey or sugar, and the flavoring ingredients. For calorie counters, coffee, vanilla, and lemon yogurts contain about 60 calories less per cup than fruit-flavored varieties.

QUICK BLINTZ

Trim tough crust from a thin slice of whole-grain bread for each blintz. Flatten with a rolling pin. Make an aisle of 1 tablespoon cottage cheese along the center, add a few raisins, and drizzle with honey. Sprinkle with cinnamon. Bring sides of bread together in center to cover filling, dip briefly in milk, and fry in hot butter until golden on both sides, about 1 minute per side.

Serve with a dollop of plain yogurt and a bit of jam.

Each blintz furnishes approximately 100 calories and 6.2 grams protein.

NOODLES AND CHEESE

Yes, for breakfast.

½ pound (2 cups) uncooked broad noodles, preferably whole wheat
1 pound cottage cheese
2 tablespoons butter

Cook noodles in boiling water until tender, about 10 minutes. Divide cottage cheese into serving bowls; top with hot noodles and a pat of butter. Best plain, but you can add a spoonful of honey and cinnamon if you like, or even some chopped nuts.

Makes 4 servings, each furnishing 390 calories and 22.5 grams protein.

Noodles and Cheese

COTTAGE CHEESE AND VEGETABLES

For a comforting winter breakfast, warm Cottage Cheese and Vegetables over gentle heat.

Allot ½ to 1 cup cottage cheese per person depending on appetites. Combine the cottage cheese in a bowl with lots of chopped green pepper, minced scallion, sliced radish, grated carrot, diced celery, adding or eliminating to suit your taste. Top with a heaping spoonful of yogurt. Some people add a few raisins for variety, and the smart ones add a thick topping of wheat germ.

COTTAGE CHEESE AND FRUIT PLATTER

Put together any array of fresh fruit that makes a colorful arrangement. Serve with a mound of cottage cheese and a sprinkling of raw cashews and pumpkin seeds.

Pleasing combinations include:

* Sliced oranges, sweet cherries, pineapple chunks, and melon balls
* Apricot halves, grapefruit sections, and green and purple grapes
* Whole strawberries, quartered plums, and sliced banana.

ROLLED CHEESE

Use thinly sliced Muenster, Swiss, Edam, or other mild-flavored yellow or white variety. Spread each slice with a thin layer of jam or peanut butter, roll, and serve 2 or 3 per person.

APRICOTS À LA LITTLE MS. MUFFET

Diced dried fruit in a sauce of sweet curds and whey. This delicacy is prepared in the evening and is worth waiting the night for.

1 cup (4 ounces) dried apricots
2 cups milk
1 tablespoon honey
½ tablespoon lemon juice

Cut apricots in quarters and place in serving bowl. Bring milk to boil, add honey, and pour over apricots. Stir in lemon and cool to room temperature. Cover and refrigerate overnight.

Makes 4 servings, each furnishing 155 calories and 6 grams protein.

COTTAGE-CHEESE CAKES

2 cups pot cheese or well-drained cottage cheese
2 eggs
¼ teaspoon salt
2 tablespoons honey
½ cup whole-wheat flour
1½ tablespoons butter

Puree cheese in food mill or by pressing through a sieve. Beat in eggs, salt, honey and flour. Melt butter in skillet, then drop batter by the tablespoon into hot butter and brown on each side. Turn when spatula slips readily underneath, after about 5 minutes. Serve with jam.

Makes 16 cakes, each furnishing 70 calories and 5 grams protein.

BROILED TOMATO AND CHEESE

4 medium tomatoes
2 cups cottage cheese
1 cup shredded cheese (Cheddar, Swiss, Gouda, or Provolone)
salt, pepper
2 tablespoons wheat germ

Slice each tomato into three thick slices. Broil on one side. Turn. Combine cheeses and season to taste. Pile in mound on ungrilled side of tomato. Sprinkle with wheat germ and broil until cheese bubbles.

Allow 2 to 3 slices tomato per serving.

Makes 12 slices, each furnishing 90 calories and 8 grams protein.

BROILED PEACHES AND CHEESE

Prepare as for Broiled Tomato and Cheese, using 6 peaches, split, pitted, and broiled. For the shredded cheese choose Muenster, Jack, or mozzarella.

Each peach half furnishes 101 calories and 7.7 grams protein.

BAKED AVOCADO

Split two avocados, remove pit, and season with salt and lemon juice. Fill with cottage cheese filling used to top Broiled Tomato and Cheese, sprinkle with wheat germ and sesame seeds, and bake in a 375° oven 15 minutes.

Each avocado half furnishes 414 calories and 25 grams protein.

FRIED CHEESE, ITALIAN STYLE

8 ounces mozzarella cheese
1/3 cup whole-wheat flour
1 egg, lightly beaten
oil

Cut cheese into eight cubes. Dredge with flour, dip in beaten egg, and coat with flour again. Make sure cheese is well coated with egg and flour. If convenient this can be done ahead and the coated cheese refrigerated until cooking time. Heat oil to cover surface of skillet generously. When hot, quickly brown cheese on all sides, about 3 minutes per side, remove from heat, and serve.

Furnishes approximately 1256 calories and 62 grams protein; makes 3 to 4 servings.

FRIED CHEESE, UKRAINIAN STYLE

Prepare Fried Cheese as above, substituting 8 ounces farmer cheese, cut in slices. Saute in 2 tablespoons hot melted butter.

This dish will have about 616 calories and 51 grams protein.

FRIED CHEESE, ORIENTAL STYLE

Prepare Fried Cheese as above, but omit cheese and replace it with one square tofu (soybean cake) per person. Slice the tofu as you would the cheese.

BAKED CUSTARD

Prepare a day or evening in advance for custard lovers. If you do not have ovenproof custard cups, an oiled muffin tin can be used.

½ cup plus 2 tablespoons nonfat dry milk powder
hot water
3 eggs
¼ cup honey *or* molasses *or* pure maple syrup
1 teaspoon vanilla
salt

Combine milk powder with enough hot water to make 2 cups and stir to dissolve. Beat eggs with sweetening and gradually add hot milk. Stir in vanilla and a pinch of salt. Pour into 6 custard cups, place in a pan of hot water that comes halfway up the custard cups, and bake in a 325° oven about 50 minutes, until a knife blade inserted in center comes out clean but custard is still soft.

Cool to room temperature, then chill.

Makes 6 ½-cup servings, each furnishing 124 calories and 7 grams protein.

Peanut-Butter Custard: Prepare as for Baked Custard, using only 2 eggs and adding ½ cup peanut butter.

Creamy Cheese Custard: Prepare Baked Custard using only 2 eggs and 1½ cups milk and adding 1 cup cottage cheese. Puree the ingredients in blender until smooth, pour into custard cups, add a few raisins to each, and bake 40 to 50 minutes.

Baked Custard with Fruit: Slice ¾ pound peeled fruit into a pudding dish, pour in custard mixture, and bake as for Baked Custard.

Baked Custard with Fruit

weekend dairy dishes

CHEESE PUDDING

If you find it more convenient you can assemble the Cheese Pudding an evening in advance and refrigerate it until morning. You can then put it in the oven first thing and prepare the rest of breakfast while it bakes.

12 slices stale whole-grain bread
12 ounces cheese, sliced or grated
4 eggs
2 cups milk
1 teaspoon salt
½ teaspoon dry mustard powder
1 tablespoon butter

Arrange pieces of bread over the bottom of a greased, shallow 2-quart baking dish. Cover with cheese and repeat the layers, ending with bread. Beat eggs, add milk and seasonings. Pour over bread and cheese and dot top with butter. Bake in a 350° oven

20 minutes. Let set 5 minutes and serve.

Makes 6 servings, each furnishing 450 calories and 28 grams protein.

BAKED MATZOH BLINTZ

4 eggs
2 tablespoons milk
6 matzohs
1 pound cottage cheese
¼ teaspoon salt
1 tablespoon honey
½ teaspoon cinnamon
¼ cup raisins, optional

Beat 2 eggs with the 2 tablespoons milk. Break matzohs into quarters and soak in beaten eggs. Let stand while blending remaining eggs and seasonings into cottage cheese. Grease a 2-quart casserole and arrange alternate layers of matzoh and cheese, beginning and ending with the matzoh. Bake in a 350° oven 30 minutes, until brown.

Serve plain, with honey or your favorite syrup, or with stewed dried fruit.

Makes 4 servings, each furnishing 265 calories and 25 grams protein.

COTTAGE CHEESE FONDUE

A Cottage Cheese Fondue served with fresh fruits for dipping is a fine idea for company breakfasts and informal breakfast buffets in particular.

2 tablespoons butter
2 cups (1 pound) cottage cheese
3 tablespoons milk
2 tablespoons honey
1 teaspoon grated lemon rind
¼ teaspoon cinnamon
⅛ teaspoon nutmeg

Melt butter in saucepan. Add cottage cheese, ½ cup at a time, and stir over moderate heat until cheese becomes liquidy and curd separates out. After all the cheese is added and the mixture is soft, but lumpy, transfer to a blender container and process at low speed until smooth and creamy. Pour into a fondue pot and set over the warmer. Add the milk, honey and grated lemon rind and stir until smooth and warmed through. Sprinkle with cinnamon and nutmeg. To serve, skewer tangerine sections, whole strawberries, pineapple chunks and other fruits of your choice on fondue forks and coat with the creamy cheese mixture.

Makes approximately 2½ cups fondue; ½ cup furnishes 166 calories and 12.5 grams protein.

SOFT FRESH CHEESES—MAKING YOUR OWN

Yogurt and cottage cheese are the two most important breakfast cheeses. They are the lowest in fat and calories and the highest in nutritive value. Mild in flavor and creamy in texture, they are adaptable to sweet and savory service.

yogurt

Plain, unflavored yogurt is the best, for it leaves you the freedom to add flavor as you choose and control the amount of sweetening that goes into it. Both whole and part-skim-milk yogurts are available commercially, but many people find it simple and more economical to prepare their own. In this way you can produce all-skim-milk yogurt as well. Following are two variations on yogurt-making, practical with or without a heat-regulating yogurt-maker.

Though satisfactory yogurt can be made without any special equipment, the yogurt-maker makes the process much easier and encourages frequent use of yogurt, which, in the long run, saves money.

NONFAT DRY-MILK YOGURT

Nothing could be easier than this yogurt-making process using nonfat dry-milk powder and any commercial or homemade yogurt as a starter. Use of an extra concentration of milk powder makes the yogurt rich and sweet and much higher in protein than store-bought varieties.

1 cup nonfat dry-milk powder *or* 1-quart envelope
2½ cups warm water
¼ cup unflavored yogurt, commercial or homemade

Beat milk powder with water until all granules are dissolved. Pour into the container of yogurt-maker or heavy glass casserole and beat in yogurt. Cover and incubate according to directions on yogurt-maker or using one of the insulating techniques outlined below. Do not move the apparatus unnecessarily during this time or the yogurt will separate. A fresh, active starter will produce a thick, sweet yogurt within 3½ hours. Chill several hours before using.

Makes 3 cups yogurt; ½ cup furnishes 54 calories and 5.3 grams protein.

FRESH-MILK YOGURT

When you prepare yogurt from fresh, fluid milk, whole or skim, pasteurized or raw, you must first scald the milk to destroy any bacteria that might interfere with the growth of the yogurt culture. Next, you must be sure to let the milk cool sufficiently so that the heat does not kill the yogurt-forming bacteria in the starter.

1 quart skim or whole milk
½ cup nonfat dry-milk powder
¼ cup unflavored yogurt, commercial or homemade

Combine milk and dry-milk powder in saucepan, heat just below boiling, remove from heat, and cool to lukewarm, about 15 minutes. Add a small amount of lukewarm milk to unflavored yogurt and beat lightly with a fork or wire whisk. Add to remaining cooled milk and beat briefly. Pour into yogurt-maker or glass casserole, cover, and incubate according to directions on yogurt-maker or using one of the

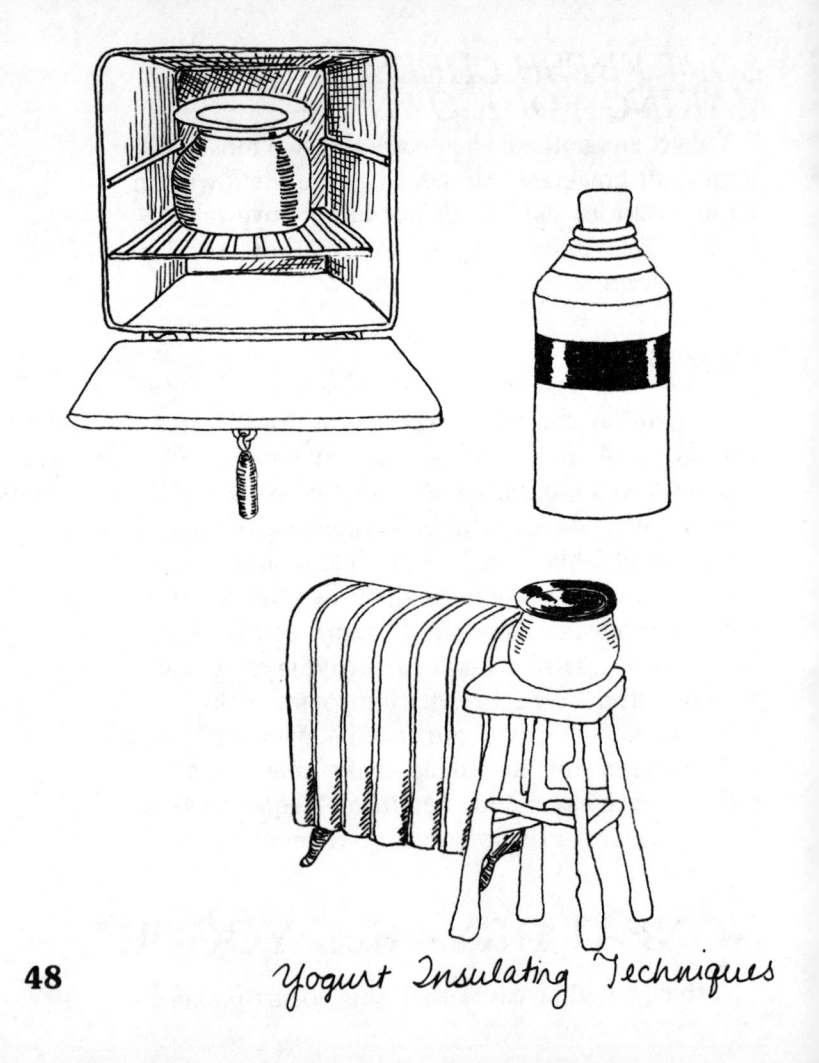

Yogurt Insulating Techniques

insulating techniques outlined below. Chill several hours before using.

Makes 1 quart yogurt; ½ cup furnishes 100 calories (65 calories if made with skim milk) and 6.3 grams protein.

Insulating techniques: If you do not have a yogurt-maker, try incubating the culture in an oven with a pilot light, a Thermos bottle, or an earthenware crock wrapped in a blanket or nestled in a styrofoam chest. In winter set the yogurt near a radiator or heating duct.

Note: Always save ¼ cup yogurt from the last culture to start the next batch. However, if you find it takes more than 3½ hours to set, begin again with a fresh commercial starter.

FLAVORED YOGURT

Flavoring should always be added after yogurt has set.

Plain yogurt can be quickly flavored with peanut butter; honey; fresh, canned, or softened dried fruit diced or pureed; your choice of jam; frozen juice concentrate; or anything else that strikes your fancy.

cottage cheese

Cottage cheese and its sister cheeses, pot and farmer cheese, are the first soft curds attained in cheesemaking. To produce other cheeses these curds may be drained, pressed, and fermented, but the delicate, soft, highly perishable curds that come from the initial separation of the milk should be included on your breakfast table without restraint.

The primary difference among cottage cheese, pot cheese, and farmer cheese is in the milk and cream. Traditional cottage cheese, generally marketed as "creamed cottage cheese," is made from skim milk to which cream and salt are added. Skim-milk or pot-style cottage cheese has no cream added. Pot cheese is a form of skim-milk cottage cheese with a larger, drier curd and neither salt nor cream added. Farmer cheese is similar to skim-milk cottage cheese, only pressed into block form.

Should you wish to make cottage cheese at home the process is uncomplicated, but unless you have access to large quantities of milk inexpensively it can be fairly costly. If you use nonfat dry milk the cost of homemade cottage cheese will approximate the cost of store-bought varieties, and thus you can eliminate the salt and addition of cream if you wish.

HOMEMADE COTTAGE CHEESE

Add 3 tablespoons lemon juice or cider vinegar to 1 quart skim milk or reconstituted nonfat dry milk and let stand 10 minutes to sour. Heat gently until soft curds form, about 15 minutes. Pour carefully into a cloth-lined sieve and let drain thoroughly. Break into fine pieces, season to taste, and, to make creamed cottage cheese, moisten with cream or yogurt.

One quart milk makes 4 ounces, or ½ cup, cottage cheese.

sour cream and cream cheese

Both these cheeses are relished for their appealing texture and slightly tart taste. But since they offer little in the way of nutritional benefits and are appallingly high in calories and saturated fat, they should be reserved for breakfasts that contain a good supply of protein from other sources. As alternatives to these fat-filled cheeses, yogurt and cottage cheese are invaluable. For example, yogurt can be used as a topping wherever you might use sour cream. In baking, yogurt, and also buttermilk, can replace sour cream with excellent results.

Another creamy topping, comparable to sour cream, can be made by pureeing cottage cheese in the

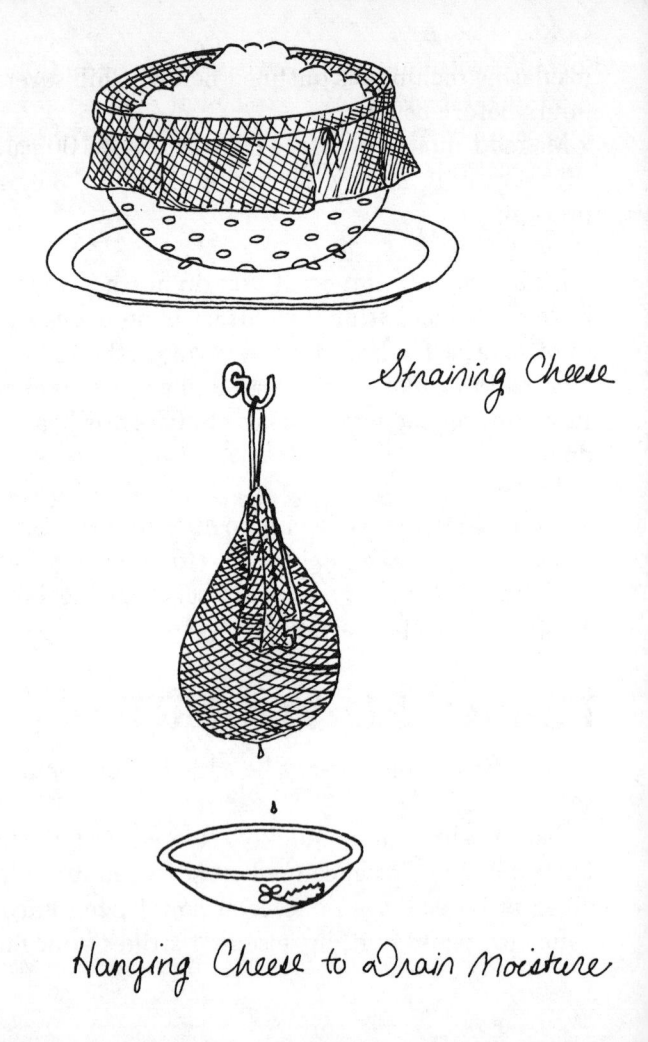

Straining Cheese

Hanging Cheese to Drain Moisture

blender with milk to make it as thick or as thin as you like. Or buttermilk can be left at room temperature until it separates, and then skimmed for a thick, sour-creamlike sauce. This can be used as is, or combined in a ratio of 2 or 3 to 1 with sour cream, and should be chilled before using.

To make a spread similar to cream cheese, cottage cheese can be mashed with a little milk, or at least used half and half with cream cheese. The following recipe for Arab Cheese can also replace cream cheese for a skim-milk cheese with the texture of the high-fat spread and a pleasing tart taste.

ARAB CHEESE (LABANI)

Hang unflavored yogurt in a linen bag or several layers of cheesecloth about 12 hours, until moisture has drained out and a firm, creamy cheese remains. Season to taste with salt, allowing about 1 teaspoon per 2 cups yogurt. Add caraway seeds or chives for variety.

2 cups yogurt makes 5 ounces Labani.

soy cheese

For those who do not use animal products and others who would like to vary their diet, a soy cheese, similar to cottage cheese, has excellent potential. It is prepared in the same manner as homemade cottage cheese and is a good deal more economical. This cheese is crumbly, like dry pot cheese, and tastes best combined with a fruit dish or used as a spread made by mashing it with honey to taste or yogurt and savory seasonings.

SOY CHEESE

1 cup full fat soy flour
1 cup cold water
2 cups boiling water
¼ cup fresh lemon juice

Combine soy flour and cold water to form a smooth paste. Stir into boiling water and cook 10 minutes. Remove from heat, add lemon juice and let stand to cool. When solids and liquid have separated, strain through a fine cheesecloth or linen napkin draped over a colander. Hang to drain several hours, then refrigerate.

Makes 12 ounces cheese; one ounce furnishes about 25 calories and 2.2 grams protein.

MORE HOMEMADE CHEESES

For the most part, with the wide variety of natural cheeses on the market, it is not advantageous to get into cheese-making at home unless you have some special love for the art. Sometimes, however, very little work will produce a cheese you would otherwise miss.

It is still possible to buy exotic pot-style cheeses, fresh or baked, flavored with vegetables, fruits, and nuts, in communities that have Old World dairies. Similar to these are the two cheeses that follow. They can be stored in the refrigerator for about a week and are wonderful in the morning sliced thinly on toast or crackers.

QUICK KOCHKAESE (COOKED CHEESE)

A dense, caraway-flavored farmer cheese based on an old German favorite.

2 cups (1 pound) cottage cheese
2 eggs
1 quart skim milk
1 rounded teaspoon caraway seeds
1 teaspoon salt
2 tablespoons butter, optional

Combine cottage cheese with eggs, beating until smooth. Bring milk to boil; add caraway seeds, salt, and the egg-cottage cheese mixture. For a richer cheese, add the butter.

Bring the mixture to a slow boil and cook until liquid and solids separate and the mixture is chunky. Strain through a linen napkin or several layers of cheesecloth draped over a colander. Gather cloth into a bag and hang several hours until firm. Refrigerate. Slice thin to serve.

Makes 14.5 ounces; one ounce furnishes 96 calories and 8.8 grams protein.

RUSSIAN CHEESE

A richer version of this cheese is served as dessert, but this lightly sweetened, compact cheese is well suited to breakfast. It makes a fine meal when served with fresh fruit.

1 pound cottage cheese
¼ cup yogurt
2 tablespoons softened butter
1 egg
3 tablespoons honey
1 teaspoon grated lemon peel
¼ cup finely chopped almonds
¼ cup chopped raisins

Force cottage cheese through a fine sieve. Add yogurt, butter, egg and honey and beat smooth. Stir in remaining ingredients. Line a sieve or clay flowerpot that is 6 to 8 inches deep with several layers of cheesecloth or a linen napkin. Pack in cheese, cover, and place a weight on top to press out all moisture. Let stand at room temperature 24 hours, unmold, and refrigerate until serving.

Makes 8 servings, each furnishing 162 calories and 9.8 grams protein.

the value of cheese

	Amount	Calories	Protein
Cheddar Cheese	1 ounce	112	7
Edam	1 ounce	87	7.7
Swiss	1 ounce	104	7.7
Cottage cheese, creamed	1 ounce	30	3.9
	½ cup	120	16
Pot cheese	1 ounce	25	4.9
	½ cup	100	20
Cream cheese	1 ounce (2 Tbs)	105	2.2
Yogurt, made from partially skim milk	½ cup	61	4.2
Yogurt, made from whole milk	½ cup	75	3.6

THE EGGERY

No one food typifies breakfast more than the egg. To many, the egg *is* breakfast.

Eggs are one of our most nutritious foods and are especially important for growth. Just one large egg furnishes 7 grams of excellent-quality protein and a mere 88 calories. A little more than half the protein is in the white; the remainder of the protein, the fat, the vitamin A, the B vitamins, and the minerals are concentrated in the yolk. Egg yolks also contain rich supplies of lecithin and are one of the only food sources of vitamin D. Unfortunately, egg yolks also contain a higher proportion of dietary cholesterol than almost any other food (275 mg. per large egg) and, in view of the possible correlation of some forms of heart disease with elevated levels of cholesterol in the blood, the Inter-Society Commission for Heart Disorders Resources suggests that Americans limit daily cholesterol intake to 300 mg. This puts a heavy embargo on egg intake. On the other hand, many highly renowned scientists point out that most of the cholesterol in the blood does not come from food but is manufactured by the body, and the healthy individual has body mechanisms designed to help control the balance of blood cholesterol. It is asserted that with a proper diet—high in certain B vitamins (available in whole grains), lecithin, and vitamin C—a normal individual can eat a reasonable amount of egg without affecting blood cholesterol. Reasonable, in this case, is considered to be seven eggs per week, including those eaten alone and those used in prepared foods.

One way to reduce egg intake is to spread the egg out so that one egg, used in combination with cheese, milk, or grains, can feed one to two people—a method common to such foods as pancakes, French toast, breakfast shakes, and many of the high-protein recipes throughout this book.

The unique egg flavor and texture, however, can be achieved only when the egg itself is the predominant ingredient in the recipe, and consequently most egg fanciers still indulge in an "egg breakfast," although perhaps less frequently than they would have a few years ago.

FRIED, SCRAMBLED, BOILED, BAKED, POACHED, SHIRRED, OMELETED, SOUFFLEED

Although eggs can be varied in infinite ways, there are only a few basic methods for cooking them.

The critical factor in egg cookery is the time-temperature balance. The objective is to coagulate the egg protein without toughening it. If low temperatures are used, timing need not be precise; but if high heat is employed, timing must be controlled or the eggs will be rubbery and unpalatable and difficult to digest.

EGGS IN THE SHELL

Many people are satisfied to let eggs bump around in rapidly boiling water, so all too often "boiled" eggs are thought to be a most unpleasant food. For mild-flavored eggs with tender whites and delicate yolks, they should be cooked just below the boiling point.

HARD-COOKED EGGS

Place eggs in pot with enough water to cover completely and bring to boil. When actively boiling, cover tightly, and remove from heat. Let stand 20 minutes, then cool quickly under cold running water. Peel for immediate eating or refrigerate in the shell for future use.

MEDIUM-COOKED (OR 4-MINUTE) EGGS

For eggs with a soft-cooked white and a runny yolk, slip eggs into boiling water to cover, reduce heat, and simmer gently 4 to 4½ minutes. For a yolk that is soft but set, simmer 5 minutes.

SOFT-COOKED (OR 3-MINUTE) EGGS

To soft-cook eggs, slip eggs into boiling water to cover, reduce heat, and simmer 3 to 3½ minutes.

Note: Since the shell retains the heat, all eggs cooked in the shell should be cooled under cold running water or opened immediately to prevent further cooking.

the joys of soft-cooked eggs

Traditionally, eggs in the shell are placed in "egg cups" specially designed to hold the egg upright. The top is whacked off with a knife or spoon, and the egg

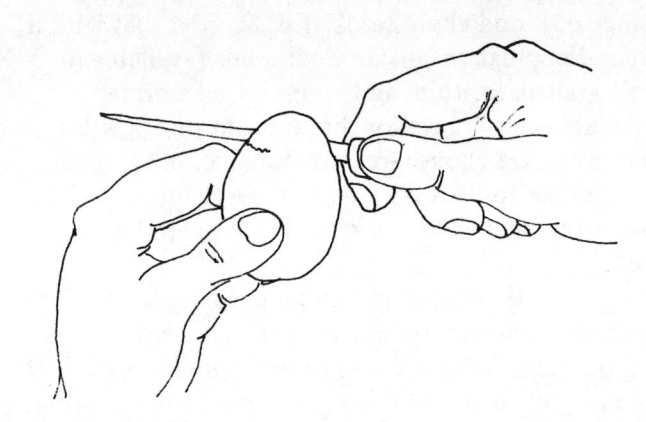

Cutting the tip off a soft-cooked egg.

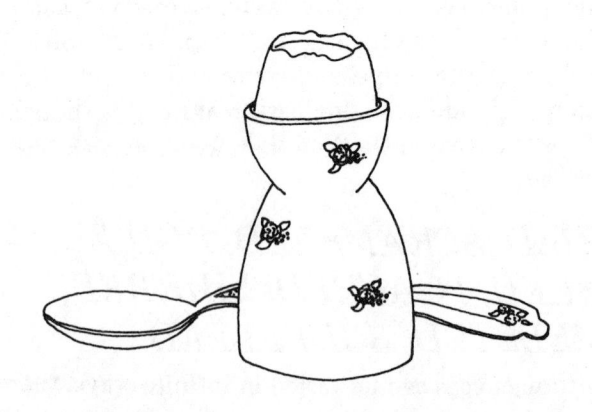

is eaten out of the shell with a spoon or by dunking strips of bread or toast. (Dunkers should try Cheese Sticks; see Index.)

Three- and Four- Minute Eggs can also be scooped out of the shell onto toast or muffins or into a cup. In the latter case scatter pieces of bread or toast on top of the egg to soak up the yellow.

the joys of hard-cooked eggs

EGG SALADS

In making hard-cooked eggs into salad, moisten the mixture with mayonnaise, avocado, or yogurt, and add any of the following as you like:

- wheat germ
- bran
- ground nuts
- sesame seeds
- olives
- chopped celery
- minced onion
- sprouts
- chopped green or red pepper
- caraway seeds
- mushrooms

GOLDEN EGGS

Hard-cooked eggs are also popular served in a sauce, as in this brunch favorite.

1 tablespoon butter
½ tablespoon cornstarch or potato starch
1 cup milk
4 hard-cooked eggs
salt, pepper, paprika

Melt butter over low heat. Stir in cornstarch to form a smooth paste. Gradually add milk, stirring until smooth, and cook, stirring occasionally, until mixture thickens and begins to boil. Remove from heat, peel and slice eggs and add to sauce. Season to taste and return to heat for about 3 minutes until warmed through. Serve on toast, toasted muffin halves or potatoes.

Makes 4 servings, each furnishing 156 calories and 9 grams protein.

POACHING EGGS

Once broken open, eggs can be cooked in either liquid or in fat. The method of cooking eggs in simmering liquid is called poaching and the resulting dish is similar in flavor and consistency to eggs cooked in the shell. Only the freshest eggs, with upstanding yolks and compact whites, can be successfully prepared in this manner. A little salt (½ teaspoon per quart of water) or vinegar (1 tablespoon per quart of water), added to the poaching liquid, will help the egg keep its shape. The vinegar, however, may impart an undesirable flavor.

POACHED EGGS

Fill a shallow cooking vessel (a large straight-sided skillet, for example) with water to a depth of 1½ inches. Bring liquid to boil, break eggs into a cup or ladle, and, one at a time, slip them into the water. It is essential that the yolk stay intact. *Regulate heat so water is just below boiling.* As the egg cooks, carefully spoon a little of the hot liquid over the top surface, and in two or three minutes, when the white has become opaque and enveloped the yolk, remove the egg carefully with a perforated spoon.

Poached eggs are generally served on toast but are just as good on English muffins or corn muffins that have been split and toasted. Poached eggs also make a tasty topping for pureed beans, brown rice, cracked wheat, cornmeal mush, or other grains.

Vary the Medium: One reason poaching is preferred to cooking in the shell is the opportunity it affords to introduce additional flavor to the egg. This is done by varying the poaching medium, choosing, for example, milk, a thin white sauce, or tomato sauce rather than water. This liquid is then served along with the egg; you can further enhance the dish by cooking vegetables into the sauce or melting a slice of cheese over the egg. These principles are demonstrated in Spanish Eggs.

SPANISH EGGS

1 small can (1⅔ cup) tomatoes
½ cup diced onion
½ cup diced green pepper
½ slice whole-wheat bread
salt and pepper
4 eggs
Cheddar cheese

Empty canned tomatoes into a 10-inch skillet. Add onion and green pepper, bring to boil and simmer gently 10 minutes. Crumble in the whole-wheat bread and season to taste with salt and pepper. When just boiling slip in the eggs, breaking them first carefully into a ladle or small shallow cup, and poach until set, about 5 minutes. When just about ready, sprinkle with Cheddar cheese and cover to finish cooking.

Serve on toast or rice.

Plan on 1 egg for small eaters, 2 eggs for big eaters, and if necessary double the recipe and prepare in a 12-inch skillet.

BAKING EGGS

Baking eggs holds several advantages over other methods of egg cookery. Eggs cook quickly in the oven and use almost no fat. What is particularly nice is that they need little attention, leaving you free to prepare the rest of your breakfast. Since baked eggs are prepared in individual orders they are convenient to make even when breakfast is served in shifts; they can also be adapted to personal preferences.

BAKED EGGS

Rub the surface of custard cups or other small heatproof casseroles lightly with butter or oil. Slip in the eggs, allowing one or two eggs per baking dish. Bake in a 325° oven 8 to 10 minutes, depending on how well cooked you want them. Since the eggs are served right in the hot casserole they will continue to cook even after removal from the oven, so take them from the heat when slightly underdone.

Salt at the table.

For additional flavor a tablespoon or two of minced cooked meat, grain, vegetables, or beans can be placed as a cushion underneath the eggs, and cheese can be grated on top to melt in the oven. A hollowed-out roll, or Toast Cups (see Index), can serve as an edible baking dish in place of custard cups.

For family service, a single baking dish can be employed and the eggs dished out gingerly onto serving plates. Choose an 8-inch baking dish for 4 eggs, a 9-inch dish for 6 eggs, and a 9 by 13-inch dish for 8 to 12 eggs. Baking time increases with the number of eggs. For multiple servings allow 10 to 15 minutes baking time.

BAKED EGGS WITH CHEESE

2 Spanish onions, minced
2 tablespoons oil
3 cups grated cheese
8 to 12 eggs
salt and pepper
2 tablespoons butter
yogurt, optional

Saute onion in oil until limp, about 5 minutes. Spread over bottom of oiled 9 by 13-inch baking pan. Sprinkle with half the cheese, make slight depressions in the cheese at intervals, and carefully slip in the eggs. Season. Dot with butter, cover thickly with remaining cheese, and bake in a 325° oven 10 to 15 minutes. Spoon onto serving plates and top with yogurt, if desired.

Makes 8 servings. When made with 8 eggs, each serving furnishes 325 calories and 18 grams protein; with 12 eggs each serving furnishes 370 calories and 22 grams protein.

FRYING EGGS: SUNNY SIDE UP, OR OVER EASY

The caloric value of eggs is greatly elevated by the addition of fat, which, for fried eggs, should be plentiful enough so that the egg almost swims in it. If you are sparing, one tablespoon of fat will be sufficient in a small one-or two-egg pan, but for a 10-inch skillet up to three tablespoons of fat will be needed. Overbrowned fried eggs are highly indigestible.

FRIED EGGS

Heat oil, butter, or a combination in a skillet to cover generously. When hot, add eggs and, when almost done to your liking, quickly turn "over easy" if you wish to cook any remaining loose egg. Novice egg flippers should slip eggs onto a plate and flip eggs back into pan. Drain off fat to serve.

MARY JANES

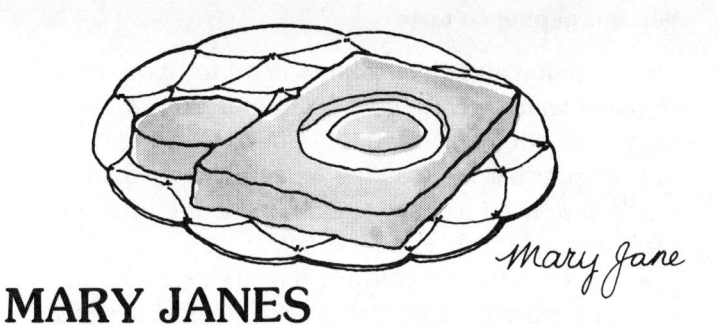

With a shot glass or cookie cutter, cut a small hole in the center of a slice of whole-grain bread. Brown the bread lightly on one side in hot fat, turn the bread over, and break an egg into the center hole. Cook until yolk begins to set on the bottom, flip, and cook briefly to set. Don't forget to saute the small round of bread that has been removed—the "dunky" —along with the egg. Use it to sop up the yolk.

SCRAMBLING EGGS

The best scrambled eggs, whether dry or loose, are cooked over very gentle heat. The amount of fat needed will depend on your frying pan. Generally one tablespoon of fat is needed for every two eggs, but by using a well-seasoned skillet (see Omelets) you can easily reduce the fat by half.

SCRAMBLED EGGS

Break desired number of eggs into a bowl and add 1 tablespoon water or milk for every 2 eggs. Beat lightly and season with salt and pepper. Heat oil or butter in skillet, turning so as to grease sides, add eggs, and reduce heat to medium-low. When eggs begin to set on bottom, stir by drawing a spoon from edge of eggs across the pan to form large, soft curds. Eggs can be made as soft or dry as you like by extending the cooking time, but they will always remain tender and mild tasting if you keep the heat low.

For more protein a few spoonfuls of wheat germ or nonfat dry-milk powder can be beaten into the eggs before scrambling without altering the flavor. Any number of taste changes can be effected by adding onion, mushrooms, peppers, or other diced vegetables, caraway seeds, bits of meat or fish, beans, or cheese. Meat should be precooked and vegetables sauteed lightly in the pan before adding the eggs. Scrambled egg favorites include:

SCRAMBLED EGGS AND COTTAGE CHEESE

4 scallions, minced
1 tablespoon oil
1 tablespoon butter
½ cup cottage cheese
8 eggs

Saute scallions briefly in oil. Add butter and, when it has melted, stir in cottage cheese until creamy. Beat eggs lightly, season to taste, and pour into hot pan. Lower heat and cook, stirring as egg sets, until eggs are soft, but set.

Makes 4 servings, each furnishing 270 calories and 18 grams protein; or 6 servings, each furnishing 180 calories and 12 grams protein.

SCRAMBLED EGGS WITH EVERYTHING

1 medium onion
¼ cup chopped green pepper
1½ tablespoons oil
1 cup sliced fresh mushrooms
1½ tablespoons butter
8 eggs
1 chopped tomato
½ cup diced cheese
2 tablespoons wheat germ
salt and pepper to taste

Saute onion and green pepper in oil until onion is limp and transparent, about 5 minutes. Add mushrooms and cook 2 to 3 minutes longer. Add butter and, when it has melted, add remaining ingredients which have been beaten together and cook over low heat, stirring as for scrambled eggs.

Makes 4 servings, each furnishing 315 calories and 21 grams protein; or 6 servings, each furnishing 210 calories and 14 grams protein.

MATZOH SCRAMBLE

4 eggs
¼ cup milk
½ teaspoon salt
4 matzohs, whole wheat, plain, or onion
1 medium onion, diced
2 tablespoons oil

Beat eggs with milk and salt. Crumble in matzoh and let stand while browning onion in oil. When onion is lightly browned, add egg mixture and cook, stirring quickly with a fork.

If desired, omit onion and scramble softened matzoh mixture in 1 tablespoon melted butter. Serve with honey.

Makes 2 servings, each furnishing 495 calories and 20 grams protein; or 3 servings, each furnishing 330 calories and 13 grams protein.

SWEET SCRAMBLED RICE

Like having dessert for breakfast.

2 cups cooked brown rice
4 eggs, lightly beaten
¼ cup milk
¼ cup raisins
¼ cup sunflower seeds
½ teaspoon salt
½ teaspoon cinnamon
1 tablespoon butter

Combine all ingredients except butter. Melt butter in skillet and add egg mixture. Let brown over medium heat. Then mix quickly with a spoon until egg is completely set.

Makes 4 servings, each furnishing 222 calories and 10 grams protein.

SCRAMBLED EGGS AND BRAINS

Sounds awful but tastes good; a meal that's packed with protein and B vitamins.

2 sets calves' brains
boiling water
whole-wheat flour
2 tablespoons oil
6 eggs
3 tablespoons milk
salt and pepper

Cover brains with boiling water, cover, and let stand 5 minutes. Drain, remove membrane, and cut into cubes ½ inch thick. Roll in whole-wheat flour and saute in oil until lightly browned. Beat eggs with milk and salt and pepper to taste and pour over brains in skillet. Lower heat and cook until eggs are just set. Stir with a fork to break into small pieces and serve on toast.

Makes 6 servings, each furnishing 194 calories and 12 grams protein.

BAUERNFRÜHSTUCK (FARMER'S BREAKFAST)

A hearty German breakfast that demands some time but makes a wonderful weekend special.

vegetable oil
1 to 2 onions, thinly sliced
3 large potatoes, boiled, unpeeled and thinly sliced
½ green pepper, diced
½ cup cooked ham, diced (optional)
salt and pepper
8 eggs, beaten

Heat oil to cover surface of large skillet. Add onions and cook until wilted. Add potatoes and continue to cook over moderate heat, allowing potatoes to brown gently (about 25 minutes). Add green pepper, plus ham if desired, and season liberally with salt and pepper. Lower heat, pour eggs over vegetables, and mix with large spoon until eggs are completely set.

Makes 4 servings, each furnishing 301 calories (372 with ham) and 16 grams protein (24 with ham); or 6 servings, each furnishing 200 calories (248 with ham) and 11 grams protein (16 with ham).

OMELETS

People often shy away from omelet preparation. With the right cooking utensil and a bit of practice, however, it is an easy art to master. Reserve a special pan just for egg-making, preferably one with sloped sides and a thick bottom. If you wish you can *season* the pan, a technique that creates a supersmooth, almost permanent coating that will endure if you clean the pan only with a mild soap and a gentle pad; never use steel wool or harsh abrasives. When properly seasoned the pan will need only a minimum of fat.

To season a frying pan: Cover the surface with one tablespoon peanut or corn oil. Heat until a vapor rises. Pour off the oil and rinse immediately under cold water. Wipe dry and repeat. Cast-iron skillets should be dried over low heat and rubbed lightly with oil to prevent rusting.

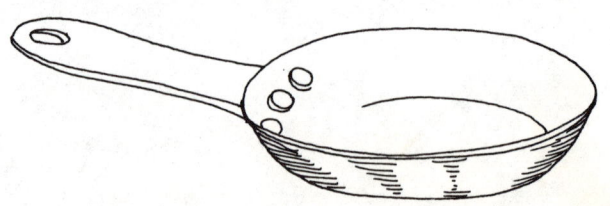

Omelet Pan with Gently Sloping Sides

Although there are several different schools of omelet making, all have the same basic techniques in common:

* Though the eggs should be mixed thoroughly, they should never be beaten with a rotary beater, an electric mixer, or a blender.
* Allow 1 to 2 eggs per serving and do not prepare more than 6 eggs at a time in one omelet pan. A successful omelet is impossible in a pan that is too full.
* The smaller the omelet the easier it will be to handle, so practice with individual omelets made in a 7-inch pan. A 3-egg omelet, made in a 7- or 8-inch pan, will serve two. A 6-egg omelet can be accommodated in a 10-inch skillet and will serve three to four.
* Do not overdo the amount of fat. Use just enough to coat the pan evenly, or about one tablespoon for every four eggs.
* The pan must be good and hot, with the fat just sizzling, before receiving the eggs. You may continue to cook the omelet quickly over high heat (but then you must tend it carefully) or lower the heat and proceed gently.
* Serve the omelet as soon as it has set.

CLASSIC FRENCH OMELETS

Beat eggs lightly with salt and pepper, allowing 1 to 2 per person. Melt 1 tablespoon butter (or oil) in pan for every 4 eggs. When fat begins to sizzle add the beaten eggs, and, as the omelet begins to set, lift edge gently and tilt the pan so that the uncooked egg can run underneath, allowing the omelet to cook in layers. Repeat two or three times if necessary. When the omelet is no longer liquidy, shake the pan to loosen omelet, fold in half, and slide onto serving plate. Any filling should be added just before folding.

If the pan is sufficiently heated, the entire process will take only 1 to 2 minutes, the eggs will remain soft, and the bottom will still be quite yellow.

Wire Whisk

AMERICAN OMELETS

Melt fat in pan. Add beaten, seasoned eggs to hot fat as for French Omelets. Stir once and cook, keeping heat fairly high, until bottom is set and lightly browned. Flip over or slip onto a plate, invert back into pan, and brown the other side. Vegetables can be sauteed in the pan before adding the eggs and will become set in the omelet. Sliced or grated cheese can be sprinkled on the top cooked surface while the bottom is browning. Cover pan to melt cheese.

FLUFFY OMELETS

Separate the eggs. Beat the yolks with seasonings and whip the whites until soft peaks form. Fold the whites gently into the yolks, pour into pan which has been heated with the fat, and cook until bottom is set. To finish cooking place pan under broiler or in a 400° oven for about 5 minutes, until puffed.

omelet fillings

To fill an omelet use any of these alone or in fanciful combination. Plan to add ¼ to ½ cup filling per 3- or 4-egg omelet.

grated cheese
jam or jelly
chopped cooked chicken liver
cooked vegetables, diced or pureed
applesauce
cottage cheese
sliced peaches
drained crushed pineapple
cooked rice, kasha, or cracked wheat
mashed white or sweet potato
sweetened berries

In addition to salt and pepper, minced chives, scallions, caraway seeds, and parsley, among others, can be used in seasoning.

CLEAN-UP

To wash dishes and silverware that are coated with egg, soak them first in *cold* water. Egg yolk tends to tarnish silverware and should be washed or soaked off as soon as possible.

MEAT, FISH, AND EVEN POULTRY FOR BREAKFAST

Although North Americans comprise only 7 percent of the world population, they consume 30 percent of the supply of animal protein. The United States Department of Agriculture estimates that the average American consumes 10 to 12 percent more protein than he can use, including 212 pounds of meat and poultry per person yearly—by far the largest chunk of the family food budget.

There is no question that the trio of meat, poultry, and fish is overemphasized in our diets, and at precisely the wrong time of day, for it is in the morning, when we are trying to get going, that a good supply of protein, fat, and calories is important—not in the evening when we are soon to put our bodies to rest. High concentrations of fat and protein are taxing to the digestive system, particularly when it is in a prone position. When our energies are high, however, with physical and mental stimulation, blood circulates freely through our system and the digestive apparatus can handle food much more effectively.

Thus, it appears, if you plan to eat meat, fish, and poultry it would be more sensible to incorporate them into the breakfast menu and forgo them at dinner.

Meat, fish, and poultry are all abundant in protein. They also help us meet the daily requirement for iron and B vitamins. Although meat is often touted as "nonfattening," when you consider how much meat you are likely to consume in a sitting this may not necessarily be so. The Table of Meat and Fish Values at the end of this chapter presents calorie, protein, and fat content of 3½ ounces of raw meat. Though, at breakfast time, 3½ ounces will probably fill you up (and provide anywhere from 10 to 28 grams of protein), most people consider twice this amount an ample dinner portion.

FISH

On a pound-for-pound basis, fish is higher in protein and lower in fat than most other animal foods. Fish has the added advantage of being quickly and easily prepared and mild enough in taste to be accommodated to the breakfast table.

prepared fish and other breakfast specialties

Anyone who has been to England has no doubt encountered kippers for breakfast, a strong-smelling form of herring, salted and smoked. Canned cooked kippers are widely available; fresh kippers cooked in the following manner are a superb breakfast dish served plain or with eggs.

FRESH-COOKED KIPPERS

Split fish, remove backbone, then fold back into shape. Brush with oil and grill on each side about 3 minutes; or saute in a hot frying pan that has been lightly covered with oil or butter. Serve topped with a pat of butter or a wedge of lemon.

Allow one to two kippers, or ½ pound, per serving.

KIPPERS ON PUMPERNICKEL

The classic combination according to some.

Prepare kippers as above and serve with scrambled eggs and pumpernickel.

For those on a low-salt diet, bloaters, which are smoke-cured herrings without the salt, can be cooked just like kippers, but since they are highly perishable they must be very fresh to be worthwhile.

Finnan Haddie, or lightly salted and smoked haddock, is a Scottish import. It is quick to prepare in the following ways:

BROILED FINNAN HADDIE

Rub fish with oil or melted butter and broil on each side about 5 minutes. Serve with butter and lemon.

POACHED FINNAN HADDIE

Cut skinned, boned fish into several manageable pieces. Heat milk to a depth of 1 inch in skillet and, when just about to boil, add fish, cover, and simmer gently 10 to 15 minutes. Season to taste with salt, pepper, and nutmeg, and spoon over toast, milk and all.

Among the other prepared fish varieties that you can introduce at breakfast time, smoked sturgeon, whitefish, sable, and chubs, lox (salt-cured salmon), Nova Scotia salmon (smoked salmon), pickled herring, and sardines need no special preparation; just a nice hunk of black bread or a fresh bagel.

more fish specialties
PICKLED FRESH FISH

Cut 2 pounds boned raw fish into bite-size pieces and arrange in a large glass or pottery casserole. Cover surface with 1 thinly sliced lemon and 1 thinly sliced onion. Pour over the marinade (below) and, when cool, cover tightly and refrigerate. The fish will be ready to serve in 24 to 48 hours and will keep in the refrigerator for several weeks.

Marinade:

Enough for two pounds carp, cod, haddock, mackerel, salmon, or raw herring.

1 cup cider vinegar
2 tablespoons honey
¼ cup water
1 teaspoon salt
2 bay leaves

2 cloves garlic or 12 peppercorns

Combine ingredients and boil 3 minutes.

Serve Pickled Fish with black bread and cream cheese. To make Pickled Fish in Cream Sauce add yogurt or sour cream at serving time.

SALMON SAUSAGE CAKES

2 cups canned salmon
  (the cheapest variety available)
½ cup wheat germ
2 eggs, lightly beaten
¾ teaspoon salt
¼ teaspoon paprika
whole-wheat flour
oil for cooking

Combine salmon, wheat germ, eggs, and seasoning. Form into 8 patties. Dredge with whole-wheat flour. Heat oil to cover surface of skillet or griddle and saute the fish cakes until browned, 3 to 5 minutes per side.

FISH SAUSAGE CAKES

Prepare as for Salmon Sausage Cakes, using cooked fish of your choice. A good way to use leftovers.

FISH PANCAKES

Don't let the name deter you. These pancakes are very tender, with an appealing, creamy interior. Makes great use of leftover fish.

2 cups cooked fish (any kind), flaked
¾ cup milk
3 tablespoons oil
¼ cup whole-wheat flour
¼ cup wheat germ
1 egg
1 teaspoon salt
½ teaspoon cinnamon, optional

Puree fish with milk in blender to consistency of mashed potatoes. Turn into bowl and beat in remaining ingredients with a fork until smooth. Heat enough oil to cover surface of griddle or large skillet and, when hot, drop on fish batter by soupspoonfuls. Brown on bottom and, when spatula slides under easily without breaking the cake and mixture appears to be setting on top, turn and brown the other side. Do not rush. Cooking time will be about 10 minutes in all. Serve hot, at room temperature, or cold; plain or with mayonnaise.

Makes 16 2-inch cakes, or 4 servings.

FISH HASH

When made with an inexpensive variety such as cod or haddock, Fish Hash is economical as well as good tasting. Only minutes to prepare.

1 pound white-fleshed fish, filleted
4 tablespoons fresh bread crumbs
2 tablespoons oil
1 teaspoon salt
½ teaspoon sugar
dash of pepper
¼ cup yogurt

Cut fish fillets into bite-size pieces. Saute fish and bread crumbs in oil, stirring until fish separates easily into flakes. This will take, at the most, 10 minutes. Add seasonings, remove from heat and stir in yogurt. Serve plain or on toast.
Makes 4 breakfast servings.

SARDINE SPREAD

1 can (about 3¾ ounces) sardines
2 tablespoons cottage cheese
2 teaspoons lemon juice
¼ teaspoon mustard

Mash together all ingredients and spread on crackers or toast. Serve cold, or better still, broil quickly, about 1 minute, to heat through.
Makes about ½ cup spread; enough for 8 crackers or 2 pieces of toast.

"GOTHIC" BRUNCH

Gets rave reviews served over hot biscuits, English muffins, or small baked potatoes.

2 cups canned salmon (1 pound)
skim milk
2 tablespoons chopped onion
2 tablespoons oil
2 tablespoons cornstarch
pepper
1½ cups cottage cheese

Drain liquid from salmon and add enough milk to it to equal 1 cup. Saute onion in oil until tender and transparent. Remove from heat and, using a wire whisk, stir in cornstarch to make a smooth paste. Add liquid and stir over moderate heat until thickened, 5 to 10 minutes. Season with pepper, stir in cottage cheese, and heat, stirring gently, until cheese melts. Add salmon, stir, warm, and serve immediately.
Makes 4 servings.

basic fish cookery

In addition to the preceding breakfast fish specialties, you shouldn't discount just plain fish for breakfast.

Fish that is fresh need not be "fishy" in flavor or smell. Avoid overcooking and it will be tender; become overzealous and it will be tough and dry. To test for doneness, when fish becomes opaque probe flesh gently with a fork; if it separates readily from the bone or peels off in flakes it is ready to be eaten. A large fillet can be pressed gently as you would test a cake; if fingermarks remain, more time is needed; as soon as the flesh bounces back it is sufficiently cooked.

The following fish are well suited to all the basic methods of quick fish cookery outlined below:

cod	flounder	haddock
halibut	perch	pike
salmon	sole	trout
turbot	scrod	

For an ample breakfast portion figure ¾ pound whole dressed fish per person, ½ pound fish steaks, or ⅓ pound fillets.

steaming

Steaming permits you to cook fish with no fat at all and is the most effective way to preserve the natural fish flavor. Steaming can be done effectively with any adjustable vegetable steamer.

Arrange fish in a single layer on steamer and place over boiling water in a pot with a tight cover. Do not let water come in contact with the fish. If fish is less than one inch thick, steam 4 to 5 minutes. Fish one to two inches thick needs 8 to 10 minutes' steaming. To steam whole fish allot 10 minutes per pound.

Steaming Fish

pan frying

Use this method for fillets, steaks, or small whole fish.

Dry surface, dip in beaten egg or milk, and coat with seasoned wheat germ, whole-wheat or rye flour, or cornmeal, used separately or in combination. For extra flavor and protein add finely ground almonds, peanuts, or sunflower seeds to the flour. Heat oil to cover surface of skillet and, when it begins to sizzle, brown fish quickly on both sides, allowing 3 to 5 minutes per side for fillets and 4 to 6 minutes per side for larger, thick pieces.

Pan Frying Fish

Fish Steaks on a Broiling Rack

grilling

Grilling (or broiling) requires less fat than pan frying and is also suitable for steaks, fillets, and small whole fish.

Dry surface and place fish skin side down on a rack with a drip pan beneath. Brush with oil or melted butter and season with salt, pepper, and other seasonings to taste. Paprika will enhance browning. If fish is whole, score gashes across the surface so skin does not burst and heat can penetrate interior before the surface dries out. Broil at medium temperature, or 3 to 4 inches from heat, allowing 7 to 8 minutes for thin fillets, 8 to 12 minutes for larger pieces, and 10 to 15 minutes if fish is more than ½-inch thick. Turn only if fish falls into this last category.

baking

This last method is less convenient for breakfast but is suitable for brunch or mornings when the oven is already in use.

Season fish and place in greased baking dish. Add a shallow layer of milk, cover, and bake in a 375° oven 10 to 20 minutes, or allow 10 minutes per pound.

Cooked fish can be garnished in the traditional manner with lemon wedges or, perhaps even better for breakfast, with orange or grapefruit sections.

MEAT AND POULTRY: DINING FOR BREAKFAST

In September 1973, *The New York Times* related the story of a family of nine with a unique approach to breakfast. "At 6:50 A.M., an Entire Family Sits Down to Dinner Together," the caption proclaimed. The "dinner" on that September morning included meat loaf, baked potatoes, and broccoli, but on other mornings might just as likely be "roast chicken, spaghetti, and even lamb curry."

Though it is a rare household indeed that is willing to rise at 6 A.M. just to dine together, the principle of having such a hearty meal at the start of the day can be followed without sacrificing sleep.

In choosing a meat dish for breakfast, try to plan leftovers of beef, veal, lamb, pork, and poultry when cooking other meals. You can also turn your attention to meat products that require little cooking. Many of the variety cuts, like liver, kidneys, brains, and sweetbreads, can be cooked in less than 20 minutes; in addition they are a rich source of B vitamins, iron, and protein.

If you can tempt your family with a roast in the morning, by all means try the Overnight Roast, which cooks by itself in the oven from bedtime to breakfast.

bacon

Bacon is perhaps America's favorite breakfast meat and, along with sausage, one of the few that is consistently chosen for breakfast service. Most commercially sold bacon, however, is only aroma and taste. As the Table of Meat Values indicates, it is a poor source of protein, with a calorie:protein ratio of 72:1. One pound does not go very far, for as much as half the weight may cook out in the form of fat. Most significantly, it is cured not by the traditional smoking process but with the aid of curing chemicals, among them sodium nitrite, a chemical salt that may react in the body to form cancer-causing agents.

Should you still continue to eat bacon, however, you might as well prepare it in the most efficient manner. Remember, raw bacon can be stored in the refrigerator up to one week before risking rancidity.

MAKING BACON

Start bacon in a cold pan and cook slowly over very low heat. (Rubbing the bacon with ice will help prevent curling.) As the bacon cooks, the slices can be separated. Pour off fat as it accumulates. Turn the bacon often.

As an alternate method, bacon can be broiled on a

rack set over a drip pan and placed 4 inches from the source of heat. Broil 2 or 3 minutes per side, draining off excess fat to prevent a flash fire.

canadian bacon

Unlike American-style bacon, which comes from the fatty regions along the sides and back of the pig, Canadian bacon is made from boned pork loins. Though considered quite a luxury because of its cost, this bacon has considerably less fat than American bacon and goes a lot further in service.

Canadian bacon can be sliced ⅛ to ¼ inch thick and cooked like other bacon by pan frying or broiling. Alternately, the whole roast can be prepared in a 350° oven, allowing 25 minutes per pound, or cooking to an internal temperature of 160° F.

variety meats

Variety meats—which include liver, kidneys, sweetbreads, heart, and brains—are, surprisingly enough, easily accepted at breakfast, where they can be disguised in a batter of egg and flour or a rich sauce. Serve variety meats on toast or as an accompaniment to eggs or pancakes.

CRUNCHY SWEETBREADS AND BRAINS

Soak sweetbreads and/or brains in cold water, rinse, and remove membrane. Steam over boiling water in a vegetable steamer 10 minutes. Dice into small pieces, dredge with seasoned whole-wheat flour, and broil or saute in hot fat 3 to 5 minutes per side.

BRAIN AND SWEETBREAD FRITTERS

Soak and steam as for Crunchy Sweetbreads and Brains. Dice, coat with a batter of 1 cup whole-wheat or rye flour, 1 egg, and ⅓ cup milk, and saute in hot oil that measures ½ inch in skillet.

Canadian Bacon

GRILLED KIDNEYS

Remove tough white membranes; then wash. (Be sure to proceed in this order and you will not be faced with the strong ammonia odor associated with cooking kidneys.) Cut into slices ½-inch thick, brush with oil, and broil 3 to 5 minutes on each side, until brown. Or dredge with seasoned whole-wheat flour and saute.

SAUTÉED LIVER FOR SIX

¼ cup oil
2 onions, sliced
2 pounds calves' or chicken liver, cut in strips
½ teaspoon pepper
½ teaspoon marjoram

Saute onions in oil until golden. Add liver and seasonings and saute, stirring, for 3 to 4 minutes. Serve on toast. Salt at the table to taste; this keeps liver from becoming tough. If desired, top with a spoonful of plain yogurt or sour cream.

LIVER PANCAKES

As a friend put it, "these are a great improvement on liver."

Serve with marmalade or applesauce.

¾ pound beef liver
½ cup fresh bread crumbs
1 egg
2 tablespoons milk
2 tablespoons minced onion
1 teaspoon salt

Cut liver into pieces, then puree a few at a time in the blender. Transfer pureed liver to a mixing bowl, add remaining ingredients and beat well. Preheat griddle or frying pan with a light covering of oil. Drop batter by the heaping soupspoonful onto hot pan, and brown 2 minutes on each side.

Makes 12 pancakes or 3 to 4 servings.

other quick-cooking meat dishes

CHOPPED-BEEF TOAST

Toast whole-wheat bread under broiler on one side. Spread untoasted side with butter; then cover completely with chopped beef seasoned to taste with salt and onion. Broil 5 to 6 minutes.

One-half pound ground beef will cover 4 slices of bread.

MEAT PATTIES

1 pound ground liver, veal, or chicken
½ cup wheat germ
¼ cup yogurt
2 teaspoons grated onion
1 clove minced garlic, optional
½ teaspoon salt
¼ teaspoon paprika
¼ teaspoon pepper

Combine all ingredients and shape into 6 flat cakes. Place on oiled baking pan and bake in a 350° oven about 15 minutes. Or broil by placing directly on oiled broiler pan and browning about 8 minutes on one side, 5 minutes on the other. Serve with ketchup if you wish.

Makes 6 patties.

Chopped-Beef Toast

EXTENDED MEAT BURGERS

To each pound ground meat add ½ cup wheat germ, fresh whole-wheat bread crumbs, or ground, cooked soybeans. Season to taste, shape into patties and cook by either of the following methods:

Broiling: Place on rack over drip pan 4 inches from heat. Broil 6 to 8 minutes, turn, and broil 4 to 5 minutes longer.

Pan broiling: Place in a cold skillet and cook, without added fat, 3 to 4 minutes per side. If meat is very lean you can add 1 tablespoon oil.

One pound meat, when extended, will make 4 to 6 patties.

DUTCH STEAK

Rub 4 small steaks with pepper on both sides. Heat 3 tablespoons butter in skillet and quickly saute meat on both sides. Remove from pan, add 2 tablespoons milk, and stir up brown bits clinging to pan. Serve this sauce over meat. Season to taste at the table.

BROILED HAM STEAK

To prepare uncooked ham slices less than 1 inch thick, broil 3 inches from heat, or pan broil in an ungreased skillet, about 7 minutes per side. For ham slices 1 inch thick or thicker, increase time to about 10 minutes per side.

let breakfast cook while you sleep

OVERNIGHT ROAST

This method of cooking meat at a low temperature for a long period of time results in a very tender product with the added advantage that the effortless roast "cooks itself" while you sleep. It is recommended for beef (particularly the less tender cuts), ham, leg or shoulder of lamb, turkey, and large veal roasts. A meat thermometer is your guide to doneness.

Preheat oven to 300°. Place meat fat side up on rack in an open roasting pan. If lean, brush surface with oil. Insert meat thermometer into thickest part of roast, making sure it is not touching a bone or fat. Cook meat for one hour at 300°, then lower heat to correspond to the desired internal temperature of the finished roast (see table below). When thermometer indicates appropriate temperature the roast will be done. Approximate cooking time at the reduced temperature is given below. Unlike traditional roasting procedures, if the roast is allowed to remain in the oven an extra half hour, little damage will be done.

Meat	Internal temperature when done (in degrees)	Approximate cooking time per pound at 165°
Beef		
Standing ribs	140° (rare)	1 hour
	155 (medium)	1½ hours
	170 (well done)	1½ hours
Rolled rib	140	1 hour, 40 minutes
	155	2½ hours
	170	2½ hours
Standing rump	155	1½ hours
Rolled rump	155	1½ hours
Pork, fresh		
Loin	185	2 hours
Shoulder	185	1½ hours
Boned Shoulder	185	2¼ hours
Ham	185	1½ hours
Pork, cured		
Ham, whole	160	1 hour
half	160	1¼ hours
Shoulder butt	170	1¾ hours
Lamb		
Bone in	170	1½ hours
Boned	170	2 hours
Veal		
Leg	170	1¼ hours
Loin	170	1½ hours
Rib	170	1½ hours
Shoulder	170	1¼ hours
Boned	170	2 hours
Turkey	180	1 hour

using leftover cooked meat

DEVILED POULTRY SLICES

Spread cooked chicken or turkey slices with mustard on both sides. Roll in wheat germ seasoned to taste with salt and pepper and broil on both sides until golden, about 5 minutes per side.

SAUTÉED HAM AND APPLES

Trim fat from roast or baked ham and melt in skillet; or heat oil to cover skillet. Dice ham. For each 2 cups prepare 1 cup thinly sliced apples. Saute ham and apples together in the hot fat until apples are tender and ham slightly browned, about 10 minutes. Very aromatic with a sprinkling of cinnamon.

SAUTÉED HAM AND PINEAPPLE

Omit apples from Sauteed Ham and Apples. When ham is almost cooked, add pineapple chunks, fresh or well-drained canned, and heat through.

HAM-AND-CHEESE ROLLS

For each roll, place 1 slice Swiss cheese to cover 1 slice boiled ham. Roll like a jelly roll, ham on the outside, secure with a toothpick, and broil or pan fry about 2 minutes, until ham begins to brown and cheese melts.

DEVILED MEAT SPREAD

¼ cup mayonnaise
1 cup diced cooked ham, turkey, or chicken
¼ cup walnuts
1 slice onion
¼ teaspoon salt
½ teaspoon dry mustard

Combine all ingredients in blender container and process about 30 seconds, until evenly mixed. Add additional mayonnaise, if necessary, to spreading consistency.

Makes 1½ cups spread, enough for 4 sandwiches.

MEAT PORRIDGE

Guaranteed to warm you on a bleak morning. This porridge can be made with any amount of leftover meat. The suggested proportion is one to two cups meat per cup of uncooked grain.

Cook your favorite whole-grain cereal (cornmeal, cracked wheat, oatmeal) as usual. When near done add leftover chicken, beef, or veal torn into shreds, and cook until almost all liquid is absorbed. Then whip, preferably with an electric mixer, until meat is indistinguishable from grain. Season with salt and pepper, spoon into serving bowls, and top with melted butter.

The following two cold meat salads were suggested in a USDA publication on meat.

HAM-AND-MELON SALAD

2 cups diced cooked ham
1½ cups seedless grapes
2 cups cantaloupe or honeydew cubes (replace in winter with diced apple)
½ cup diced celery

Combine all ingredients and moisten with the following dressing:

½ cup yogurt
½ cup pineapple juice
2 tablespoons honey

Makes 6 1-cup servings.

FRUITED VEAL SALAD

2 cups diced cooked veal
1 cup seedless grapes
½ cup minced celery
¼ teaspoon salt
1½ cups sliced banana
¼ cup chopped almonds

Combine all ingredients and moisten with the following dressing:

½ cup mashed banana
2 tablespoons mayonnaise
2 tablespoons nonfat dry milk powder
1 tablespoon water

Makes 6 ¾-cup servings.

BREAKFAST HASH, DINER STYLE

Hash, too, can be made with any leftover meat (or even fish) and cold cooked potato.

Chop leftover cooked meat with one-half to an equal amount of boiled potato. Add 1 teaspoon grated onion per cup, or 1 small chopped onion per panful. Season with salt and pepper to taste and add enough skim milk or water for mixture to stick together. Heat oil to cover surface of skillet, pack in hash, and fry over medium heat until bottom is golden and a thin crust forms, about 20 minutes. Do not stir. Fold over like an omelet and serve.

Baked Hash: Prepare as outlined above, pack mixture into an oiled baking dish, and bake 30 minutes in a 325° oven. If desired, depressions can be made on the surface of hash to hold one egg per person. Slip in egg during last 10 minutes.

English-Style Hash: Heat milk to a depth of ½ inch in skillet, add hash mixture, and poach 10 minutes. Serve on toast.

sausage

Sausage, like bacon, although very popular, is too high in fat and food additives to be considered a good breakfast. If you can find an untainted brand of sausage—and some do exist—you need not eliminate it from the menu, but neither should it be depended on for great nourishment, except perhaps for thiamine, in which pork is rich.

Because it is laden with fat and highly seasoned, sausage does not freeze well. It should not be kept for more than 7 days in the refrigerator.

sausage-making

Though we have never attempted to make our own sausage, we offer you the following suggestions if you are so inclined. Extensive research, rather than experience, is the basis for these recommendations, and without a doubt, those who get into it will have a real feeling of accomplishment when they are done.

The trick to sausage-making, it seems, is in the seasoning; however, since it is dangerous to eat uncooked pork, you must learn by preparing a sample batch and experimenting until you are satisfied with the result. Salt, pepper, sage, and thyme are among the traditional spices, although sausage that is made with all pork will not need much salt. Garlic may be added or not, to taste.

The basic pattern for sausage-making is 2 parts ground meat to 1 part hard fat. The meat can be all pork, all beef, or a mixture of beef, pork, and veal. The meat is finely minced, the suet grated, and the two blended with the appropriate seasoning. The mixture is then packed *loosely* into sausage casings, tied into 6-inch lengths, pricked well with a needle to prevent bursting, and either fried in hot fat for immediate eating or plunged into boiling water for 15 minutes and stored in the refrigerator to be sauteed, broiled, or baked as needed.

Sausage Cakes

As an alternative to the sausage casings, the meat can be shaped into small cakes, dredged in whole-wheat flour, and sauteed.

If desired, the meat can be extended by adding ½ pound combined bread crumbs and wheat germ for every 2 pounds of meat.

One pound of sausage will be sufficient for four servings.

About sausage casings: Sausage casings can be purchased salted or unsalted. The salted kind keeps indefinitely in the refrigerator. To use, soak in water 5 to 10 minutes, then run warm water through by fitting end onto faucet. To make handling easier cut into 4-foot lengths.

PREPARING SAUSAGES FOR THE TABLE

To fry: Heat a little fat in frying pan and brown sausages evenly, turning two or three times if encased and only once if shaped into patties. Pour off fat as it accumulates and cook until sausage is no longer pink inside. Apples sauteed along with the sausage make a good complement.

To broil: Place on rack above drip pan and broil 5 minutes on each side.

To bake: Place on rack in open pan and bake in a 400° oven 25 to 30 minutes.

TABLE OF MEAT & FISH VALUES

Food (3½ ounces raw)	Calories	Protein (grams)	Fat (grams)
Beef			
Chuck	257	18.7	19.6
T-bone steak	397	14.7	37.1
Club steak	380	15.5	34.8
Sirloin	313	16.9	26.7
Ground, regular	268	17.9	21.2
Brains	125	10.4	8.6
Carp	115	18.0	4.2
Chicken			
Light meat	117	23.4	1.9
Dark meat	130	20.6	4.7
Breast	110	20.8	2.4
Drumstick	115	18.8	3.9
Cod	78	17.6	.3
Finnan Haddie	103	23.2	.4
Haddock	79	18.3	.1
Halibut	97	19.8	4.4
Heart			
Beef	108	17.1	3.6
Calf	124	15.0	5.9
Pork	113	16.8	4.4
Chicken	134	18.6	6.0
Lamb	162	16.8	9.6
Herring			
Atlantic	176	17.3	11.3
Pacific	98	17.5	2.6
Canned in tomato sauce	208	19.9	13.6
Pickled	176	15.8	10.5
Kippers	211	22.2	12.9
Bloaters	196	19.6	12.4
Kidneys			
Beef	130	15.4	6.7
Calf	113	16.6	4.6
Pork	106	16.3	3.6
Lamb	105	16.8	3.3
Lamb			
Leg	222	17.8	16.2
Loin	293	16.3	24.8
Liver			
Beef	140	19.9	3.8
Calves'	229	26.4	10.6
Chicken	129	19.7	3.7
Mackerel			
Atlantic	191	19.0	12.2
Pacific	159	21.9	7.3
Perch, white	118	19.3	4.0
Pike	88	18.3	1.1
Pork			
Bacon	588	8.2	61.3
Ham, fresh	308	15.9	26.6
Ham, cured	282	17.5	23.0
Ham, boiled	434	19.0	17.0

	Calories	Protein (grams)	Fat (grams)
Salmon			
Atlantic	217	22.5	13.4
Pink	119	20.0	3.7
Canned	141	20.5	5.9
Smoked	176	21.6	9.3
Sardines, canned	203	24.0	11.1
Sausage			
Bologna, all meat	277	13.3	22.8
Brown-&-serve	393	13.5	36.0
Country-style	345	15.1	31.1
Frankfurter, all meat	296	13.1	25.5
Salami	311	17.5	25.6
Shad	170	18.6	10.0
Sole (and flounder)	79	16.7	.8
Sturgeon, smoked	149	31.2	1.8
Sweetbreads			
Beef	207	14.6	16.0
Calf	94	17.8	2.0
Lamb	94	14.1	3.8
Hog	242	14.7	19.9
Trout	101	19.2	2.1
Tuna, canned			
In water	127	28.0	.8
In oil	288	24.2	20.5
Turkey			
Light meat	116	24.6	1.2
Dark meat	128	20.9	4.3
Veal			
Chuck	173	19.4	10.0
Loin	181	19.2	11.0
Rib	207	18.2	14.0
Whitefish, smoked	155	20.9	7.3

THE BREAD IN YOUR BREAKFAST

The basic theme of grains ground into flour, blended with liquid to a dough, and baked, extends into nearly every culture to make bread the primary source of food energy throughout the world. It is an injustice, however, to consider bread as merely carbohydrates and calories, for breads made with whole grains are a basic source of B vitamins, iron, trace minerals, roughage, and supplementary protein. Moreover, when served with *complementary* foods rather than crowding them out, good breads can offer the most economical basis for nourishing meals.

Bread has always been the mainstay of the morning meal, but it deserves to be more than a sandwich wrapper or a palette for butter and jam. Therefore, in addition to the sandwiches and other fancy breads you can make with the fillings and spreads in this chapter, there is a section devoted to main dishes that use bread to its best advantage and represent economic savings by making use of every last bread crumb.

As important as what you do with the bread, however, is what kind of bread you begin with—a bread-based breakfast built around a loaf of white bread will be inferior to the meal in which a whole-grain bread is the focal point. If you are not baking the bread yourself take full advantage of the brands that list ingredients and choose those which are made with one-hundred-percent whole-wheat flour, or a combination of whole-wheat flour with other whole grains such as rye, millet, soybean flour, cracked wheat, wheat germ; at the least, if white flour is present, it should be unbleached. Also, avoid breads that make use of calcium or potassium sorbate as preservatives (or "fresheners"), mono- and diglycerides, and dough conditioners, since these chemicals may have undesirable aspects and add no food value. Full ingredient disclosure is always given on the label of all but standard white, rye, and whole-wheat breads, which may or may not have ingredient labeling.

Take advantage, too, of the simple breakfast sandwiches that appear in this chapter. Probably the fastest form of prepared food known, the sandwich can be very rewarding, especially with the fillings and spreads provided at the end of this section.

BREAD-BASED MAIN DISHES

french toast

There is nothing new about French Toast, but its food value is often underestimated. Made according to any of the following four recipes, just one slice of toast furnishes 5 or more grams of protein.

BASIC FRENCH TOAST

2 eggs
½ cup milk
1 teaspoon honey
pinch salt
⅛ teaspoon vanilla
8 slices whole-grain bread
1 tablespoon butter

Beat eggs with milk, honey, salt, and vanilla. Soak both sides of bread in egg mixture and, when saturated, saute in melted butter in *hot* skillet or griddle until browned on both sides. To prepare large quantities at one time, or to reduce fat and calories, French Toast can be broiled or baked as described below.

Each slice furnishes 100 calories and 5 grams protein.

To broil: Omit butter, place soaked bread on rack

above broiler pan, and brown on each side, about 5 minutes.

To bake: Omit butter. Place soaked bread on wire rack over baking sheet and bake in 450° oven 10 minutes. Turn slices and bake an additional 5 minutes. Since this French Toast, although crisp, does not brown, you might want to sprinkle it with cinnamon for color.

EGG-RICH FRENCH TOAST

4 eggs
¼ cup milk
1 teaspoon honey
pinch salt
⅛ teaspoon vanilla
8 slices whole-grain bread
1 tablespoon butter

Beat eggs with milk, honey, salt, and vanilla. Soak bread on both sides and saute, broil, or bake as described in Basic French Toast.

Each slice furnishes 120 calories and 6.5 grams protein.

BATTER-COATED FRENCH TOAST

2 eggs
¼ cup milk
¼ cup wheat germ
1 teaspoon honey
pinch salt
⅛ teaspoon vanilla
6 slices whole-grain bread
1 tablespoon butter

Beat eggs with milk, wheat germ, honey, salt, and vanilla. Soak bread on both sides until all batter is absorbed. Any batter that is left should be spooned over French Toast as it cooks. Saute in butter, or broil or bake as described in Basic French Toast.

Each slice furnishes 120 calories and 6.5 grams protein.

EGG-FREE FRENCH TOAST

A surprising taste.

4 tablespoons soy flour
4 tablespoons sesame paste (tahini)
½ cup water
1 teaspoon honey
pinch salt
6 slices whole-grain bread
1 tablespoon oil

Beat together soy flour, sesame paste, water, honey, and salt until creamy, adding more water if necessary to make batter the consistency of heavy cream. Soak bread on both sides until batter is completely absorbed. Saute in hot oil, or broil or bake as described in Basic French Toast.

Each slice furnishes 125 calories and 5 grams protein.

FRENCH-TOAST FONDUE

French toast can be served to a crowd with ease when everyone cooks their own. With a variety of sauces, jams and syrups on the table breakfast becomes a very festive meal. In order to be successful be sure to cut bread into cubes long enough in advance for them to dry out or they will not be secure on the fondue forks; stale bread works well here.

1 pound loaf whole-grain bread, unsliced
egg batter from any of the preceding French
  toast recipes, doubled
corn oil

Cut bread into 1½-inch cubes and let stand out to stale slightly. If bread seems too fresh, dry in a warm, 250° oven, for about 10 minutes. Pour oil to a depth of at least 2 inches into fondue pot or saucepan. Heat to 350°, place over warmer, and set on the serving table surrounded by a bowl of batter and a platter of bread cubes. Now each person can spear a bread cube onto a fondue fork, dip it in the egg batter and deep fry it to perfection.

BREAD CAKES

French toast ingredients, pancake style.
10 slices whole-grain bread
water
1 cup skim milk
2 eggs, lightly beaten
1 teaspoon honey
pinch salt
2 tablespoons wheat germ

Soak bread in water (to cover) a few minutes until soft. Drain, squeezing out all moisture. Mash with a fork, add remaining ingredients, and drop by soupspoonful onto skillet or griddle that has been heated with 1 tablespoon butter. Cook as for pancakes, turning once when top begins to set and bottom is lightly browned.

Makes 12 3-inch pancakes, each furnishing 83 calories and 4.2 grams protein.

RAISIN SCRAMBLE

A children's favorite, recommended when the toast is more popular than the eggs.

4 slices raisin bread
1 teaspoon butter
4 eggs
2 tablespoons wheat germ
½ cup milk
salt
2 tablespoons oil or butter

Toast bread, spread lightly with the butter, and dice. Beat eggs with wheat germ, milk, and salt to taste. Heat oil or butter in skillet, add eggs, and, when they begin to thicken, add toast cubes and stir until set.

Makes 4 children's-size servings, each furnishing 240 calories and 10.5 grams protein.

BAKED BREAD PUDDING

Bread pudding is a well-respected American favorite that disposes of all leftover bread. This version is served cold and can be kept as long as five days if refrigerated. A pleasing main dish for breakfast.

½ tablespoon butter
2 cups whole-grain bread cubes
½ cup berries or drained crushed pineapple
2 cups skim milk with 2 tablespoons nonfat dry-milk powder added
2 eggs
¼ cup honey or molasses
pinch salt
1 teaspoon vanilla
1 tablespoon wheat germ
¼ teaspoon cinnamon

Butter a loaf pan, reserving any remaining butter. Combine bread and fruit in the pan. Beat together milk, eggs, honey, salt, and vanilla and pour over bread. Dot with reserved butter, sprinkle with wheat germ and cinnamon, and bake in a 350° oven about 45 minutes, until a knife inserted 1 inch from center comes out clean. Cool to room temperature, then refrigerate. Slice like a loaf of bread to serve. (If preferred, 6 greased custard cups can be used instead of the loaf pan; place them in a pan of hot water and bake about 30 minutes.)

Makes 6 servings, each furnishing 185 calories and 8.7 grams protein.

SKILLET BREAD PUDDING

2 cups diced whole-grain bread (about 4 slices)
1 tablespoon butter
1 egg
1 cup skim milk
1 tablespoon nonfat dry-milk powder
1 tablespoon honey

Melt butter in skillet and saute bread cubes until lightly browned, 3 to 5 minutes. Meanwhile, beat together remaining ingredients. Remove skillet from heat and add milk mixture, stirring vigorously until pan stops sizzling. Return to low heat until liquid is absorbed, 2 to 3 minutes. Serve plain or with jam or honey.

Makes 3 generous servings, each furnishing 195 calories and 9 grams protein.

SWEET MATZOH BRIE

Matzoh, an unleavened bread, is the basis of this pan-size cake.

To serve an adult or two children:

1 matzoh (preferably whole wheat)
2 tablespoons raisins
hot water
1 egg, lightly beaten
pinch salt
butter
¼ cup cottage cheese
1 teaspoon turbinado sugar

Break matzohs into small pieces in a bowl, add raisins, and pour on hot water to cover. Let soften several minutes, then drain well, squeezing out all moisture. Add egg and salt and mix thoroughly. Melt butter in skillet, using ½ tablespoon in a small skillet for one or two servings and 1 tablespoon in a large skillet for more than two people. Pour the egg mixture into the hot fat and flatten to form one large pancake. Cover and cook 3 to 5 minutes until bottom is lightly browned. Shake pan to loosen pancake, slip onto a large plate, invert back into pan, and brown quickly. Divide onto serving plates and, while hot, top with cottage cheese and sugar. Serve with additional cottage cheese if desired.

Each adult-size serving furnishes 362 calories and 17 grams protein.

CHEESE AND BEAN RAREBIT

A heavy meal to combat chilly mornings.

2 cups cooked kidney or pinto beans
1 cup skim milk
1¼ cups grated Cheddar cheese
½ teaspoon salt
¼ teaspoon paprika
8 slices whole-grain toast

Puree beans in food mill or blender, adding a little of the milk to moisten. Add remaining milk, cheese, and seasonings, and heat gently, stirring, until cheese melts and sauce is just warm. If beans are unseasoned additional salt may be needed. Serve over toast, two slices per serving.

Makes 4 servings, each furnishing 424 calories and 26 grams protein.

JAPANESE TOAST

High in protein, high in polyunsaturates. Intriguing.

4 tablespoons sesame paste (tahini)
1 to 2 tablespoons soybean paste (miso)
1½ cups water
homemade whole-grain bread

Beat first three ingredients to a smooth sauce. Warm gently and serve over thick slices of homemade bread.

Makes 1½ cups sauce furnishing 230 calories and 10 grams protein; enough for 3 to 4 servings.

bread and sauce

A slice of whole-grain bread or toast bathed in a creamy milk sauce provides both a nourishing and a filling breakfast. The following Quick Sauce Mix can be prepared in quantity and stored in a closed container at room temperature. To make a quick breakfast, just combine the mix with water, heat, and season to taste; or stir in any cooked meat, vegetables, or even fruit you would like to "cream," and breakfast is ready.

QUICK SAUCE MIX

2½ cups nonfat dry-milk powder
1 cup whole-wheat or unbleached white flour
1½ tablespoons salt

Combine all ingredients in a jar, cover, and shake to distribute evenly. To prepare 1 cup of sauce combine 6 tablespoons of the mix with ⅓ cup cold water and stir until smooth. Add ⅔ cup hot water, place over medium heat, and cook, stirring, until mixture is thickened and begins to boil. Lower heat and simmer 2 to 3 minutes. Stir in any of the additional ingredients suggested below, adjust seasonings to taste, and spoon over bread or toast. Each time you make a sauce be sure to shake the dry mix first so the milk and flour are well blended.

One cup sauce furnishes 150 calories and 12 grams protein and is enough for 2 to 3 servings. The addition of cheese or meat to the sauce will increase both the protein and calorie content.

Suggested Variations:

* To each cup of sauce add ¼ to ½ cup grated cheese.
* To each cup of sauce add ½ to 1 cup chopped cooked ham, chicken, fish, or canned salmon.
* To each cup of sauce add 1 cup sliced straw-

berries, peaches, diced pineapple, or other fruit of your choice, and ¼ cup shredded mild cheese.

SANDWICH BREAKFASTS

If lack of time is your reason for meaningless breakfasts, your days of breakfast boredom can easily be ended, as the creative possibilities of a sandwich are endless. No meal could be faster to prepare. Put children in charge of sandwich breakfasts and their vivid imagination will perk up the breakfast menu in no time; if you have a big family to get out in the morning, assigning breakfast sandwiches to youngsters will allow you more mobility.

Here are some obvious and less obvious sandwich ideas to set an example. Sandwiches for breakfast are best served open-faced; that way you get half as much bread per sandwich, or twice as much nutritious filling on two slices of bread.

the cheese sandwich

The basic cheese sandwich, particularly when served on a whole-grain bread, is a simple yet fulfilling breakfast. There are hundreds of variations, hot and cold.

cold

* The Big Cheese: Moisten your favorite bread with mustard or mayonnaise. Cover with lettuce and thin slices of your favorite cheese, and top with tomato. By varying the bread and the cheese you can have a different breakfast sandwich every day of the week.
* Moisten bread with apple butter. Cover with cheddar cheese and sprinkle with chopped walnuts. Grill if you like.
* For each sandwich mash ¼ cup cooked beans with ½ tablespoon ketchup and 1 tablespoon wheat germ. Spread on rye or cornbread and top with sliced cheese.
* Spread soft whole-wheat bread with equal parts cream cheese and cottage cheese. Cover with grated walnuts.
* Combine cottage cheese with equal parts figs, prunes, or softened apricots and sunflower seeds.
* Blend pot or cottage cheese with half as much yogurt. Top with favorite preserves.
* Combine cottage cheese with chopped stuffed olives. Spread on thinly sliced dark bread.
* Spread a mixture of equal parts cottage cheese and cream cheese on date-nut or other fruit bread. This same spread can be used on toasted

Cinnamon Loaf (see Index).
* Mash together pot cheese, chopped dates, minced nuts. Moisten with pineapple juice. Spread.
* Combine ½ cup cottage cheese with 2 tablespoons orange juice, 1 teaspoon grated orange rind, ¼ cup raisins, and 2 tablespoons chopped pecans.
* Toast 2 slices bread, spread each with jam, and put together with a thick slice of farmer cheese in the middle.
* Spread pumpernickel bread liberally with cottage cheese. Top with chopped scallions and thinly sliced radish.
* Pile cottage cheese in a mound on toasted English muffin. Top with alfalfa sprouts, tomato, or what have you.
* Spread any dense whole-grain bread with ricotta cheese. Top with a slice of ham and a slice of tomato.

hot

* Grilled Cheese, Luncheonette Style: Place thin slices of cheese between two slices whole-wheat bread. Add ham or tomato if desired. Butter bread on the outside and brown sandwich on both sides in hot skillet or griddle. After the first side is toasted, and as the second side cooks, press down on the sandwich with the back of a spatula

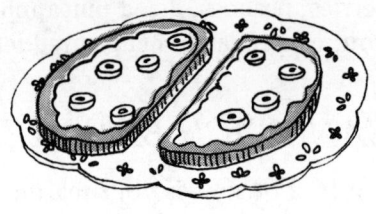

Apple Butter, Cheddar Cheese and Walnuts.

Cottage Cheese and Olives on Dark Bread

to flatten and melt cheese. Experiment with your choice of cheese, trying Gouda, Edam, Provolone, Cheddar, Swiss or Jack.
* Toast Cinnamon Loaf, Raisin Pumpernickel, or any "tea" or dark bread. Top with cottage cheese, sprinkle with wheat germ, and broil until cheese is bubbly and pale gold.
* Top buttered or peanut-buttered whole-wheat bread with two halved apricots, cover with mild cheese like Muenster or Jack, and bake in a 375° oven or toaster oven until cheese melts, about 7 minutes.
* Halve Mideastern bread (pita) and fill pockets with your favorite cheese. Warm in a 350° oven or toaster oven until cheese melts, about 7 minutes.
* Halve Mideastern bread and fill pockets with ricotta cheese seasoned with salt, chopped scal-

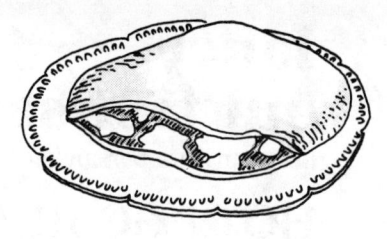

English Muffin with Cottage Cheese, Tomato and Sprouts

Toasted Pita with Melted Cheese

lions, diced tomato, and a slice of mozzarella cheese. Bake in a 350° oven or in a toaster oven until cheese is creamy, about 10 minutes.

peanut-butter "and" sandwiches

The simple peanut-butter sandwich is especially high in stature, and protein value, when served on whole-grain bread and accompanied by a glass of milk. Make the peanut butter crunchy with a sprinkle of wheat germ. For a change from jelly, here are some companions you might not have considered.

* Spread both halves of toasted English muffin with peanut butter. Cover with a thick layer of alfalfa sprouts and serve open-face.
* Spread any whole-grain bread, sweet or plain, with peanut butter. Top with slices of banana, pear, or pineapple, and sprinkle with wheat germ.
* Combine equal parts peanut butter and fresh or dried fruit butter.
* Top peanut-buttered bread with sliced ham, mashed beans, or cheese.

cold egg sandwiches

If you keep some hard-cooked eggs in the refrigerator you'll have time to try some of these.

* Mash together equal portions of avocado and hard-cooked egg yolks. Moisten with lemon juice and season with salt to taste.
* Chop together olives, hard-cooked eggs, and walnuts; add mayonnaise to smooth spreading consistency.
* Make egg salad, adding chopped celery, chopped green pepper, and chopped onion or scallions to taste. Moisten with mayonnaise, or try yogurt for a change. Fortify with wheat germ.
* Don't forget sliced egg, lettuce, and tomato.

cold meat or fish sandwiches

Any meat or fish left over from dinner can be used for a cold breakfast sandwich. Try cold meat loaf (with ketchup), cold sliced poultry, cold fish with mayonnaise dressing, sliced ham topped with crushed pineapple, or roast pork with apple butter. Or be bold and try some fancier combinations.

* Chop leftover chicken with raw cashews; moisten with yogurt and season to taste.
* Shred leftover chicken; add one-fourth the volume of diced peaches or grapes and enough sour cream or buttermilk to bind.
* Combine diced, cooked turkey with chopped almonds, shredded unsweetened coconut, and mayonnaise.
* Combine canned salmon or leftover cooked fish with drained crushed pineapple, chopped pecans, a dash of lemon juice, and enough yogurt to bind.
* Make a spread of flaked salmon or cooked fish, finely diced apple, chopped walnuts, and mayonnaise to moisten.
* For each sandwich mash ¼ cup cooked beans with 1 tablespoon applesauce. Put together with one slice ham, cold roast pork, or veal between two slices rye bread.

fancy, but fast sandwiches
(To captivate persnickety eaters).

HOT EGG ROLLS

Cut lids from hard rolls, scoop out soft centers (and save for making bread crumbs). Put a layer of finely minced leftover meat or beans in the bottom, slip in an egg, and bake in a 400° oven 5 to 7 minutes, until egg just begins to set. Sprinkle with salt, top with 2 tablespoons shredded cheese, and bake 2 to 3 minutes longer. Replace lid and serve immediately.

HOT EGG-AND-CHEESE NESTS

For each sandwich, spread any dark bread lightly with mustard. Top with a slice of Swiss cheese, Edam, or Gouda. Separate an egg, taking care not to break the yolk. Whip the white with a dash of salt until stiff peaks form, pile onto cheese, make a slight depression in the center and set in the yolk. Bake in a 400° oven until white is lightly browned and yolk barely set, 8 to 10 minutes.

Hot Egg Rolls

CHEESE MELT

Cover whole-grain bread slices with mashed avocado seasoned with salt and lemon juice. Spread cottage or ricotta cheese over avocado and top with alfalfa sprouts. Cover with a slice of Cheddar, Swiss, or Monterey Jack cheese, sprinkle with sesame seeds and broil, or brown top in toaster oven, until cheese melts. If desired, toast uncovered side of bread under broiler first.

FRENCH-TOASTED SANDWICHES

Any sandwich made on soft whole-grain bread can be French toasted. Use 2 eggs beaten with ½ cup milk for dipping 4 sandwiches. Brown in butter on both sides as you would French Toast. Serve plain or with syrup. When filled with ham and Swiss cheese the French call it Croque Monsieur. When chicken replaces the ham it becomes Croque Madame.

TOASTS

When the rest of the meal contains high-protein foods you can afford to use bread more decoratively.

CLASSIC CINNAMON TOAST

Toast bread on one side. Spread untoasted side with 1 teaspoon butter or peanut butter, 1 teaspoon honey, and ¼ teaspoon cinnamon. Broil until bubbly.

BANANA TOAST

Arrange sliced banana on each piece of lightly buttered or peanut-buttered toast. Spread with honey and broil until honey bubbles.

PECAN TOAST

Toast bread on one side. Spread untoasted side with a thin layer of butter and honey. Add crushed pecans on top, and broil until brown.

CHEESE TOAST

Toast bread. Butter lightly and cover buttered surface with grated cheese. Broil until cheese begins to bubble.

MELBA TOAST

Slice stale bread as thin as possible and place on an ungreased baking sheet in a 250° oven until completely dry. Store in an airtight container. Keeps for months.

TOAST CUPS

These Toast Cups are also used in the section on coffee cakes as Miniature Tarts, since they are so simple and versatile they can be filled with almost anything. For a high-protein breakfast accompaniment fill with cheese sauce or spread, nut butter, fresh fruit in thick honey-sweetened yogurt, seasoned cottage cheese, scrambled eggs, Sardine Spread, or Deviled Meat Spread. You will need 1 heaping tablespoon filling for each Toast Cup.

Brush muffin tin with oil. Trim crusts from any sliced, commercial whole-grain bread, flatten lightly with a rolling pin, and press gently into each muffin cup. Brush surface of bread with oil and bake in a 400° oven 10 to 15 minutes, until toasted and golden.

SPREADS FOR BREADS

For years butter, jam, and jelly have been the most popular breakfast bread accompaniments. Butter, with its high concentration of saturated fats and calories, is now losing its status among educated eaters; jams and jellies, because of the predominance of sugar, are being replaced with spreads of some nutritional worth.

jams and alternatives to jam

instant jam

When you need something sweet to top off butter, peanut butter, cottage cheese, or cream cheese try one of these instant jams:

* Drained canned crushed pineapple
* Banana, sliced or mashed, with a sprinkling of lemon or orange juice
* Unsweetened or honey-sweetened applesauce
* Dried fruit, diced, soaked, and moistened with honey
* Sliced pears, apples, dates, or raisins
* Freshly grated apple or pear

* Diced fresh orange
* A tablespoon of fruit juice mashed in with the cheese or nut butter and a sprinkling of grated orange rind

no-cook sweet spreads

HALVAH SPREAD

Blend three parts sesame paste (tahini) with one part honey to spreading consistency.

SEED SPREAD

For 2 cups of spread combine:

1/3 cup grated unsweetened coconut
1/2 cup peanut halves
1/2 cup sunflower seeds
1/3 cup chopped dried figs
3/4 cup sweetened condensed milk

Store this mixture in the refrigerator and use as a spread for toast, crackers, biscuits, and so forth.

Each tablespoon of spread furnishes 58 calories and 2 grams protein, more protein yet half the calories of a cup of rice crispies.

DATE-NUT SPREAD

Grind 1/4 cup almonds in blender. Add 1/3 cup pineapple juice, turn blender to puree (low), and process, gradually adding 1/2 cup chopped pitted dates. Blend until mixture is of spreading consistency.

Makes 1/2 cup.

CREAMY FRUIT SPREAD

Puree in blender:

1/2 cup fresh or softened dried fruit
1 teaspoon lemon juice
1/4 cup honey
1/4 teaspoon cinnamon

Beat in about 1/4 cup nonfat dry-milk powder to thick spreading consistency.

Makes 3/4 cup.

cooked sweet spreads

DRIED-FRUIT BUTTER

Combine 1 cup chopped dried figs, prunes, or dates with ½ cup hot water. Cook over moderate heat, stirring occasionally, about 8 minutes, until thick. Add 1 teaspoon lemon juice and cool. Stores indefinitely in refrigerator.

Makes ¾ cup.

FRESH-FRUIT BUTTER

fruit (apples, pears, strawberries,
   peaches, plums)
¼ cup water
honey
lemon juice

Dice unpeeled fruit and cook in covered saucepan with water until soft, about 10 minutes. Puree in food mill, return to saucepan and cook, uncovered, 20 minutes. Measure, and for each cup of pulp add ¼ to ⅓ cup honey, according to taste, and 1 tablespoon lemon juice. Cook to desired thickness; about 30 minutes longer will give a nice spreading consistency. To improve color, add a few cranberries.

Three pounds fresh fruit makes about 2 pints fruit butter. Fruits can be combined for interesting variations.

BANANA FRUIT BUTTER

Prepare Fresh Fruit Butter but eliminate the precooking. Mix the mashed banana with honey and lemon juice and cook over low heat to desired consistency.

CRANBERRY-ORANGE JAM

4 cups cranberries
2 cups water
grated rind of 1 orange
1½ cups honey

Wash cranberries. Combine with water and orange rind and boil 10 minutes. Puree in food mill, return to boil, add honey, and boil gently 10 minutes. Pour into sterilized jelly jars and seal.

Makes 4 half-pint jars.

nut butters

Peanut butter is too often reserved for children's menus and peanut-butter-and-jelly sandwiches. Peanut butter, and other nut butters as well, provide inexpensive protein that is of excellent quality when eaten at the same meal with milk, whole-grain breads and cereals, eggs, or cheese. A tablespoon of peanut butter furnishes 94 calories and 4 grams protein. Though peanut butter is high in fat, this fat is primarily unsaturated.

The finest peanut butter is made from ground peanuts, with salt the only added ingredient. Cheap commercial varieties add hydrogenated (saturated) oil, sugar, and dextrose. If you cannot find pure, high-quality peanut butter, make your own.

HOMEMADE PEANUT BUTTER

2 cups unsalted peanuts
2 to 4 tablespoons peanut or safflower oil
¼ teaspoon salt

Grind peanuts to a powder in the blender. Gradually add the oil, one tablespoon at a time, blending thoroughly. Stop blending from time to time to push the mixture away from the sides of the blender. Add as much oil as you need for a soft spreading consistency, but remember, the mixture will become firmer as it chills. Stir in salt. Store in a covered jar in the refrigerator.

Two cups peanuts makes about 1½ cups peanut butter. Do not try to make more than 3 cups at a time to avoid straining your blender.

While prepared peanut butter and sesame butter (tahini) are available commercially, more exotic nut butters are reserved for those curious enough to make them at home.

MORE NUT BUTTERS

Grind any of the following nuts alone or in combination in the blender. Add oil as needed for spreading consistency, a pinch of salt, and honey to taste.

raw cashews	blanched almonds
sunflower seeds	roasted soy beans
walnuts	pumpkin seeds

If desired, wheat germ can be added to the ingredients in the blender, but we prefer simply to sprinkle the wheat germ on top of the spread at serving time.

savory spreads

All very high in vitamins and minerals.

PINEAPPLE-AVOCADO BUTTER

Mash 1 small ripe avocado (about 1 cup pulp) and add to it ½ cup drained crushed pineapple, 2 teaspoons fresh lemon juice, ½ teaspoon salt, and 2 tablespoons yogurt.

Makes about 1½ cups.

CARROT BUTTER

Puree in food mill, or mash with a fork, 1 cup cooked carrots. Beat until smooth with 2 tablespoons peanut butter, 1 teaspoon honey, and ¼ teaspoon salt.

Makes ¾ cup.

CHEESE BUTTER

Can be prepared with any leftover cheese ends you'd like to use up.

¼ pound cheese (1 cup grated)
¼ cup cashew nuts
4 to 6 tablespoons yogurt

Grate cheese finely in blender; transfer to a mixing bowl. Grind nuts in blender to a powder. Combine ground nuts with cheese and add yogurt, mashing with a spoon, until mixture is of stiff spreading consistency. Store in refrigerator and use like butter on bread or crackers.

Makes 1 cup.

MISO BUTTER

Beat 3 parts sesame paste (tahini) with 1 part soy bean paste (miso) until smooth; gradually beat in a small amount of water to smooth spreading consistency.

GRIDDLECAKES AND WAFFLES

The use of the griddle and waffle iron dates back to the early days of cookery when fuel was scarce. Both griddlecakes and waffles provided a hot bread when time and economics prevented the use of the baking oven. In America such breadstuffs are closely associated with rustic life.

While in the early days griddlecakes and waffles appeared on the table as only one element in a traditionally large breakfast spread, today they are the focal point of many breakfast menus. Consequently, only the most nourishing raw materials should be used, or the caloric content of the meal will far outweigh its food value.

GRIDDLECAKES

Griddlecakes, also known as pancakes, hotcakes, and flapjacks, are the product of simple batters that can be mixed in a few minutes. The batter can be made in the morning, or it can be prepared the night before and stored in the refrigerator.

The consistency of the batter will determine the

quality of the cakes. Since the moisture content of flours varies, you might find it necessary to add a little flour if the batter seems too thin, or more liquid if it is too thick. To avoid toughness, flour batters are best mixed as little as possible, just enough to moisten all dry ingredients. Ignore the lumps. They'll smooth out during cooking.

A large flat griddle is a great convenience for making quick griddlecakes since you can cook about eight at one time, but any frypan with enough room will do. A "well-seasoned" griddle or skillet needs only a light surface oiling to keep the cakes from sticking. Be sure you preheat the cooking surface first. To test for proper heat, sprinkle a few drops of cold water. When the droplets bounce the griddle is ready. If the water sits on the surface the pan is not hot enough; if the water vanishes immediately it is too hot.

Griddlecakes are ready to be turned when bubbles begin to cover the surface. A spatula should slip right under and you may peek to make sure they are sufficiently browned. Turn only once, though, or they'll turn out heavy. The second side will cook in about half the time it took to cook the first side.

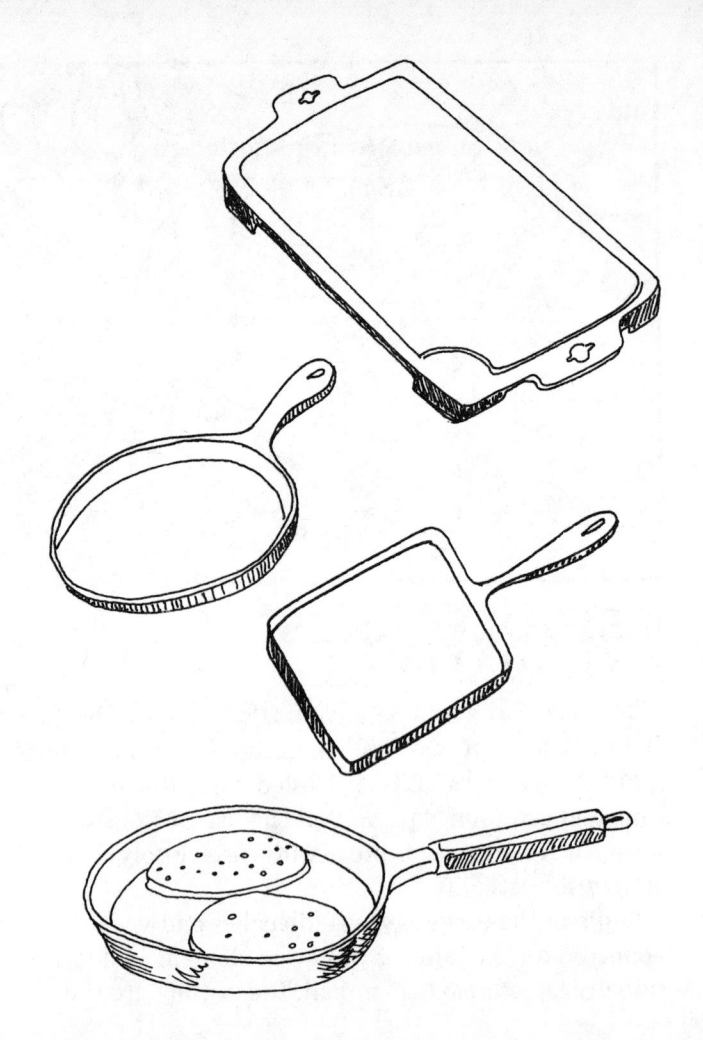

Serve griddlecakes at once. If they will not be eaten immediately stack them in an oven warmed to 250°, separating them with a cloth towel or napkin. The cloth protection will keep them from becoming rubbery.

To get uniform pancakes without making a mess, ladle out batter from the mixing bowl or pour it from a pitcher.

BASIC WHOLE-WHEAT GRIDDLECAKES

¾ cup whole-wheat flour
2 tablespoons wheat germ
2 teaspoons baking powder
½ teaspoon salt
6 tablespoons nonfat dry-milk powder
1 cup water
1 tablespoon honey
1 egg, lightly beaten
1 tablespoon oil

Mix dry ingredients. Add water, honey, beaten egg, and oil, and mix just enough to moisten all ingredients. Pour batter onto preheated, lightly oiled griddle or skillet, allowing about ¼ cup batter per pancake. When bubbles appear, turn and brown other side.

Makes 10 3-inch pancakes, each furnishing 78 calories and 3.5 grams protein.

Eggless Griddlecakes: A nice, light pancake with less fat.

Follow recipe for Basic Whole-Wheat Griddlecakes, but add ½ teaspoon baking powder and 2 tablespoons soy flour to the dry ingredients and eliminate the egg.

Each Eggless Griddlecake will furnish 71 calories and 3 grams protein.

Peanut-Butter Griddlecakes: Substitute 2 tablespoons peanut butter for each tablespoon oil in Basic Whole-Wheat Griddlecakes.

Each Peanut-Butter Pancake will furnish 85 calories and 4.5 grams protein.

Griddlecakes with Fruit or Nuts: Add ¼ cup chopped walnuts, raw cashews, peanuts, pumpkin seeds, or sunflower seeds, or ¼ cup sliced fresh banana, peaches, berries, or well-drained canned crushed pineapple to Basic Whole-Wheat Griddlecakes.

Sour Milk Griddle Cakes: If you buy unpasteurized milk and it goes sour before you have a chance to finish it, be sure to make these pancakes.

Prepare as Whole-Wheat Griddlecakes but reduce baking powder to ½ teaspoon and add ½ teaspoon baking soda. Substitute 1 cup sour milk for nonfat dry-milk powder and water.

SOUR-DOUGH GRIDDLECAKES

Mix the batter at night for these special pancakes in the morning.

1 tablespoon yeast
2 cups warm water
2 cups whole-wheat flour
1 teaspoon salt
1 tablespoon honey
2 eggs
½ teaspoon baking powder dissolved in
   1 tablespoon water

Using a *large* bowl, dissolve yeast in water. Add flour and beat well. Cover and let stand at room temperature overnight. In the morning beat in remaining ingredients and cook, as for all pancakes, on a preheated, lightly oiled griddle or skillet, allowing ¼ cup batter per pancake.

Makes 16 pancakes, each furnishing 65 calories and 3 grams protein.

BUCKWHEAT CAKES

Buckwheat cakes are particularly tasty with a yogurt-based syrup. For egg counters, these are egg free.

1 cup buckwheat flour
½ cup whole-wheat flour
3 teaspoons baking powder
¼ teaspoon salt
½ cup nonfat dry-milk powder
1½ cups water
1 tablespoon oil
2 teaspoons molasses

Combine dry ingredients. Add water, oil, and molasses, and mix to moisten all ingredients. Cook on a preheated, lightly oiled griddle or skillet, allowing ¼ cup batter per cake.

Makes 12 3-inch cakes, each furnishing 71 calories and 3 grams protein.

RAISED BUCKWHEAT CAKES

Prepare the batter in the evening, refrigerate overnight, and have old-fashioned, one-hundred-percent-buckwheat cakes for breakfast.

¾ teaspoon yeast
2 cups warm water
1½ cups buckwheat flour

½ cup nonfat dry-milk powder
¼ teaspoon baking soda
½ teaspoon salt
1 teaspoon molasses

Dissolve yeast in warm water. When completely dissolved beat in flour and milk powder. Let stand at room temperature up to one hour, then cover and refrigerate overnight. (Batter will be thin.)

Before breakfast, remove from refrigerator and beat in baking soda, salt, and molasses. Drop by ¼ cups onto hot, lightly oiled griddle or skillet, leaving a few inches between pancakes, since batter spreads.

Makes 16 pancakes, each furnishing 45 calories and 2 grams protein.

SKILLET CORNCAKES

Also known as ash cakes, hoe cakes, and Johnny cakes. This is one version of the first native bread the settlers learned from the Indians.

1 egg
¾ cup skim milk or buttermilk
1 cup cornmeal
½ teaspoon salt

Beat egg with milk. Stir in dry ingredients. Drop batter by the soupspoonful onto well-oiled, preheated griddle or skillet. Cook over moderate heat until golden brown and crisp on both sides, turning only once. A spatula will slip underneath without any trouble when they are ready to be turned.

Serve hot with honey or maple syrup, alone, or as an accompaniment to a fish breakfast.

Makes 10 small cakes, each furnishing 58 calories and 2.4 grams protein.

SOY PANCAKES

Surprisingly delicate, low in calories, and high in protein.

1 cup cooked soybeans
2 eggs
¼ cup milk, whole or skim

Combine all ingredients in blender container and puree until smooth. Pour batter onto preheated, lightly oiled griddle or skillet, allowing ¼ cup batter per pancake. When bubbles form on surface and bottom is lightly browned, turn and cook until the other side is set.

Serve with jam or syrup.

Makes 10 3-inch pancakes, each furnishing 48 calories (44 calories with skim milk) and 3.8 grams protein.

RICE PANCAKES

These are thin pancakes, crisp on the outside, light and tender on the inside, and easily prepared in the blender.

1 cup cooked brown rice
1 egg
½ cup milk, skim or whole
½ cup (2 ounces) chopped Muenster cheese

Combine rice, egg, and milk in blender container and puree 60 seconds. Add cheese and puree 15 seconds longer. Mixture will be lumpy. Heat 1 tablespoon oil on griddle or skillet and, when hot, pour batter using ¼ cup per pancake. After about 2 minutes, when edges are crisp and spatula slides under easily, turn pancakes and cook until bottom sets, about 1 minute longer. Lumps will be gone.

Serve with salt or jam.

Makes 10 pancakes, each furnishing 57 calories (53 calories with skim milk) and 3 grams protein.

SEED PANCAKES

At last, pancakes that are low in carbohydrates, high in protein, and packed with vitamins and minerals.

¼ cup sunflower seeds
¼ cup sesame seeds
¼ cup wheat germ
2 eggs
½ cup milk

Grind seeds and wheat germ to a fine powder in blender. Add eggs and milk and puree at low speed until batter is smooth. Pour onto a hot, lightly oiled griddle or skillet and cook as for other pancakes, turning when bubbles begin to break on the surface and a spatula slides under easily.

Serve sweet with jam or syrup or savory with soy sauce.

Makes 10 cakes, each furnishing 70 calories and 4 grams protein.

POTATO BLINI

Tiny soft potato pancakes that can be served as a main dish or along with fried or poached eggs. So light you can down ten without thinking.

1 egg
½ cup whole-wheat flour

2 tablespoons wheat germ
5 tablespoons nonfat dry-milk powder
1 cup water
¾ teaspoon salt
3 medium potatoes, peeled and diced
2 tablespoons oil

Combine egg, flour, wheat germ, milk powder, water, and salt in blender container and process until smooth, about 30 seconds. Add potato, a few pieces at a time, and continue to process at low speed until all are blended into batter. Heat a thin layer of oil in a large skillet or griddle and drop batter by soupspoonful. Brown on both sides as for other pancakes.

Serve plain, with eggs, or with applesauce and yogurt, cottage cheese, or sour cream.

Makes 40 2-inch pancakes, each furnishing 25 calories and 1 gram protein.

BAKED-APPLE PANCAKE

A fine weekend selection. You might try this with bananas or peaches as well.

3 cups sliced apple (2 large or 3 medium apples)
2 tablespoons oil
1 tablespoon butter
1 teaspoon cinnamon
6 eggs
1 tablespoon honey
¼ teaspoon salt
⅔ cup whole-wheat flour
⅔ cup skim milk

Saute apples in oil in large ovenproof skillet until tender, about 8 minutes. Add butter and cinnamon. Beat together remaining ingredients, pour over apples, and cook over medium heat until bottom begins to set, 3 to 5 minutes. Transfer to a 400° oven for 10 minutes to finish cooking.

If you wish to double the recipe and do not have a skillet large enough to accommodate the pancake, transfer the cooked apple to a greased 9-by-13-inch baking dish, pour on the egg batter, and bake in a 400° oven 10 minutes; reduce heat to 350° and bake until set, about 10 more minutes.

To serve, cut in wedges and top with cinnamon sugar, molasses, or your favorite syrup.

Makes 4 servings, each furnishing 385 calories and 15 grams protein.

WAFFLES

Although shaped differently, waffles are essentially a rich version of pancakes containing more fat and eggs in the batter. The recipes here are more conservative than most conventional waffle mixtures to keep them within the calorie-protein ratio called for to qualify as a good protein breakfast.

Like the griddle or skillet used in making griddlecakes, the waffle iron must be preheated to the point at which droplets of water dance about on the surface. If you break in the waffle iron by heating it with oil before it is used you will need only a light surface oiling each time you make waffles. The iron can be cleaned after each batch by wiping off any crumbs and rubbing the grid with an oil-dampened paper towel or cloth.

If the waffle batter is prepared ahead of time, do not add the beaten egg whites until the last minute. Waffles are ready to serve soon after steam ceases to escape from the sides of the waffle iron. They should be eaten at once to retain their crispness.

In general, the preparation and cooking time for waffles is longer than for griddlecakes, so do not attempt a waffle breakfast if you are pressed for time.

WHOLE-WHEAT WAFFLES WITH YOGURT

2 eggs, separated
1 cup yogurt
2 tablespoons oil
1 cup whole-wheat flour
1 teaspoon baking soda
½ teaspoon salt

Beat egg yolks, yogurt, and oil until smooth. Beat in flour and baking soda. Whip egg whites with salt until stiff peaks form and fold into batter. Pour by ⅓ cups onto preheated, lightly oiled waffle iron.

Makes 6 8-inch waffles, each furnishing 160 calories and 6.5 grams protein.

RYE WAFFLES

1 cup rye flour
¾ cup cornmeal
½ teaspoon salt
6 tablespoons nonfat dry-milk powder
4 teaspoons baking powder
2 eggs, separated
1 tablespoon oil
1½ cups water

Mix together dry ingredients. Beat in egg yolks, oil, and water. Whip egg whites until soft peaks form and fold into batter. Pour by ½ cups onto preheated, lightly oiled waffle iron.

Makes 7 8-inch waffles, each furnishing 146 calories and 6 grams protein.

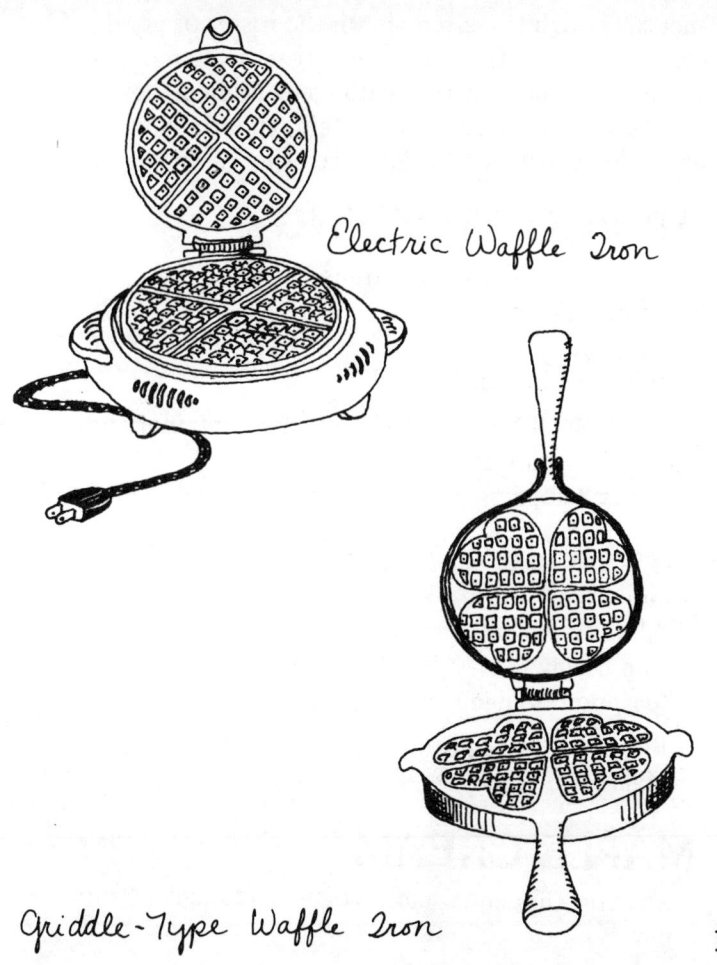

Electric Waffle Iron

Griddle-Type Waffle Iron

CRUNCHY NUT WAFFLES

1½ cups whole-wheat flour
2 teaspoons baking powder
½ teaspoon salt
½ cup wheat germ
3 eggs, separated
¼ cup oil
1¾ cup skim milk
¼ cup raw cashews, chopped
½ cup sunflower seeds, chopped

Combine flour, baking powder, salt, and wheat germ. Beat egg yolks, oil, and milk together and add, all at once, to dry ingredients. Mix until all ingredients are moistened. Fold in nuts. Beat egg whites until stiff and fold into batter. Pour onto preheated, lightly oiled waffle iron, using a scant ½ cup per waffle.

Makes 10 8-inch waffles, each furnishing 220 calories and 9.5 grams protein.

SAVING THE LEFTOVERS

Any leftover griddlecakes or waffles should be frozen for later use since they freeze well and can provide a superior breakfast in minutes.

Before wrapping, separate the cakes with pieces of waxed paper or aluminum foil so they can be removed easily one at a time.

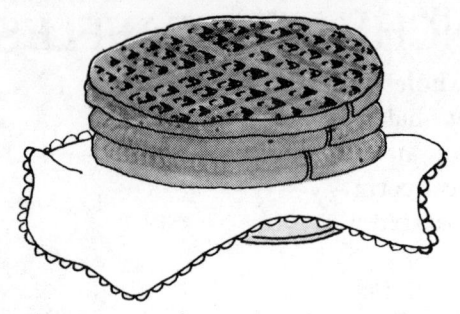

To reheat, place in a single layer on a baking sheet in a 400° oven for about 3 to 5 minutes. Or, for smaller, individual servings, toast on a light setting.

Toasted waffles are perfectly crisped and one leftover waffle is enough to provide a small (or children's-size) main dish. Even lone pancakes are worth freezing to use singly or in pairs in place of bread with eggs, dairy, or other nonstarchy main dishes. If you build up a large enough reserve of frozen griddlecakes and waffles you can defrost a variety and serve them "mixed grill" one morning.

SYRUPS AND TOPPINGS

The traditional maple syrup, honey, and molasses that enhance griddlecakes and waffles all add quick energy to the morning meal, but they also add calories without any protein, vitamin, or mineral enrichment. Though these remain on the roster of good griddlecake, waffle, and French-toast toppings, you can expand the selection with some homemade syrups that do offer some protein, vitamin, and mineral value and lots of unique flavoring variations.

APRICOT TOPPING

1 cup apricots (fresh or softened dried)
6 tablespoons honey
1 cup yogurt
thin slice of lemon

Combine all ingredients in blender container and puree until smooth.
Makes 2 cups.

ORANGE SYRUP

1 cup yogurt
2 tablespoons orange juice
¼ cup honey
1 teaspoon orange rind

Beat with an egg beater or wire whisk until frothy.
Makes 1⅓ cups.

MAPLE CREAM

Mix together equal parts yogurt and maple syrup. Yum.

LEMON-MOLASSES SYRUP

1 cup molasses
⅓ cup lemon juice
2 tablespoons butter

Bring molasses to boil. Remove from heat and add lemon juice and butter.
Makes 1⅓ cups.

ORANGE-MOLASSES SYRUP

Prepare as for Lemon Molasses Syrup, substituting orange juice for lemon juice.

BERRY SYRUP

2 cups berries
¼ cup honey
½ teaspoon vanilla

Crush berries with a fork or the back of a spoon, add honey, and simmer gently 5 minutes. Stir in vanilla.
Makes 1½ cups.

CRANBERRY SYRUP

1 cup cranberries
1 cup honey
2 tablespoons butter

Combine cranberries and honey and cook over moderate heat about 5 minutes, until berries pop. Add butter.
Makes 2 cups.

MORE FRUIT TOPPINGS

A very simple banana topping can be made by combining chunks of banana with a little orange juice in the blender and pureeing until creamy. Or, dried fruits can be soaked to soften in apple juice or pineapple juice and then the softened fruit and the soaking liquid can be pureed in the blender until smooth and creamy. If need be, these pureed fruit toppings can be sweetened with honey to taste.

storing the sauce

Leftover syrups keep quite well if they are refrigerated. When yogurt is part of the recipe they have a limited life span—about 4 days—but otherwise they can remain in a tightly covered jar for several weeks.

To reheat syrups select a heat-resistant jar for storage (such as a canning jar) and stand the syrup-filled container in a pot surrounded by hot water for several minutes before serving. If you store maple syrup or honey in the refrigerator you can use this same method to get the chill out, but unless the weather is particularly warm, they last indefinitely at room temperature.

SOUP FOR BREAKFAST

Soup for breakfast?

While most of us immediately associate the word "porridge" with a hot breakfast cereal, the word originally described any vegetable or grain cooked in liquid. So, though many of us would reject the idea of soup for breakfast, hot soup and hot cereal are actually very similar.

Though almost any hot soup can provide a warming breakfast, and any cold soup presents the possibility of a light, energizing meal in hot weather, some soups in particular are more appealing to the morning palate. These preferred soups tend to be creamy in texture, either savory or lightly sweetened, but never highly seasoned. Leftover bean, pea, potato, or vegetable soups, when pureed with milk, all lend themselves to breakfast service. Such a breakfast is very convenient, since it takes only seconds to warm the soup over moderate heat. (Soups made with milk must be watched, though, for they curdle easily.)

In addition to the "leftover" soups, there are other porridges that are geared to breakfast demands: mild in flavor, easy to digest, and simple and quick to prepare. They come in handy in combating breakfast boredom.

CREAM CORN PORRIDGE

Takes less than 1 minute to prepare.

2 cups corn kernels, fresh or frozen
4 cups rich skim milk (see Index)
2 slices whole-wheat bread
1 thin slice onion
2 teaspoons salt

Combine all ingredients in blender container and process at high speed for 20 seconds. Warm gently over moderate heat.

Makes 6 servings, each furnishing 132 calories and 9 grams protein.

FRIJOLES COLADES (STRAINED SWEETENED BEANS)

This recipe comes from Peru; it is a porridge that resembles sweet, thick milk more than it does beans.

4 cups cooked kidney beans
3 cups rich skim milk (see Index)
3 tablespoons honey
Toasted sesame seeds

Puree kidney beans with the fine blade of a food mill or in the blender. Combine pureed beans with milk and honey and boil gently until thickened. Sprinkle each serving with sesame seeds.

Makes 6 servings, each furnishing 280 calories and 18.5 grams protein.

GREEK TAHINI SOUP

6 cups water
2 teaspoons salt
½ cup couscous or pastina
½ cup sesame paste (tahini)
juice of ½ lemon

Bring 5½ cups water to boil; add salt and couscous and cook 5 minutes, until grain is tender. Beat tahini with remaining ½ cup water and pour into hot soup, stirring constantly. Add lemon juice.

If tahini is not available, substitute peanut butter.

Makes 4 servings, each furnishing 236 calories and 10 grams protein.

SAUCE KARTOFFLE (POTATO SAUCE)

2 tablespoons oil
1 onion, chopped
6 medium potatoes, peeled and diced
1 teaspoon salt

Sauce Kartoffle

pepper
1½ cups milk
1 tablespoon chopped parsley

Heat oil and saute potatoes and onion, stirring frequently, until onion is limp and about to brown, about 10 minutes. Add seasonings and milk, cover, and boil gently until potatoes are tender and sauce is thickened, about 15 minutes longer. If desired, top with cooked sausage.

Makes 6 servings, each furnishing 160 calories and 4.5 grams protein.

CARROT CREAM

This smooth, thick puree of carrots can be made with leftover cooked or canned carrots and is an ideal way to get vitamin A onto the breakfast table.

1½ cups diced cooked carrots
2½ cups skim milk
2 teaspoons honey
2 tablespoons wheat germ
pinch of salt

Carrot Cream

Puree all ingredients in blender until smooth. Cook over gentle heat until warmed through; do not boil. Pour into serving bowls and serve with additional milk, or yogurt, and a sprinkling of sunflower seeds.

Serve cold, without cooking, in warm weather.

Makes 4 servings, each furnishing 98 calories and 7 grams protein.

BUTTERMILK SOUP

1 quart buttermilk
3 tablespoons molasses
¼ teaspoon cinnamon
¼ cup wheat germ
¼ cup raisins
grated lemon rind, optional

Combine all ingredients except lemon rind, which is used as a garnish. Serve cold, or warm gently in winter. *Do not boil.* Sprinkle with brown sugar to taste.

Makes 4 servings, each furnishing 180 calories and 11 grams protein.

Buttermilk Soup

Apple-Buttermilk Soup: Beat ½ cup applesauce into ingredients for Buttermilk soup.

Pineapple-Buttermilk Soup: Omit raisins from Buttermilk Soup and add 1 cup crushed pineapple.

Extra-rich Buttermilk Soup: Beat two eggs, or two egg yolks, into any of the Buttermilk Soup recipes above.

FRUIT SOUP

From the Catskills.

1 cup diced fresh fruit (apple, pear, berries, peach, melon, pineapple)
1 cup orange juice
2 cups unflavored yogurt
½ cup berries *or* halved grapes *or* halved, pitted sweet cherries
8 whole-wheat or whole-rye crackers

Combine diced fruit and orange juice in blender container and process at high speed to liquify. Add yogurt and process at low speed until smooth. Stir in berries, grapes, or cherries, and pour into serving bowls. Crush crackers into each bowl.

Makes 3 cups soup, or 4 servings, each furnishing 158 calories and 6 grams protein.

GARNISHING BREAKFAST SOUPS

Pureed vegetable soups are well suited to a topping of chopped peanuts or almonds. Creamy bean purees can be enhanced with sesame or sunflower seeds, or a sprinkling of grated coconut. Split-pea soup is favored with fresh mint in the morning.

All soups are delicious when topped with yogurt, which provides additional protein and a pleasing contrast in texture and temperature.

MILK AND MAIN-DISH BEVERAGES

Milk is both a phenomenal and a fatal food. Praised for its high protein, calcium, riboflavin, phosphorous, and vitamin A content, it is equally damned for its overgenerous contribution of saturated fat and cholesterol to the diet. How one deals with the situation is largely a personal matter. Many people still follow the adage that milk is nature's most perfect food and drink it by the quart. More prudent milk-lovers have switched from whole to skim milk, and even to nonfat dry milk. Where there is access to goat's milk and unpasteurized, unhomogenized milk, these are often the preferred choice. Still others, shunning the animal by-product completely, have turned to soy, nut, and seed milks to fill the same nutritional needs.

Just how these various alternatives compare in terms of food value will be illustrated shortly. In cooking they are hardly distinguishable. Therefore, skim milk, and particularly the less costly nonfat dry milk, are the most economical choices for baked products and combination dishes, where they add few calories and little or no fat. They offer, too, a multiple of vitamins, minerals, and valuable protein that acts as a "body builder" itself in addition to containing an excess of the amino acids needed to elevate grain protein.

If you prefer to stay away from the animal product, soy, nut, and seed milks provide a laudable alternative. On the average they offer more protein and calories per cup, plus several vitamins and minerals, although they are not so well endowed with vitamin A, calcium, or riboflavin. With the exception of soy milk, vegetable milks are also deficient in certain essential amino acids; they are, however, of excellent value when consumed along with grain protein and therefore highly acceptable in baked goods, cereals, and combination dishes. Vegetable milks are also an important source of unsaturated fat.

For straight drinking you will undoubtedly detect the differences and therefore must decide for yourself which form of milk is the best choice for you. Perhaps this table comparing their food values will be of some help. The nutritive content for each vegetable milk is based on the recipes given in this chapter.

TABLE OF MILK VALUES

Food	Measure	Calories	Protein grams	Total Fat grams	Saturated Fat grams	Linoleic Acid grams	Cholesterol milligrams	Carbohydrate grams	Calcium milligrams	Iron milligrams	Sodium milligrams	Potassium milligrams	A International Units	Thiamin milligrams	Riboflavin milligrams	Niacin milligrams	C milligrams
Whole milk	1 cup	159	8.5	8.5	5	trace	27	12	288	.1	122	351	340	.07	.41	.2	2
Skim milk	1 cup	88	8.8	.2	0	0	7	12.5	296	.1	127	355	10	.09	.44	.2	2
Buttermilk	1 cup	88	8.8	.2	0	0	—	12	296	.1	318	343	10	.10	.44	.2	2
Soy milk from beans	1 cup	160	12.6	6.5	trace	3	0	15.8	83	3.1	2	618	30	.40	.12	.8	—
from flour	1 cup	142	11.9	6.6	1	3	0	9.8	64	2.7	trace	538	.40	.27	.10	.7	0
Almond milk	1 cup	292	8.6	25.0	2	5	0	13.3	108	2.2	2	356	0	.11	.42	1.6	trace
Peanut milk	1 cup	257	11.6	21.5	5	6	0	9.1	32	1.0	2	310	—	.14	.06	7.6	0
Cashew milk	1 cup	207	6.3	16.8	3	1	0	10.8	14	1.4	6	171	40	.16	.09	.7	0
Seed milk	1 cup	266	10.1	21.4	3	12	0	13.4	186	3.7	18	386	20	.76	.10	2.4	0
Sprout milk	1 cup	26	2.9	trace	0	0	0	4.9	14	1.0	4	166	20	.10	.10	.5	14
Rich skim milk	1 cup	108	10.8	.2	0	0	7	15.4	369	.1	157	452	10*	.11	.54	.2	2

*Applies to unfortified product

120

rich skim milk

Although the formula for reconstituting nonfat dry-milk powder is given on the box it comes in, you can increase the protein value and achieve a richer consistency by adding an extra tablespoon of dry-milk powder for each cup of milk you prepare. As a general rule use 1¼ cups nonfat dry-milk powder for each quart of milk. To maximize flavor, chill reconstituted dry milk at least 4 hours before drinking.

buttermilk

Because it is a skim-milk derivative, buttermilk is a popular commodity for those trying to reduce calorie or fat intake. True buttermilk, the liquid residuals of the butter-making process, is available today only through the farmer who churns butter. Store-bought cultured buttermilk is produced commercially by reworking stale milk. Because cultured buttermilk is dependent on the addition of salt to disguise any residual off-taste, it is unsuitable to many people. But despite this problem, it is still sought after, for its fermented nature is pleasing to both the digestive system and the taste buds. One way of circumventing some of the adverse characteristics is to culture your own buttermilk, much as you might make your own yogurt. This is also quite economical, since a quart of cultured buttermilk costs about twice as much as this homemade version.

HOMEMADE CULTURED BUTTERMILK

To make Homemade Cultured Buttermilk, shake ¼ cup commercial cultured buttermilk with 1 quart reconstituted nonfat dry milk. Let stand at room temperature until thickened. Depending on how warm it is, this incubation period will last from 12 hours to 3 days. If you have a yogurt-maker you can prepare buttermilk in several hours in the heat-controlled container. When the desired consistency and degree of pungency have been attained, refrigerate the culture. To start the next batch always save ¼ cup from the previous quart and you will never have to purchase the commercial form again.

soy milk

Soybean powder designed especially for the preparation of soy milk is available in many natural-food stores. If you cannot purchase this milk powder you can use one of the following methods for preparing soy milk from the dried beans or the flour.

SOYBEAN MILK

Soak 1 cup soybeans in plenty of cold water to cover, all day or overnight. Discard soaking water and combine beans with 5 cups cold water in blender, processing at high speed until smooth. It will probably take two shifts to accommodate this volume. Simmer bean liquid for 15 minutes, add 1 tablespoon honey (or to taste), and return to blender. Strain milk through a cheesecloth or fine sieve, pressing out as much moisture from the residue as possible, and chill. Save residue for baking or extending ground-meat dishes.

SOY-FLOUR MILK

Using a wire whisk or rotary beater, gradually beat 4 cups water into 1 cup soy flour until smooth. Pour through a cheesecloth or fine sieve into saucepan and cook, stirring occasionally, 15 minutes. Sweeten to taste with honey (about 1 tablespoon is right) and chill. For mineral enrichment you can omit honey and process milk in blender with 1 tablespoon raisins plumped in water or apple juice.

ALMOND MILK

1⅓ cups almonds, blanched
4 cups water
1 to 2 tablespoons honey or molasses

To blanch almonds pour boiling water over nuts and let stand 1 minute. Drain and slip skins off; pat dry.

Grind nuts to a powder in blender container. Gradually add water and continue to blend at high speed until smooth. Strain through a cheesecloth, pressing out all moisture. Return pulp and a little of the "milk" to blender, sweeten to taste, reprocess and strain once more. Chill. Reserve nut pulp for baking, for preparing vegetable patties, or for use on top of cereal.

PEANUT MILK

1⅓ cups peanuts
4 cups water

Grind nuts to a powder in blender container. Gradually add water and continue to blend at high speed until smooth. Strain as for almond milk, one or two times.

CASHEW MILK

Because the cashew nut is soft, it can be completely broken down in the blending process, and thus this milk need not be strained. Cashew milk is the mildest of the nut milks and makes quite a pleasurable drink.

1½ cups raw cashews
4 cups water
1 teaspoon honey

Grind nuts to a powder in blender. Add water gradually and process at high speed until smooth.

Add honey during last few seconds of blending. Chill.

SEED MILK

1 cup sunflower seeds
⅓ cup whole sesame seeds
4 cups water
1 tablespoon honey

Grind seeds to a powder in blender. Add water gradually and process at high speed until smooth. Strain once or twice as for Almond Milk and sweeten.

SESAME MILK

1 cup sesame paste (tahini)
3½ cups water
honey

Using a rotary beater or wire whisk, beat water gradually into sesame paste until smooth. Sweeten to taste.

SPROUT MILK

3 cups mung-bean sprouts
3 cups water

Combine sprouts and water in blender container and process at high speed until smooth.

handling milk

The perishability of cow's milk is well known to all, and there is no need to stress the importance of refrigeration for keeping milk fresh-tasting and free from bacteria. Unpasteurized milk that has soured is excellent for baking. Pasteurized milk, however, is more likely to spoil than sour and should be discarded.

If sour milk is called for in a recipe and you have only pasteurized milk on hand, it can be suitably soured by the following method:

SOURING MILK

Add 1 tablespoon plain or cider vinegar or 1 tablespoon lemon juice to each cup (8 ounces) of milk. Let the mixture stand at room temperature about 10 minutes.

Vegetable milks are also highly perishable and should be made fresh for drinking. Vegetable milk can be held under refrigeration but should not be kept for more than a few days. Shake before pouring if milk separates.

FLAVORED MILK

One method widely employed to entice children to drink milk is the addition of flavoring, chocolate being the most popular. Unfortunately, chocolate is not among the foods that promote good health, and it actually may hinder it, since chocolate is high in saturated fat, contains a stimulant similar to caffeine, and is also naturally high in oxalic acid, which, ironically, inhibits the absorption of calcium. As an alternative you can add a variety of other flavoring ingredients that not only enhance the taste of the milk but add to the vitamin and mineral content as well. While any "milk" can be so flavored, these ideas are especially good for improving the taste of reconstituted nonfat dry milk.

BANANA MILK

Rich in potassium.

1½ cups milk
1 large banana
1 tablespoon honey
½ teaspoon vanilla extract
nutmeg, optional

Puree in blender; or mash banana, add remaining ingredients, and shake in a tightly covered container. Pour into serving glasses and sprinkle with nutmeg, if desired.

Serves 2.

APRICOT, PRUNE, OR RAISIN MILK

A good source of iron.

1½ cups milk
½ cup softened dried fruit
¼ cup cracked ice
2 teaspoons molasses

Puree all ingredients in blender until smooth. Makes 2 10-ounce servings.

BUTTERMILK SHAKE

2 cups buttermilk
½ cup orange juice, pineapple juice, or unsweetened applesauce
dash of lemon juice
1 teaspoon molasses

Puree all ingredients in blender or shake in a tightly covered container. Makes 2 10-ounce servings.

TAFFY MILK

1 cup milk
1 to 2 teaspoons molasses

Beat with rotary beater or wire whisk, or use shaker.

VANILLA MILK

1 cup milk
1 to 2 teaspoons honey
½ teaspoon vanilla extract

Beat with rotary beater or wire whisk, or use shaker.

CAROB MILK

1 cup milk
2 teaspoons carob powder
1 to 2 teaspoons honey
¼ teaspoon vanilla

Beat with a rotary beater, or wire whisk, or use shaker.

yogurt drinks

Instead of serving milk with the morning meal, many people prefer the health-giving properties of yogurt, which is as high in protein as milk, more easily digested, and a catalyst for B-vitamin synthesis in the intestine. As an accompaniment to the meal, a yogurt shake can offer a pleasant change from the daily routine of milk.

YOGURT FRUIT SHAKE

½ cup yogurt
½ medium banana
1 small peach, preferably skinned
1 teaspoon honey
1 ice cube

Whip all ingredients in blender until smooth. Makes 1 cup, or 1 serving.

ORANGE FROSTED

¾ cup yogurt
¼ cup orange juice
1 to 2 teaspoons honey
2 ice cubes

Whip all ingredients in blender until smooth. Makes one 10-ounce serving.

Orange Frosted

MAIN-DISH DRINKS

The meal-in-a-glass concept has become so popular at breakfast time that several food companies manufacture powdered mixes to add to milk which have "the nutrition of a bacon-and-eggs breakfast." Though they do offer a breakfast of good protein value (14 to 17 grams per serving), over half the nutrients come from the milk you add yourself. The bulk of the product is nonfat dry milk, sugar, vegetable gums, corn syrup solids, artificial coloring and flavoring, and synthetic nutrients.

With the aid of a blender, or in some cases just a tightly covered container, you can whip up a breakfast shake from scratch in seconds. Thus you can control the amount of sweetening and obtain vitamin and mineral enrichment from natural fruit sources. The recipes that follow for Main-Dish Drinks are geared to the most conservative palates. You can boost their food value on your own by adding additional nonfat dry-milk powder or 1 to 2 teaspoons of brewer's yeast per serving. Replacing half the milk with an equal amount of yogurt creates an unusual, more pungent beverage. For those who make a daily habit of meal-in-a-glass breakfasts it is advisable to eliminate the egg white, since it contains a substance known as avidin which, in large doses, prevents the absorption of the B vitamin biotin.

The fruit you choose for preparing these milk drinks determines the predominant flavor. Peaches, bananas, apples, berries, pineapple, cantaloupe, oranges, and all softened dried fruits are easily transformed into drinking consistency in the blender.

Most of the recipes here are based on the use of whole or skim milk and are well suited to reconstituted as well as fresh fluid milk. If a nondairy drink is preferred, substitute any of the vegetable milks. Naturally, the nutritive values will be altered by these changes and if you are curious they can be computed from the Table of Milk Values (p. 120).

THE BASIC EGGNOG

1 cup milk
1 egg
2 teaspoons honey
½ teaspoon vanilla

Mix in blender or shaker.

Makes 1 large or 2 smaller servings; furnishes 216 calories with skim milk (267 with whole milk) and 15.5 grams protein.

Orange Eggnog: Omit honey and vanilla in Basic Eggnog recipe and add 3 tablespoons frozen orange-juice concentrate. Blend or shake to mix.

Mixed-Fruit Nog: Add ½ cup diced fruit, fresh or softened dried, to Basic Eggnog, and puree in blender until smooth.

Golden Glow: Omit vanilla in Basic Eggnog recipe, add ½ cup diced raw carrot (1 medium), and puree in blender until smooth.

Buttermilk Nog: Substitute buttermilk for milk in Basic Eggnog and increase honey to 1 tablespoon. Replace vanilla with a squirt of fresh lemon juice if desired.

ORANGE MILK SHAKE

1 cup orange juice
¼ cup nonfat dry-milk powder
¼ teaspoon vanilla extract
1 ice cube

Puree in blender or whip with rotary or electric beater.

Makes 1 serving furnishing 199 calories and 10.5 grams protein.

RICH ORANGE MILK SHAKE FOR TWO

Prepare Orange Milk Shake, doubling the ingredients and adding 1 egg.

Makes 2 servings, each furnishing 244 calories and 14 grams protein.

PRUNE FLIP

Looks and tastes like whipped iced coffee.

2/3 cup prune juice
1 1/3 cups milk
1 teaspoon lemon juice
1 egg
2 ice cubes

Mix in blender or shaker until ice is completely melted.

Makes 2 servings, each furnishing 165 calories with skim milk (209 calories with whole milk) and 10 grams protein.

TOMATO BREAKFAST

3/4 cup tomato juice
1 egg
pinch salt
2 tablespoons nonfat dry-milk powder

Mix in blender or shaker.

Makes 1 serving, furnishing 162 calories and 12 grams protein.

CREAMY FRUIT SHAKE

1 cup milk
1 tablespoon nonfat dry-milk powder
1 cup berries (or other fruit)
2 teaspoons honey
1/2 cup creamed cottage cheese

Puree in blender.

Makes 2 servings, each furnishing 155 calories with skim milk (192 calories with whole milk) and 13 grams protein.

ALL-IN-ONE BREAKFAST SHAKE

1 cup milk
1/2 cup orange juice
1 egg
2 tablespoons nonfat dry-milk powder
1/4 cup wheat germ
1 small banana
1 tablespoon honey

Puree in blender.

Makes 2 servings, each furnishing 265 calories with skim milk (300 calories with whole milk) and 15 grams protein.

HIGH-PROTEIN MORNING SNACKS

It's just about impossible to ignore the demand for pastries and other sweet things in the morning—foods that provide quick energy and can be eaten on the run. We have found that the most sensible way to cope with this demand is to provide tempting sweets that also offer protein and vitamin value, and which, when combined with milk, can actually constitute a good breakfast. As the Table of Breakfast Sweets reveals, most of the traditional sweet morning favorites offer very little protein in relation to calorie intake. Compare these food values with the nutritional contribution of the homemade sweets that follow and you'll know why it makes sense to prepare your own cakes, cookies, and candies for breakfast desserts, breakfast-on-the-run, or portable treats. You will astound your coworkers at coffee-break time.

Most of the recipes you'll find in this chapter take from 5 to 10 minutes to assemble and from 10 to 35 minutes to bake; they can all be prepared well in advance and in large enough quantity to provide several days' worth of breakfast and after-school goodies.

table of breakfast sweets*

Food	Amount	Calories	Protein (grams)	Calorie/Protein Ratio
Eclair	1	316	7.6	42:1
Iced coffee cake	4½" segment	196	3.9	50:1
Cinnamon bun	1	158	3.1	51:1
Danish pastry	1 small	148	2.6	57:1
Plain doughnut	1	124	1.9	65:1
Jelly doughnut	1	226	3.4	66:1
Oatmeal cookie	3"	63	.9	70:1
Pop tarts	1	210	3.0	70:1
Sugar doughnut	1	151	2.1	72:1
Cupcake, no icing	1	146	1.8	81:1
Pound cake	slice 3x3x½"	142	1.7	84:1
Chocolate graham	1 (41/lb.)	58	.6	91:1
Chocolate-chip cookie	1 (43/lb.)	51	.5	94:1
Oreo	1	50	.5	100:1
Fig Newton	1	55	.5	110:1

Note: In addition to poor calorie-protein ratios, the above items provide no significant amount of vitamins or minerals.

*Source: Bowes, Anna dePlanter and Charles F. Church, *Food Values Of Portions Commonly Used*, Eleventh Edition, Revised by Charles Frederick Church and Helen Nicols Church (Philadelphia: J. B. Lippincott Company, 1970).

SOY SPICE CAKES

3 tablespoons safflower oil
¾ cup molasses
1 egg
2 cups cooked soybeans
1½ cups whole-wheat flour
¼ cup turbinado sugar
3 teaspoons baking powder
½ teaspoon baking soda
½ teaspoon cinnamon
½ teaspoon nutmeg
½ teaspoon ginger
¼ cup nonfat dry-milk powder
½ cup water

Puree oil, molasses, egg, and soybeans in blender until smooth. Combine flour, sugar, baking powder, baking soda, spices, and dry-milk powder and add to pureed bean mixture alternately with water, beating until smooth. Pour into a well-oiled 9-by-13-inch baking pan and bake in a 350° oven 30 minutes, until done. Cool in pan and cut into 16 3-by-4-inch "squares."

Makes 16 "squares," each furnishing 156 calories and 5 grams protein.

CARROT CUPCAKES

Soft, light cupcakes that are high in both protein and vitamin A.

3 eggs, separated
⅓ cup honey
½ cup grated carrot (about 2 medium)
½ cup finely chopped walnuts
½ cup soy flour
½ teaspoon cinnamon

Beat egg yolks with honey until thick. Add carrot, nuts, soy flour, and cinnamon. Beat egg whites until stiff and fold into carrot batter. Spoon into well-oiled or paper-lined muffin cups and bake in a 350° oven 25 minutes.

Makes 12 cupcakes, each furnishing 94 calories and 3.6 grams protein.

CHEESECAKE COOKIES

If you prefer, oil can be used instead of butter.

¾ cup whole-wheat flour
2 tablespoons wheat germ
¼ cup turbinado sugar
¼ cup butter
¼ cup chopped sunflower seeds
¼ cup chopped pumpkin seeds
1 cup cottage cheese
¼ cup honey
1 egg
1 tablespoon juice
grated lemon rind
¼ teaspoon nutmeg

Combine flour, wheat germ, sugar, and butter with pastry blender or fork until crumbly. Add chopped seeds. Reserve ¾ cup of the mixture and press remainder over bottom of an oiled 9-inch-square baking pan. Bake in a 350° oven 12 minutes. Meanwhile, mash cottage cheese with a fork and beat in remaining ingredients. Pour over baked crust, sprinkle with reserved crust mixture, and return to oven 25 minutes. Cool and cut into 9 bars. If not consumed within 24 hours store in refrigerator.

Makes 9 bars, each furnishing 210 calories and 8 grams protein.

40-SECOND CASHEW COOKIES

Nicknamed *Coney Island Cookies*, these smell just like the roasted nuts sold along the boardwalk years ago.

1 cup raw cashews
2 eggs
¼ cup turbinado sugar
½ teaspoon vanilla
3 tablespoons wheat germ

Chop nuts coarsely in blender and reserve. Puree eggs, sugar, and vanilla at low speed in blender for 15 seconds. Add wheat germ and chopped nuts and process 25 seconds. Drop by teaspoonful onto oiled baking sheet and bake in a 300° oven 15 minutes. Cookies will be firm but pale. Cool on wire rack. For long-term storage keep refrigerated. If desired, toast lightly to recrisp.

Makes 20 cookies, each furnishing 50 calories and 2 grams protein.

BANANA COOKIES

¾ cup sunflower seeds
¼ cup oats
1 banana
1 egg
1 tablespoon oil
2 tablespoons honey

Grind the sunflower seeds and oats in the blender until powdery. Mash banana with a fork, then beat in the rest of the ingredients. Drop by rounded teaspoonful onto an oiled cookie sheet and bake in a 350° oven 15 to 20 minutes, until lightly browned on the bottom. Transfer to a wire rack and cool.

Makes 16 cookies, each furnishing 64 calories and 2 grams protein.

Peanut Snaps with Jam

PEANUT SNAPS

A non-sweet cookie that can be topped with a dollop of jam before baking, if you like. Excellent also with cheese.

⅓ cup cornmeal
¼ cup nonfat dry-milk powder
½ teaspoon salt
¾ cup water
2 cups ground peanuts (use blender)

Combine cornmeal, dry-milk powder, salt, and water, and cook, stirring constantly, until thick and dry, about 5 minutes. Cool slightly and stir in ground nuts. Place dough between two sheets of waxed paper and roll ¼ inch thick. Cut into 1½-inch rounds with a cookie cutter or the rim of a glass dipped in cold water. Using a spatula, transfer cookies to an oiled baking sheet and bake in a 350° oven 20 minutes, until crisp. Peanut Snaps will keep for weeks.

Makes 24 cookies, each furnishing 74 calories and 3.8 grams protein.

PEANUT-BUTTER SHORTBREAD

A chilled dough that can be stored in the refrigerator and sliced and baked as needed.

Peanut-Butter Shortbread

1 cup whole-wheat flour, sifted
½ teaspoon salt
2 tablespoons oil
¼ cup peanut butter
¼ cup nonfat dry-milk powder
¼ cup honey
½ teaspoon vanilla
2 tablespoons water
1 tablespoon milk
2 tablespoons sesame seeds *or* 3 tablespoons chopped nuts *or* 36 nut halves

Stir salt into flour. Cut in oil and peanut butter with a fork or pastry blender. Work in milk powder, honey, vanilla, and water, using your hands if necessary to form a dough. Shape into a log 1 inch in diameter and 9 inches long. Chill. Cut into slices ¼ inch thick, place flat on oiled baking sheet, brush with milk, and press seeds or nuts into surface. Bake in a 400° oven 10 minutes.

Makes 36 cookies, each furnishing 40 calories and 1.2 grams protein.

PEANUT CLUSTERS

6 tablespoons sesame paste (tahini)
4 tablespoons honey
½ teaspoon cinnamon
½ cup chopped peanuts
1 cup oatmeal or rolled oats

Beat tahini and honey until smooth. Add remaining ingredients and shape, a teaspoonful at a time, into compact balls. Place on oiled baking sheet and flatten slightly. Bake in a 350° oven 12 to 15 minutes. Peanut Clusters will keep for weeks in a covered container.

Makes 20 cookies, each furnishing 65 calories and 2.3 grams protein.

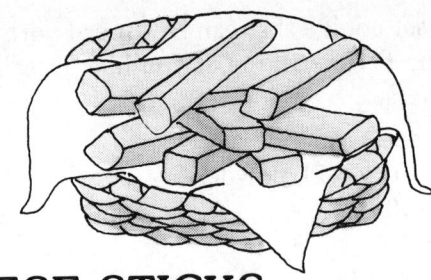

CHEESE STICKS

1 cup grated Cheddar cheese
¾ cup unbleached white flour
¼ cup wheat germ
1 teaspoon baking powder
½ teaspoon salt
¼ teaspoon paprika
1 egg, beaten
2 to 4 tablespoons milk

Combine cheese, flour, wheat germ, baking powder, salt, and paprika. Add beaten egg and mix well. Add milk to make a stiff dough. Roll on well-floured board to ⅛ inch thickness and cut into sticks 3 inches long and 1 inch wide. Place on oiled baking sheet and bake in a 450° oven 10 minutes.

Makes 45 sticks, each furnishing 24 calories and 1.3 grams protein.

PEANUT CROQUETTEN

Shaped like miniature hot dogs, these can be eaten warm, cold, or at room temperature. Good plain or with ketchup, mustard, or in the European tradition, with mayonnaise.

1½ cups whole-wheat bread crumbs (made in the blender from stale bread)
½ cup wheat germ
1 cup peanuts, ground in blender
½ cup grated cheese
½ teaspoon salt
1 egg yolk
1 cup skim milk
¼ cup wheat germ, for rolling

Combine all ingredients except the wheat germ for rolling. Using a heaping soupspoonful at a time, shape into logs about 1 inch in diameter and 3 inches long. Roll in reserved wheat germ and refrigerate until ready to cook. Bake on oiled baking sheet in a 350° oven for 20 minutes, or broil 5 minutes on each side until browned. Store what you don't eat in the refrigerator and serve cold, or reheat if desired.

Makes 14 croquetten, each furnishing 125 calories and 7.2 grams protein.

FRUIT STRIPS

1¼ cups whole-wheat flour
¼ cup wheat germ
¼ cup nonfat dry-milk powder
2 teaspoons baking powder
¼ teaspoon salt
2 tablespoons turbinado sugar
3 tablespoons oil
2 cups blueberries
⅓ cup honey
½ teaspoon cinnamon
1 cup yogurt
½ cup skim milk
1 teaspoon vanilla

Combine flour, wheat germ, milk powder, baking powder, salt, and sugar. Add oil and mix until evenly distributed. Press crumbs onto bottom of oiled jelly-roll pan or a 9-by-13-inch baking dish. Bake in a 400° oven 5 minutes while you beat together remaining ingredients. Pour over partially baked crust, reduce oven to 375°, and bake 25 minutes longer. When cool cut into strips 1 by 3 inches.

Makes 45 strips; 2 strips furnish 83 calories and 2.3 grams protein.

Variation: Replace berries with 1 can (20 ounces) well-drained crushed pineapple, reduce honey to ¼ cup, and omit cinnamon.

...E-AND-CHEESE
...RES

...ep for a week in the refrigerator and taste
...chilling.

1½ cups unsweetened applesauce (if sweetened, eliminate honey)
⅓ cup honey or pure maple syrup
1 teaspoon cinnamon
1 cup grated Cheddar, Edam, or Gouda
1¼ cups oats
1¼ cups wheat germ
¼ teaspoon salt
¼ cup chopped walnuts
1 tablespoon turbinado sugar
¼ cup additional grated cheese

Combine applesauce, sweetening, cinnamon, and cheese. Combine oats, wheat germ, and salt. Spread half of oat mixture over bottom of an oiled 9-by-13-inch baking dish, cover with applesauce, and top with remaining oat mixture. Sprinkle with walnuts, sugar, and remaining cheese. Cover and bake in a 350° oven 30 minutes, remove cover, and bake 10 minutes longer.

Makes 12 portions, each furnishing 197 calories and 8.2 grams protein.

FIG MILTONS

1 cup whole-wheat flour
¾ cup unbleached white flour
3 teaspoons baking powder
½ teaspoon salt
1 tablespoon oil
2 tablespoons honey
about ½ cup skim milk
1 cup chopped figs
2 eggs
2 tablespoons wheat germ
cinnamon

Combine dry ingredients, add oil, and mix with fork until thoroughly blended. Add honey and enough milk to form a dough that can be handled. If too dry add more milk. Divide dough into two portions and roll or pat into two 9-inch squares. Place one-half dough in an oiled 9-inch-square baking pan. Combine figs, eggs, and wheat germ and spread over dough. Top with remaining dough, brush with additional milk and sprinkle with cinnamon. Bake in a 450° oven for 12 minutes, until browned. When cool cut into 16 one-inch squares.

Makes 16 squares, each furnishing 102 calories and 3.4 grams protein.

No cooking required for these:

SESAME ROLLS

¼ cup sesame paste (tahini)
3 tablespoons honey
½ cup wheat germ
¼ cup sunflower seeds, ground in blender

Combine all ingredients and, when thoroughly blended, form into a roll 1 inch in diameter and 12 inches long. Wrap in foil or waxed paper and store in refrigerator. Slice as needed.

One-inch slice furnishes 78 calories and 3 grams protein.

Peanut Butter Balls

PEANUT BUTTER BALLS

¼ cup peanut butter
2 tablespoons honey
¼ teaspoon vanilla
¼ cup nonfat dry-milk powder
⅓ cup chopped raw cashews
about 4 teaspoons toasted sesame seeds

Mix together peanut butter, honey, vanilla, and milk powder until evenly blended. Add cashews; if mixture is too stiff add 1 teaspoon hot water. Taking a teaspoonful at a time, form into 1-inch balls; roll in sesame seeds to coat.

Makes 10 balls, each furnishing 80 calories and 3.2 grams protein.

MOLASSES TAFFY

2 tablespoons molasses
¼ cup peanut butter
3 tablespoons coarsely chopped peanuts
¼ cup nonfat dry-milk powder

   Combine molasses and peanut butter. Add peanuts. Gradually knead in milk powder. Roll into a rope ¾ inch in diameter and 12 inches long. Wrap in waxed paper or foil and chill. Slice as needed.
   One-inch slice furnishes 70 calories and 3 grams protein.

QUICK SNACKS

   Put these together in seconds or prepare them in advance and keep in the refrigerator for quick getaways.

* Sliced apple or pear with cheese wedges
* Banana, pear, or apple slices spread with peanut butter and rolled in wheat germ. Make these fresh or store them in the freezer for a refreshing summer treat.
* Dried prunes, figs, or dates, pitted and stuffed with nut butter or cottage cheese
* Whole-grain crackers spread with peanut butter or ricotta cheese and honey, fresh fruit slices, jam, or one of the spreads in the chapter "The Bread in Your Breakfast."

YOUR OWN BREAKFAST BREADS

Whole-grain baked goods are meant to be tasted and savored. For us they are an integral part of the meal. When whole wheat, whole rye, whole-ground cornmeal, wheat germ, nonfat dry milk, honey, molasses, and other such nourishing ingredients form the basis of a loaf of bread, a tin of muffins, or a panful of biscuits you can count on your breakfast being a substantial one. You will probably find that more commercial breads pale in comparison, seeming too airy in texture and flat in taste. In addition, baked goods made with whole-grain flours are more satisfying because of their greater bulk, thus eliminating the need for three or four slices to fill you up.

YEAST BREADS

Sprouted-wheat breads, one-hundred percent whole-wheat breads, and a variety of whole-grain combination breads are sold in most food outlets. But the best bread you will ever taste is the loaf you make at home, a bread built around a framework of natural ingredients and nurtured by your efforts.

Recipes for whole-grain yeast breads are easy to come by; today's market is well stocked with books on the "old fashioned" art of bread baking. Rather than repeat what has already been written we offer here some special recipes for yeast breads particularly suited to breakfast in style, convenience, or high food value.

Though yeast breads are not difficult to make they do require a chunk of time in which they must rise once, twice, or even three times. Without exception, however, these breads remain fresh for several days, and, since they can all be successfully frozen, you can prepare them in quantity for the future.

Before trying out these recipes be sure you have read the Basic Guidelines for Making Yeast Breads.

basic guidelines for making yeast breads

When yeast is dissolved in warm liquid, its cells become active. Compressed yeast cakes are dissolved in liquid at 85°F.; if yeast is in the dry, powdered form, liquid should be 110° to 115°F. Liquid that is above 145°F. will kill the yeast. Yeast that is potent should dissolve within 10 minutes. The addition of sugar, molasses, or honey will accelerate yeast growth and also help produce a rich, brown, crusty bread. If you are certain your yeast is active you can bypass the dissolving procedure and mix the yeast right in with the other dry ingredients; add the liquid allotted for dissolving along with the remaining liquid ingredients in the recipe. You do not have to worry about killing the yeast with liquid that is too hot with this method since the flour acts as a protective agent.

To knead dough: Press it with the palms of your hands, then fold the farthest edge to the center. Repeat this motion, turning the dough as you knead it. Add flour as necessary to prevent sticking, but do not add more than is specified in the recipe or the bread will be heavy.

When sufficiently kneaded, dough will be smooth and soft. Though 5 minutes of kneading should suffice, the longer you manipulate the dough the better the texture; if you have the stamina, 10 minutes is recommended.

Place the ball of kneaded dough in a well-greased bowl and turn it so that all surfaces are coated with the oil. This will prevent the outer surface from drying out.

Cover the dough with a cloth and allow to rise as directed in a place free from drafts. Yeast dough should rise at a temperature of 75° to 85°F. If the room is too cold the bowl of dough can be set on a rack in a pan of hot water.

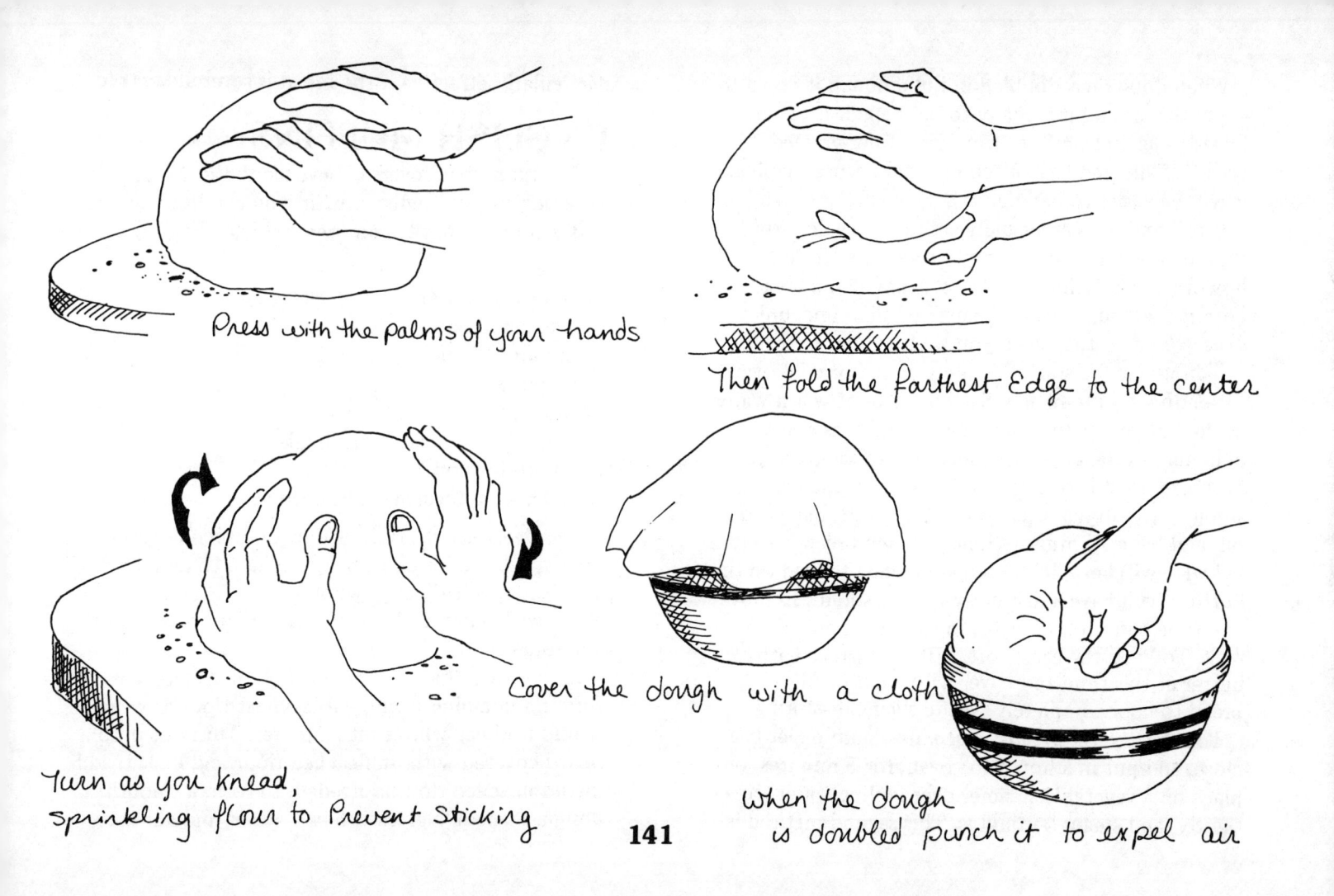

Press with the palms of your hands

Then fold the farthest edge to the center

Turn as you knead, sprinkling flour to prevent sticking

Cover the dough with a cloth

When the dough is doubled punch it to expel air

141

When dough has doubled in bulk, punch it down to expel the air and it is ready to be shaped. It can be kneaded again briefly to produce a finer-grained bread. If allowed to rest ten minutes before shaping, it will be easier to handle.

Bread and rolls are usually set to rise again after shaping but this is not entirely necessary. It does, however, greatly improve the texture of the bread. Permit the dough to rise uncovered this time, unless otherwise directed, since you want a crust to form.

Baking may be started in a preheated or cold oven depending on the recipe. Setting a pan of warm water in the bottom of the oven during baking is said to help harden the crust. Another way to secure a rich, browned crust is to take the bread from the oven when nearly done, brush the surface with butter or oil, and bake 15 minutes longer. When bread is fully baked it will be well colored and, when tapped on the bottom, will have a distinctly hollow sound. Remove from the pan soon after baking and cool on a wire rack. To keep the crust soft, rub the surface with butter at this time and cover with a cloth. Allow bread to cool completely before slicing or storing.

To reheat yeast breads: Place in a damp paper bag, close, and put in a hot, 425° oven, for 5 minutes; or place on a vegetable steamer over boiling water, cover tightly, and steam 5 minutes. This second method is particularly effective if the bread is several days old.

ENGLISH MUFFINS

English muffin lovers believe us, these are far superior to any English muffin you can buy.

3½ hours rising; 12 minutes' baking.

1 tablespoon dry yeast
¼ cup warm water
1¼ cups hot water
2 teaspoons honey
1 teaspoon salt
¼ cup nonfat dry-milk powder
3 cups whole-wheat flour, divided
3 tablespoons oil
½ to 1 cup unbleached white flour

Dissolve yeast in warm water. Combine hot water, honey, salt, and milk powder and add to dissolved yeast along with 2 cups whole-wheat flour. Beat well, cover with a damp cloth and let rise in a warm spot 1½ hours.

After dough has risen, pour in 3 tablespoons oil and fold in remaining 1 cup whole-wheat flour as you would fold egg whites into a batter. Turn out onto a board covered with unbleached flour and knead, adding unbleached flour as needed, to form a smooth dough. Place in a greased bowl, cover, and allow to until double, about 45 minutes.

To bake, place muffins on a preheated, ungreased griddle or heavy baking sheet on top of the range, lower heat, and brown on both sides, turning only once and allowing about 6 minutes per side.

To serve, split with fork and toast. To store, cool completely, wrap, and freeze.

Makes 15 muffins, each furnishing 128 calories and 4.3 grams protein.

FLAT ONION BREADS

A delicious breakfast with eggs or cottage cheese. Overnight rising; 25 minutes baking.

1 tablespoon dry yeast
2 tablespoons warm water
1 cup warm water
1 teaspoon salt
1 tablespoon honey
1 tablespoon oil
2 cups whole-wheat flour
1 cup unbleached white flour
1 egg yolk beaten with 1 tablespoon water
2 chopped onions
coarse or kosher salt

Dissolve yeast in 2 tablespoons warm water. Combine remaining 1 cup water, salt, honey, and oil. Add

English Muffins

rise until double, about 1 hour.

When dough has risen, punch down and let rest 10 minutes. Then roll ½ inch thick and cut into 3-inch rounds. A tunafish can with both ends removed makes a perfect mold. Place the muffins on a board brushed with cornmeal, cover, and allow to rise again dissolved yeast and beat in whole-wheat flour. Turn onto a board sprinkled with unbleached flour and knead, adding remaining flour, until smooth. Place in a greased bowl, cover, and set in a warm spot to rise overnight.

In the morning punch down dough, knead lightly, and divide into balls about the size of tennis balls. Roll each ½ inch thick, brush with diluted egg yolk, and sprinkle with coarse salt and onion. Prick the entire surface with a fork, place on a floured baking sheet, and bake in a 400° oven 20 to 25 minutes, until onions are golden and crust crisp.

Makes 5 breads, each furnishing 290 calories and 8.5 grams protein.

FRESH BAGELS

Bagels are individual breads that look very much like doughnuts encased in a thick crust. They are a traditional Sunday-morning breakfast in Jewish households, split and spread with cream cheese and lox. The version offered here is a good facsimile of commercially made bagels, but to be quite honest, a duplicate is almost impossible in the home kitchen.

2 hours' rising; 25 minutes' cooking.

1 tablespoon dry yeast
1 cup warm water, divided
3½ cups whole-wheat flour
¼ cup wheat germ
1½ teaspoons salt
3 tablespoons oil
2½ tablespoons honey
1 egg, lightly beaten
4 quarts boiling water
2 tablespoons sugar

Dissolve yeast in ⅓ cup of the warm water. Mix 3 cups whole-wheat flour with wheat germ and salt, then beat in remaining warm water, dissolved yeast, oil, honey, and egg. Turn onto a floured board and knead 10 minutes, adding the remaining ½ cup flour only as needed to prevent sticking. Place dough in a greased bowl, cover, and set in a warm spot to double, about 2 hours.

When dough has risen, punch down, knead briefly, and divide into 12 portions. Shape into bagels by rolling into ropes not more than ¾ inch thick and pinching the ends together to form a ring, like a doughnut.

Bring the 4 quarts of water to a boil in a large kettle, add the sugar, and drop in the bagels, a few at a time. When they rise to the surface turn them over and boil about 5 minutes, until they are light. Drain well and place on an oiled baking sheet. The bagels can be left plain or sprinkled with poppy seeds, caraway seeds, sesame seeds, or coarse salt at this point. To complete the cooking process bake in a 450° oven 15 to 20 minutes until lightly browned and crisp outside.

Makes 12 bagels, each furnishing 175 calories and 6 grams protein.

SOFT REFRIGERATOR ROLLS

This dough requires no kneading and can be stored in the refrigerator for days to make fresh, hot breakfast rolls.

4 hours' to 5 days' rising; 15 minutes' baking.

1 tablespoon dry yeast
¼ cup warm water
1 cup hot water
¼ cup oil
1½ teaspoons salt
2 tablespoons honey
¼ cup nonfat dry-milk powder
1 egg
1 cup unbleached white flour
1½ to 2 cups whole-wheat flour

Dissolve yeast in warm water. Combine hot water, oil, salt, and honey, and, when mixture is lukewarm, add dissolved yeast. Beat in milk powder, egg, unbleached flour, and enough whole-wheat flour to form a soft dough. (Dough will be too soft to handle, but as it is beaten it will just begin to pull away from the sides of the bowl when it has reached the right consistency.) Cover bowl and refrigerate at least 4 hours and up to 5 days.

To make rolls, pinch off pieces of dough with a soupspoon and place in a well-oiled muffin tin, filling each cup one-half full. Brush with melted butter and let come to room temperature, about 30 minutes in a warm spot. Bake in a 425° oven 15 minutes, until brown. Remove from pan immediately after baking.

Makes 16 rolls, each furnishing 125 calories and 3.7 grams protein.

HOT SUNSHINE BISCUITS

This refrigerated biscuit dough brings freshly baked bread to the breakfast table in half an hour. Rich in vitamin A.

3 hours' to 2 days' rising; 15 minutes baking.

1 cup grated carrot
1 cup water
1 tablespoon dry yeast
¼ cup honey

Sunshine Biscuits

¼ cup oil
1 teaspoon salt
1 cup sunflower seeds, ground in blender
3½ cups whole-wheat flour

Bring carrot and water to boil. Cool to lukewarm, add yeast, and let stand 10 minutes, until yeast dissolves and begins to bubble. Beat in remaining ingredients in the order given, adding enough flour to knead. Knead in remaining flour as necessary to make a dough that does not stick; it will be fairly heavy. Place in a greased bowl, cover, and allow to rise in a warm spot 1 to 1½ hours, until double. Punch down flat, cover, and refrigerate from 2 hours to 2 days.

To bake, remove dough from refrigerator, roll ½ inch thick, and cut with a glass or biscuit-cutter into 2-inch rounds. Place on oiled baking sheet and let rest 10 to 15 minutes while oven preheats to 400°. Bake 15 minutes.

Makes 16 2-inch biscuits, each furnishing 180 calories and 5 grams protein.

Steamed Sunshine Buns: Prepare like Hot Sunshine Biscuits but shape into small balls and steam over hot water in a vegetable steamer 15 minutes. These have a fine chewy texture.

Makes 30 steamed buns, each furnishing 96 calories and 2.8 grams protein.

CINNAMON LOAF

2 hours, 15 minutes' rising; 45 minutes' baking.

1½ tablespoons dry yeast
½ cup warm water
1 egg
2 tablespoons honey
¾ cup warm water
1 cup nonfat dry-milk powder
1 cup cornmeal
3 to 3½ cups whole-wheat flour
¼ cup oil
1 teaspoon salt

Cinnamon filling:
6 tablespoons honey
3 tablespoons peanut butter
3 tablespoons cinnamon

Dissolve yeast in ½ cup warm water. Beat egg with honey. Then stir in yeast mixture, remaining ¾ cup water, milk powder, cornmeal, and 2 cups whole-wheat flour. Cover and let stand in a warm place for 30 minutes. Fold in oil, salt, and another cup whole-wheat flour. Turn onto a well-floured board and knead 5 minutes, adding remaining ½ cup flour only as necessary to prevent sticking. Place kneaded dough in a greased bowl, cover, and allow to rise in warm spot 1 hour.

When dough has doubled in volume, punch down and roll into a rectangle that is 9 inches wide. Spread with Cinnamon Filling made by heating peanut butter and honey to form a smooth paste; sprinkle with cinnamon. Roll dough jelly-roll fashion along the 9-inch side and place in a well-oiled 9-inch loaf pan to rise 45 minutes.

To bake, place in cool oven, set temperature at 400°, and after 15 minutes reduce heat to 325°; continue to bake about 30 minutes, until golden and hollow to the tap.

Makes 1 large loaf, furnishing 3,308 calories and 109 grams protein; or 18 ½-inch slices, each furnishing 184 calories and 6 grams protein.

RAISIN BREAD

Prepare dough as for Cinnamon Loaf, kneading in ½ cup raisins along with the flour. After letting rise 1 hour, shape into an oiled 9-inch loaf pan, set to rise 1 hour, brush surface with an egg wash made by beating 1 egg with 1 tablespoon honey and 2 tablespoons milk, and bake as directed for Cinnamon Loaf.

CHEESE BREAD

An excellent source of protein that turns a sandwich into a superior meal.

2½ hours' rising; 40 minutes' baking.

2 tablespoons dry yeast
1½ cups warm water, divided
3 tablespoons honey
2 teaspoons salt
3½ to 4 cups whole-wheat flour
½ cup nonfat dry-milk powder
2 cups (½ pound) grated Cheddar cheese

Dissolve yeast in ½ cup warm water. Combine remaining water, honey, and salt and add 2½ cups of the flour, the milk powder, and the dissolved yeast. Stir until uniformly mixed, then add cheese and enough additional flour to knead. Turn onto a floured board and knead, adding more flour as necessary, for 5 to 10 minutes, until dough is smooth and fairly stiff. Place in a well-greased bowl, cover, and allow to rise until double, about 1½ hours. Punch down, shape into two loaf pans, and allow to rise 1 hour. Bake in a 375° oven 35 to 40 minutes.

Makes 2 loaves, approximately 18 ounces each, and furnishing 1,334 calories and 61 grams protein. When cut into 12 slices, each slice furnishes 111 calories and 5 grams protein.

Cheese Bread Wedges: This bread can also be made into sandwich rolls by placing dough into an oiled 9-inch pie tin instead of a loaf pan and scoring the surface with a fork to divide it into 6 equal pie-shaped wedges. In this manner it can easily be separated into segments and split for sandwiches. Reduce baking time to 25 to 30 minutes.

Makes 6 sections, each furnishing 222 calories and 10 grams protein.

HIGH-PROTEIN, NO-KNEADING, FAST-RISING YEAST BREAD

Because this bread is neither kneaded nor allowed to rise more than once, it is subject to an uneven crumb; nevertheless it is very tasty and light in texture.

1 hour's rising; 40 minutes' baking.

1½ tablespoons dry yeast
2½ cups warm water
2 tablespoons honey
1½ teaspoons salt
¼ cup wheat germ
½ cup nonfat dry-milk powder
½ cup soy flour
1 cup unbleached white flour
3½ cups whole-wheat flour
2 tablespoons oil

Dissolve yeast in warm water and let stand 5 to 10 minutes until frothy. Beat in remaining ingredients and, when well blended, divide into 2 well-oiled loaf pans. Dough will be quite soft and should fill pans only halfway. Cover with a cloth and let stand in warm spot 1 hour. Dough should now reach top of pan. Bake in a 375° oven about 40 minutes, until lightly browned. Cool 10 minutes in pan, transfer to a wire rack, and cool completely.

Makes 2 1-pound loaves, each furnishing 1,296 calories and 53 grams protein. When cut into 16 slices, each furnishes 81 calories and 3.3 grams protein.

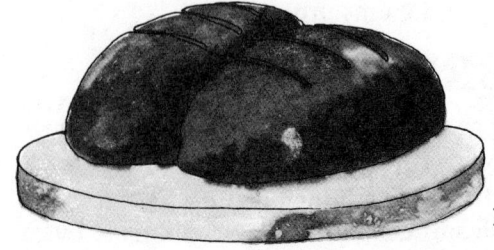

Hearty Rye

HEARTY RYE

3 hours' rising; 50 minutes' baking.

1 tablespoon dry yeast
¾ cup warm water
4 cups rye flour
6 tablespoons nonfat dry-milk powder
1 tablespoon salt
1 cup unbleached white flour
1½ cups warm water
1 tablespoon molasses
1 tablespoon oil
about ¾ cup whole-wheat flour

Dissolve yeast in ¾ cup warm water. Combine rye flour, milk powder, salt, and unbleached flour, then beat in remaining 1½ cups water, molasses, oil, and dissolved yeast. Turn onto board dusted with whole-wheat flour and knead 5 minutes, adding whole-wheat flour as needed. Place dough in greased bowl, cover, and allow to rise 2 hours. Divide in half, shape into 2 oblong loaves, and place on a well-oiled baking sheet sprinkled liberally with cornmeal. Cover and allow to rise 1 hour. Cut three diagonal slashes in surface and bake in a 375° oven 35 minutes. Brush surface with oil, increase heat to 425°, and bake 10 to 15 minutes longer.

Makes 2 1¼-pound loaves, each furnishing 1,135 calories and 40 grams protein.

Sour Rye: Proceed as for Hearty Rye, adding 1½ tablespoons white vinegar along with the 1½ cups warm water.

Caraway Rye: Prepare Hearty Rye or Sour Rye adding 1 tablespoon caraway seeds while kneading.

RAISIN PUMPERNICKEL

1 hour 45 minutes' rising; 45 minutes' baking.

2¼ cups cold water
¾ cup cornmeal
2 teaspoons salt
½ cup molasses
2 tablespoons oil
2 tablespoons yeast
1 teaspoon turbinado sugar
¼ cup warm water
3 to 3½ cups whole-wheat flour
3 to 3½ cups rye flour
1 cup raisins

Stir water into cornmeal and cook until thickened and just boiling. Remove from heat and stir in salt, molasses, and oil; cool to lukewarm. Dissolve yeast and sugar in ¼ cup warm water. Then add to cornmeal along with 2 cups each whole-wheat and rye flours. Sprinkle some of remaining flour on board and knead dough, adding flour as needed. Knead 10 minutes, adding raisins near end. Place dough in greased bowl, cover, and let rise in warm spot 1 hour. After dough has doubled, punch down, divide in half, and shape into 2 well-rounded domes. Place on well-oiled baking sheet, cover with cloth, and allow to rise 45 minutes. Bake in a 375° oven 45 minutes, or until lightly browned. Remove from oven, rub surface with butter, and cool completely on wire rack.

Makes 2 loaves, each furnishing 1,731 calories and 44 grams protein.

storing yeast breads

Freshly baked breadstuffs can be stored at room temperature if protected by an airtight wrapper such as a plastic bag or aluminum foil. After several days, however, refrigeration is recommended. Though breads lose their moisture during cold storage, refrigerated breads are fine toasted and lend themselves to other recipes, as suggested in the Chapter "The Bread in Your Breakfast."

Freezing breads allows you to plan ahead for several meals. To freeze home-baked breads, rolls, and coffee cakes, cool completely, wrap in foil, freezer paper, or polyethylene bags, seal, label and date, and place in freezer. Rolls may be wrapped individually in foil so they can be thawed in their wrapping.

Frozen breadstuffs will keep satisfactorily up to a year, but they are of highest quality if used within three or four months.

To use frozen baked goods, thaw in their wrappers at room temperature about 3 hours for serving cold. If wrapped in foil, frozen rolls and breads can be reheated in a 400° oven for about 20 minutes. If not protected by a foil wrapper place in a paper bag in a 350° oven for 15 to 20 minutes. Heat only as long as necessary to avoid drying them out. Bread slices can be toasted without thawing.

QUICK BREADS

As the name "quick breads" implies, all baked goods need not go through the lengthy rising periods of yeast-leavened breads. These quick breads, which include muffins, biscuits, and popovers, as well as sweet loaves often referred to as "tea breads," depend on baking powder, baking soda, or eggs as their leavening agent. They can be put together in less than 10 minutes. Although muffins and biscuits can be made at any convenient hour, these small breads are at their best if baked fresh for breakfast—not impossible, for they require at the most 20 minutes in the oven. For breads made in a loaf pan it is advisable to do the

Muffins Properly Beaten and Baked at Correct Temperature

Overbeaten Muffins

Oven Temperature too hot

Oven Temperature too Low

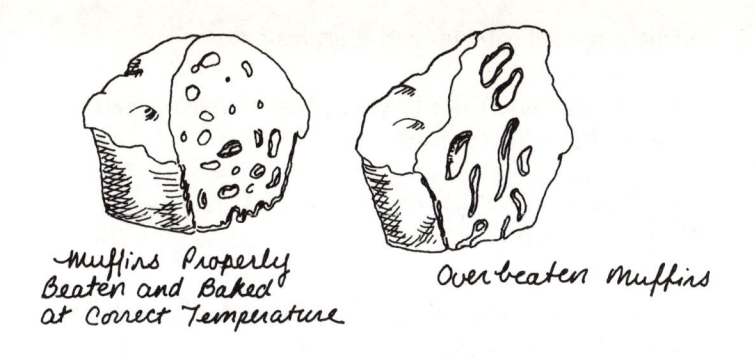

baking a day in advance so the bread has time to cool and set.

The preparation of prize-winning quick breads is considered an art. It is almost impossible to specify an exact amount of liquid to use with the flour, but you will soon learn to determine when more liquid or flour is needed by the feel of the batter. For crusty biscuits with a soft crumb, a minimum of handling is necessary; biscuits with a crumb that will peel off in flakes call for a gentle hand in kneading and thicker rolling. This enables carbon dioxide gas to become entrapped in the biscuit for greater rising, and steam to form layers between the sheets of gluten. Muffins that are large and symmetrical, with a fairly even grain that is free from "tunnels," call for mixing enough to dampen the dry ingredients but not enough to produce a smooth batter. Oven temperature must be well-controlled to produce straight-sided muffins with nicely rounded tops. If the temperature is too low the muffins will be rather flat; if too hot, the peak will be lopsided or cracked.

If all this sounds a bit foreboding, it is well to remember that you need not be a master craftsman to produce quick breads that are delicious, even if they do not look like baking-contest entries. The real test, of course, lies in the eating. Good whole-grain quick breads will be loved for their coarse, homey crumb and delicate flavor.

Although the following recipes offer good nutritional returns in addition to taste, these breads do not provide a balanced meal in themselves. Eat them in conjunction with high-protein breakfast drinks, eggs, cheeses, yogurt, or nut butters for a really worthwhile meal.

WHOLE-WHEAT MUFFINS

Although costly and ecologically offensive, the use of cupcake liners is recommended if you can't get a good heavy muffin pan that doesn't scratch or stick. For a crisp muffin use an iron muffin pan rubbed with oil and heated in the oven for a few minutes before adding the batter.

2 cups minus 2 tablespoons whole-wheat flour
2 tablespoons wheat germ
½ teaspoon salt
3 teaspoons baking powder
6 tablespoons nonfat dry-milk powder
3 tablespoons oil
1 egg, lightly beaten
1 cup water
¼ cup honey

Combine dry ingredients. Make a well in the center and add the liquid ingredients in the order given. Stir just enough to moisten, then spoon into oiled muffin cups, filling each ⅔ full. Bake in a 400° oven 15 to 20 minutes. If you do not have enough batter to fill the muffin tin add ½ inch water to each empty cup. This keeps the tin from scorching and makes the muffins nice and moist.

Makes 12 small muffins, each furnishing 105 calories and 3 grams protein; or 9 large muffins, each furnishing 140 calories and 4 grams protein.

Raisin Muffins: Fold in ¼ cup raisins before batter is spooned into muffin tin.

Corn Muffins: Substitute 1 cup cornmeal for 1 cup whole-wheat flour.

Jam Muffins: Reduce honey to 1 tablespoon and add 3 tablespoons jam.

Cheese Muffins: Add ⅔ cup grated Cheddar and ¼ cup chopped fresh apple.

Surprise Muffins

Surprise Muffins: Reduce honey to 2 tablespoons. Put 1 tablespoon batter in each muffin cup, top with 1 pitted date or softened dried apricot, and cover with additional batter.

Meat Muffins: Omit 2 tablespoons honey. Add ¾ cup well-seasoned, chopped cooked beef, ham, or chicken.

Spice Muffins: Add 1 teaspoon *each* cinnamon, ginger, and nutmeg along with dry ingredients. Add raisins or chopped apple.

EGGLESS MUFFINS

The most tender muffin of all.

1 cup unbleached white flour
1½ cups whole-wheat flour
1 teaspoon baking powder
1 teaspoon baking soda
½ teaspoon salt
2 tablespoons wheat germ
3 tablespoons oil
¼ cup honey
1½ to 2 cups yogurt

Combine dry ingredients. Make a well in center and add remaining ingredients. Stir with a fork until dry ingredients are damp. Spoon into oiled muffin cups ⅔ full, and bake in a 400° oven 20 minutes.

Makes 12 muffins, each furnishing 165 calories and 5 grams protein.

BRAN MUFFINS

2 cups bran
¾ cup whole-wheat flour
½ teaspoon baking soda
2 eggs
⅓ cup molasses
1 tablespoon oil
1½ cups sour milk* or buttermilk
¼ cup raisins

Combine dry ingredients. Beat eggs with molasses and oil and add along with milk to dry ingredients. Mix just enough to moisten. Fold in raisins. Spoon ⅔ full, into well-oiled muffin tin and bake in a 375° oven 20 minutes.

Makes 18 muffins, each furnishing 81 calories and 3 grams protein.

If chocolate-covered **cherries** are a favorite in your house try the CocoBran Muffins with blackberry, cherry, or strawberry jam.

CocoBran Muffins: Proceed as for Bran Muffins but omit raisins and add ¼ cup cocoa to dry ingredients.

*To make sour milk stir 1½ tablespoons white vinegar or lemon juice into 1½ cups milk and let stand 10 minutes.

BLUEBERRY MUFFINS

If you insist on real sweet muffins add more honey, but remember, this adds more calories, too.

2 cups whole-wheat flour
⅓ cup soy flour
½ teaspoon salt
1 teaspoon baking soda
2 teaspoons baking powder
1 egg
⅓ cup honey
4 tablespoons oil
1½ cups yogurt
½ cup blueberries

Combine dry ingredients. Beat together egg, honey, oil, and yogurt and stir into dry ingredients just enough to moisten. Fold in berries and spoon ⅔ full, into well-oiled muffin tin. Bake in a 425° oven 15 to 20 minutes, until browned.

Makes 16 muffins, each furnishing 130 calories and 4 grams protein.

biscuits

Of all the breakfast breads, biscuits are the most versatile. The Basic Drop Biscuit requires no skill, so even first-time bakers can approach them with assurance. Although less shapely than Rolled Biscuits, they have the same rich taste and are quick enough to make even for no special occasion.

BASIC DROP BISCUITS

2 cups whole-wheat flour
⅓ cup wheat germ
3 teaspoons baking powder
1 teaspoon salt
¼ cup oil
1 tablespoon molasses
1 cup milk, whole or skim

Combine dry ingredients. Cut in oil with a fork or pastry blender and, when evenly distributed, add molasses and milk all at once. Mix just until all ingredients are moistened. Drop by heaping tablespoons onto an oiled baking sheet, leaving 1 inch between. For miniature biscuits drop by teaspoons. If preferred, the biscuits can be formed into balls with a light hand.

Bake in a 425° oven 15 minutes and serve warm.

Makes 12 2-inch biscuits, each furnishing 136 calories and 4.3 grams protein; or 24 1-inch biscuits, each furnishing 68 calories and 2.1 grams protein.

ROLLED BISCUITS

For a more shapely bread, biscuits can be rolled and cut with a biscuit cutter or glass with a 2-inch diameter. Depending on the character of the flour, slightly more or less milk may be necessary so that the dough can be easily handled. If dough is too moist, work in a little flour as you roll.

Prepare as for Drop Biscuits, reducing milk to a scant ⅔ cup. Roll gently or pat dough on a well-floured board to ½ inch thickness and cut into biscuits. To prevent sticking, dip biscuit cutter or rim of glass into flour between cuttings.
For biscuits with a crisp crust bake as for Drop Biscuits. For softer biscuits place in a greased baking pan with sides of biscuits barely touching.
As an alternative to baking, Rolled Biscuits can be placed 1 inch apart on a hot, lightly oiled griddle and browned on each side about five minutes.
Makes 12 2-inch biscuits.

FLAVORED BISCUITS

Once you have the basic recipe down you can change the personality of the biscuits in any of the following ways. These suggestions are adaptable to both Drop and Rolled Biscuits.

Orange Biscuits: Add grated rind of one orange to dry ingredients. Replace ½ cup milk with ½ cup orange juice.

Cheese Biscuits: Add ⅔ cup grated cheese to dry ingredients. Reduce oil to 2 tablespoons.

Peanut-Butter Biscuits: Replace oil with ¼ cup peanut butter.

Bran Biscuits: Prepare Basic Drop or Rolled Biscuits using 1⅓ cups flour and 1 cup bran and omitting wheat germ.

Fried Egg Biscuits: Prepare biscuits adding 1 egg beaten with ½ cup milk as the liquid ingredient. Roll ½ inch thick, cut in strips 1 by 3 inches, and fry on a buttered griddle or skillet until browned and puffed. Serve with cinnamon sugar.

Shortcakes: Split biscuits; top with berries, sliced peaches, or crushed pineapple, and honey-sweetened yogurt.

Shortcake

JELLY-ROLLED BISCUITS

Biscuit dough can also be rolled jelly-roll style to make a variety of filled breads that are very impressive although they take little effort. This is the time to be a really creative baker.

Prepare biscuits replacing 1 cup whole-wheat flour with 1 cup unbleached white flour and reducing milk to ½ cup. Roll on a well-floured surface into a rectangle ¼ inch thick and 9 by 12 inches. Spread with desired filling and roll along the 12 inch side.

The jelly-rolled dough can then be placed whole onto an oiled baking sheet; or cut into ¾-inch slices and placed cut side down on the oiled baking sheet to resemble honey buns; or place dough side down for the appearance of individual strudels.

Bake as for all other biscuits in a 425° oven for 15 minutes.

Honey-Bun Filling: Spread rectangle with ¼ cup honey and ½ cup chopped nuts, sprinkle liberally with cinnamon, and roll. If left uncut, sprinkle top of roll with cinnamon as well. Because the honey has a tendency to leak it will be easier to clean up afterward if you cover the baking sheet with foil first. Experiment with an assortment of nuts, trying raw cashews, sunflower seeds, or even roasted soy beans.

Meat Roll: Fill rolled dough with 1½ cups chopped cooked meat, seasoned and moistened slightly with milk or gravy. Top rolled loaf or individual slices with bits of butter before baking.

Cheese Roll: Sprinkle rolled dough with 1 cup grated mild cheese (like Muenster) and ½ cup raisins.

Ad Infinitum: For other variations dough can be spread with peanut butter, dried fruit butter jam, honey-sweetened cottage cheese, pureed vegetables ...

SCONES

Egg-rich biscuits.

2 cups whole-wheat flour
⅓ cup wheat germ
3 teaspoons baking powder
1 teaspoon salt
2 tablespoons oil
2 tablespoons honey
2 eggs, beaten
⅓ cup milk
1 tablespoon turbinado sugar

Combine dry ingredients. Cut in oil with fork or pastry blender. Add honey, eggs, and milk to make a dough that can be easily handled. Turn onto a floured board and pat 1 inch thick. Cut into 8 squares, flatten slightly, and fold each over double. Brush with additional milk, sprinkle with sugar, and bake on oiled baking sheet in a 450° oven 15 minutes. Split and serve with jam or honey.

Makes 8 scones, each furnishing 200 calories and 7.5 grams protein.

QUICK RYE ROLLS

2 cups rye flour
¾ teaspoon salt
3 teaspoons baking powder
1 tablespoon oil
¾ to 1 cup skim milk
½ cup roasted soybeans (soynuts), ground to a powder in blender
2 teaspoons caraway seeds, optional

Combine flour, salt, and baking powder. Add oil and enough milk to form a dough that holds together. Stir in ground soybeans and caraway seeds if desired, and knead several minutes, until smooth. Shape into 6 rounds, place on an oiled baking sheet, and let rest about 20 minutes. Bake in a 350° oven 30 minutes, until light brown.

Makes 6 rolls, each furnishing 162 calories and 7 grams protein.

CORN BREAD

1 tablespoon butter
1 tablespoon oil
¾ cup cornmeal
1 egg, lightly beaten
½ teaspoon baking soda
½ teaspoon salt
1½ cups yogurt
1 tablespoon honey

Combine butter and oil in a shallow 1-quart casserole or 9-inch square baking pan. Place in a 425° oven to melt. Combine remaining ingredients, pour into hot baking dish, and return to oven for 30 minutes, until just set. Cut into 3-inch squares to serve.

Makes 9 3-inch squares, each furnishing 98 calories and 3 grams protein.

Savory Onion Squares: Omit honey in Corn Bread recipe, increase salt to 1 teaspoon, and add ⅓ cup chopped onions to batter.

NORWEGIAN CEREAL BREAD

The outside is crisp and the inside is soft, like cereal. Leftovers store well in the refrigerator and can be reheated to serve.

1 cup rye flour
½ teaspoon salt
½ teaspoon turbinado sugar
¼ cup sunflower seeds, ground to a
   fine meal in blender
1 cup skim milk
2 tablespoons oil

Combine all ingredients and pour into an oiled and floured 9-inch square baking pan. Bake in a 425° oven 30 minutes until lightly browned. Cut into 6 pieces and serve warm with applesauce, fruit butter, butter and salt, or honey, tahini, or a vegetable spread. For twice as much, double recipe and bake in a 9-by-13-inch baking pan.

Makes 6 portions, each furnishing 132 calories and 4 grams protein.

BUTTERMILK BROWN BREAD

2 cups whole-wheat flour
½ cup wheat germ
1 teaspoon baking soda
¼ teaspoon salt
½ cup molasses
1½ cups buttermilk (or 1 cup yogurt
   and ¼ cup skim milk)
¼ to ½ cup raisins

Combine dry ingredients. Beat molasses with milk

and stir into flour mixture until thoroughly blended. Fold in raisins and bake in a well-oiled 9-inch loaf pan in a 350° oven for 50 minutes.

Makes 1 large loaf furnishing 1,669 calories and 60 grams protein.

SWEET INDIAN MEAL BREAD

1½ cups cornmeal
1½ cups whole-wheat flour
1 teaspoon salt
1 teaspoon baking soda
2 cups sour milk*
⅓ cup pure maple syrup

Combine cornmeal, flour, and salt. Dissolve baking soda in sour milk and add to dry ingredients along with maple syrup. Stir until well blended, pour into an oiled 9-inch loaf pan, and bake in a 350° oven 1 hour.

Makes 1 large loaf furnishing 1,825 calories and 57 grams protein.

*To make sour milk add 2 tablespoons white vinegar or lemon juice to 2 cups milk and let stand 10 minutes.

PEANUT BUTTER BREAD

1 cup whole-wheat flour
¾ cup unbleached white flour
2 tablespoons wheat germ
4 teaspoons baking powder
1 teaspoon salt
½ cup peanut butter
3 tablespoons honey
1½ cups milk, whole or skim

Combine dry ingredients. Cut in peanut butter with a fork or pastry blender until mixture is crumbly. Make a well in center and add honey and milk. Beat thoroughly. Pour into an oiled 9-inch loaf pan and bake in a 350° oven 50 minutes.

Makes 1 large loaf furnishing 1,928 calories (1,820 calories with skim milk) and 76 grams protein.

leftover quick breads

The best way to keep muffins and biscuits that are left over is to wrap them in foil and freeze them. They can then be readied for future meals by warming them, still wrapped, in a 300° oven for 10 to 20 minutes. Unfrozen biscuits can be revived by placing them inside a dampened paper bag in a hot oven for several minutes, or by reheating them in a vegetable steamer placed over boiling water. Muffins tend to dry out with reheating but can be enjoyed the second day split and toasted.

While quick breads are generally said to "wither young," those made with honey or molasses are astonishingly long keepers. Loaf breads can be stored successfully at room temperature for several days if kept well wrapped in foil or a plastic bag. After three or four days the breads should be refrigerated and toasted as needed. If you make an extra loaf to freeze, it can be thawed in its wrapper at room temperature, or uncovered in a 325° oven for 20 to 25 minutes.

Muffins, biscuits, and "tea breads" that have become stale and dry beyond eating enjoyment make delicious cold breakfast cereals (see "Hot and Cold Cereal").

POTATOES AND OTHER BREAKFAST SIDE DISHES

Fruit for breakfast, vegetables for lunch and dinner—this has been the basic pattern of the American diet with one important exception: the potato.

Hash browns, home fries, and even French fries team up with eggs on the morning menu of most breakfast haunts. But these restaurant potatoes, although tasty, have often been reduced to a starchy pulp by being prepeeled, soaked, and left on the griddle for hours. When correctly handled, however, potatoes are a fine source of minerals and vitamins and even add significant amounts of protein when coupled with milk or milk products.

One thing that keeps potatoes off the breakfast menu in most homes is the need to preboil them before they are home fried, hash browned, and so forth—extending the cooking time far beyond the patience of most appetites. One way to get around this is to use leftovers from dinner or cook the potatoes the night before. This is not very time-consuming since quartered potatoes, left unpeeled, can be cooked in a vegetable steamer or small amount of boiling water in 15 minutes. The potatoes, which should be barely tender, can be peeled easily after cooking or left unpeeled.

HASH BROWNS

Hash browns!

3 to 4 cups diced, cooked potatoes
1 tablespoon grated onion
1 tablespoon butter
1 tablespoon oil
1 tablespoon chopped parsley
½ teaspoon paprika
¼ cup milk
salt and pepper

Combine potatoes and onion and saute in a mixture of butter and oil about 15 minutes, shaking pan to prevent sticking. Add parsley, paprika, and milk, turn potatoes with a spatula, and cook 5 minutes longer. Season to taste with salt and pepper.

Makes 4 servings.

HOME FRIES

Home Fries!

1½ tablespoons oil
1½ tablespoons butter
1 chopped onion
3 to 4 cups diced, cooked potatoes
salt and pepper

Heat oil and butter in skillet and brown onion lightly. Add potato and continue to cook, mashing potatoes into fat with the bottom of the spatula and turning occasionally, until they begin to brown, about 20 minutes. Season to taste.

Makes 4 servings.

HOME-FRIED SWEETS

High in vitamin A.

4 sweet potatoes
1½ tablespoons oil
1½ tablespoons butter
salt

Wash sweet potatoes and slice into ½-inch pieces. Place in vegetable steamer and cook over boiling water 15 minutes, until barely tender. Remove peel, dice, and cook in mixture of oil and butter over medium-high heat, stirring occasionally, until a light crust forms, about 15 minutes. Season to taste.

Makes 4 to 6 servings.

These last potato recipes have two distinct advantages—the potatoes require no advance preparation and all add high-quality protein to the meal:

Home Fried Sweets

INDIVIDUAL POTATO CAKES

Very much like potato pudding but not quite so heavy. The recipe can be halved, but if you like potatoes you'd best make a lot.

2 ounces (½ cup) Swiss cheese, grated
2 eggs
3 cups (4 medium potatoes) diced, peeled
6 tablespoons wheat germ
6 tablespoons whole-wheat flour
¼ cup minced onion
1 teaspoon salt
2 tablespoons oil

Grate cheese in blender and remove to mixing bowl. Combine eggs and potatoes in blender and puree until potatoes resemble thick applesauce. Add potatoes to cheese along with remaining ingredients, except the oil. Heat ½ teaspoon oil in each cup of a muffin tin, spoon in potato batter, and bake in a 375° oven 20 minutes, until top is firm.

Makes 12 muffins, each furnishing 105 calories and 5 grams protein.

DANISH POTATOES

2 pounds potatoes
3 tablespoons butter
3 tablespoons honey
1 teaspoon salt
cottage cheese

Quarter potatoes and steam 15 minutes, until barely tender. (Or substitute cooked, chilled potatoes.) Peel and dice into small pieces. Heat butter with honey and salt and, when melted, add potatoes, stirring over medium heat until potatoes are coated with the honey butter. Continue to cook until all butter is absorbed, about 5 minutes. Top with plenty of cottage cheese to serve.

Makes 4 to 6 servings.

IRISH POTATOES

A fine brunch choice.

3 medium potatoes, about 1 pound
1 large onion
1 tablespoon oil

¾ cup grated Cheddar
salt and pepper
1 tablespoon butter

Peel potatoes, slice paper thin, and pat dry. Slice onion very thin. Heat oil in a 10-inch skillet, then alternate layers of potato, onion, and cheese, beginning and ending with a good, thick layer of potato. Season each layer of potato with salt and pepper. Dot top with butter, cover, and cook over moderate heat until almost tender, about 20 minutes. Uncover and slip carefully onto a plate; then invert back onto skillet. It may take practice to master this flip; until you have it under control cut the potato "cake" into four wedges, slip spatula under each and turn as best you can. Cook, pressing down with the bottom of the spatula, 10 minutes longer. Cut in wedges to serve.

Makes 4 servings, each furnishing 207 calories and 7.5 grams protein.

OTHER BREAKFAST VEGETABLES

In places where potatoes are less common, other starchy vegetables take their place in the morning. Beans, for example, are the standard fare in Spanish and Arab cuisines, and plantains (cooking bananas) in Puerto Rico, grits in the southern United States, buckwheat in Russia, and rice throughout Asia appear regularly at the breakfast table. Use any of these, as you would potatoes, to accompany eggs, sandwiches, cheese, meat, or fish main dishes.

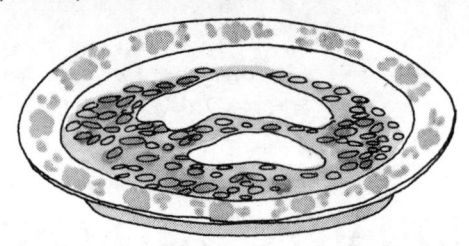

MEXICAN BEANS FOR SIX

Heat ¼ cup oil in skillet. Add 4 cups cooked pinto or kidney beans, a few at a time, mashing them into the hot fat with a fork or potato masher. Add bean liquid as necessary until all beans are mashed. Cook to a thick mush and season to taste with salt.

Mexican Beans with Cheese: Top mashed cooked beans with Monterey Jack cheese, cover, and heat until cheese melts.

Sweet Mexican Beans: Add 1 tablespoon molasses to Mexican Beans during cooking.

FUUL MUDAMMAS

The most popular breakfast in Egypt and much of the Arab world consists of a bowl of cooked fava beans seasoned with lemon and oil, topped on occasion with a cooked egg, and accompanied by a wedge of white cheese, fresh dates, and lots of sweet coffee and tea.

2 cups cooked (or canned) dried fava beans
¼ cup olive oil
1 tablespoon fresh lemon juice
½ teaspoon salt

If you cook the beans at home let them become quite tender so that they can be easily mashed. This will take 3 to 4 hours. For added flavor combine them with a few tablespoons of dried lentils.

Warm beans in a small amount of cooking liquid. Spoon into individual serving bowls. Beat together oil, lemon juice, and salt and pour over beans, mashing lightly with a fork so they absorb the dressing. Top with a poached egg or chopped hard-cooked egg if you like. The authentic way to eat Fuul is to scoop it up with mideastern bread (pita).

Makes 4 servings.

FRIED PLANTAINS

Peel plantain as you would a banana, figuring 1 plantain for every two servings. Slice on the diagonal and soak briefly in salted water. Pat dry and saute in hot oil in skillet using enough oil to keep them from sticking. Cook until brown and crisp on the outside and tender on the inside, about 10 minutes.

CARROT (OR SQUASH) CAKES

Try a Carrot Cake instead of potatoes with fried or poached eggs. A good source of vitamin A.

2 cups cooked carrot (or winter squash)
wheat germ
1 egg, lightly beaten
oil

Mash leftovers of cooked carrot (or squash) with a fork, or puree in a food mill to a thick puree. Shape into flat cakes, dredge with wheat germ, dip in egg, then coat with wheat germ again. Heat a thin layer of oil in skillet and saute the vegetable cakes until brown on both sides, about 5 minutes per side.

Makes 6 cakes, or 6 servings.

Carrot Cakes with Cheese: Add ¼ cup grated cheese per cup of mashed vegetable.

Nutty Carrot Cakes: Add 1 tablespoon peanut butter and 2 tablespoons chopped peanuts per cup of mashed vegetable.

SOUTHERN GRITS

Hominy grits is the name reserved for hulled, coarsely ground corn. Years ago the health of poor farm workers was maintained by the use of this nutritious cereal, which the farmer would grind himself or take to the village mill. Today, grits are more commonly available in the degermed enriched state, and you must go to a health-food store or mill to find them unrefined.

1 cup grits
4 cups boiling water
1 teaspoon salt
1 tablespoon butter

Pour grits into boiling salted water and simmer 1 hour. Or, bring to boil in salted water, cover, remove from heat, and let soak overnight. Then in the morning simmer 15 minutes. Top with butter to serve.

Makes 4 to 6 servings.

KASHA

Groats, like grits, are the result of hulling and coarsely grinding cereal. Buckwheat groats, or kasha, is the most common variety. Kasha is cooked in only 20 minutes and makes a side dish that is particularly rich in potassium, iron, and trace minerals.

1 egg, lightly beaten
1 cup kasha (buckwheat groats)
1 teaspoon salt
2 cups boiling water
butter

Mix egg with kasha and salt and cook, stirring constantly, in a dry saucepan until mixture is dry and each grain separate. Add the boiling water, cover tightly and cook over low heat 15 to 20 minutes until water is absorbed and grain is fluffy. If desired, top with butter to serve. Groats also team up well with wheat germ, sunflower seeds, pine nuts or pumpkin seeds; add to taste.

Makes 6 servings.

QUICK-COOKED RICE

The virtues of brown rice were extolled in the chapter "Hot and Cold Cereal." To cook rice conveniently for breakfast begin before you go to bed, using the following directions.

Combine 1 cup grain and 2 cups water in a heavy saucepan. Bring to boil and cook 5 minutes. Cover and remove from heat. Let stand until morning. Just before breakfast place over moderate heat 5 minutes, until water is absorbed and rice is soft. Serve alongside, or beneath, eggs or a creamy cheese dish.

Makes about 3 cups rice, or 4 to 6 servings.

COFFEE CAKES

Coffee cakes are the rich relatives of yeast and quick breads, thriving on the addition of extra eggs, fat, sweetening, nuts, and fruits. For breakfast entertaining there is no pleasure that can equal these oven-fresh cakes coupled with a good beverage and friendly conversation. Unfortunately, this is a rare treat, since it takes thirty minutes or more to turn out a fresh-baked coffee cake and so the baker must rise early or choose a cake that will not suffer from being prepared in advance.

In general, yeast-leavened coffee cakes are the answer, since they keep well. Most cookbooks do provide yeast coffee-cake recipes, but preparation is often quite intricate, and you rarely receive enough back in food value to warrant the effort. You will find the recipes in this section far less complicated, yet delicious. While these cakes still do not make a substantial breakfast, there is a closer relation between the energy you invest and the nourishment you receive.

Most quick coffee cakes (baking-powder leavened)

are at their peak still warm, so they are preferred with a late breakfast. The Honey-Rye Loaf is the exception here; unlike most baked goods, it stays fresh for weeks.

If you're racing the clock choose one of the ideas for transforming ready-made breads and rolls into delicious desserts.

Though none of these breakfast desserts is impressively high in protein or low in calories, they are more amply endowed with vitamins and minerals than most baked sweets and do add significant amounts of these nutrients to the meal. Cakes of refined flour, sugar, and saturated fats not only add little to the good breakfast, but actually diminish it.

Note: To produce a more delicate cake, whole-wheat pastry flour or sifted whole-wheat flour can replace the whole-wheat flour in any recipe. When sifting whole-wheat flour, return any coarse remains to the flour bin to use in bread-making.

YEAST-LEAVENED COFFEE CAKES
PRUNE-FILLED TEA RING

Prepare dough as for Cinnamon Loaf (see Index). After allowing to rise one hour as directed, divide dough in half and roll into two rectangles, each 9 by 12 inches. Spread with Prune Filling and roll along the 12-inch side. Place seam side down on oiled baking sheet, form into a horseshoe, and press ends to seal. Cut slits with a kitchen scissors to a depth of 1 inch, spacing them 2 inches apart. Let rise 45 minutes, brush surface with a mixture of 1 egg beaten with 1 tablespoon honey and 2 tablespoons milk, and bake in a 350° oven 40 minutes, until golden.

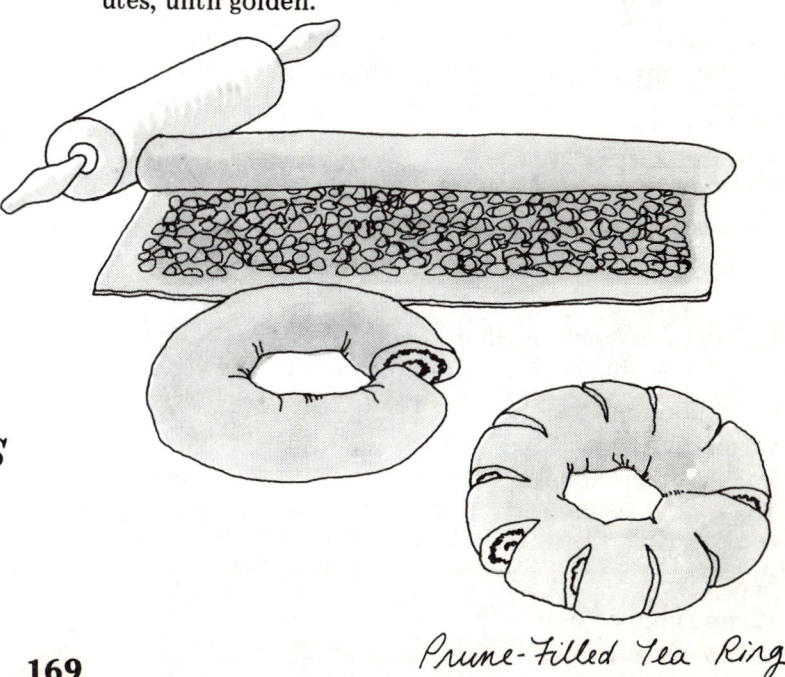

Prune-Filled Tea Ring

Prune Filling (for two tea rings):

2 cups diced dried prunes
½ cup orange juice
½ cup honey
pinch salt

Combine ingredients in a saucepan and simmer until thick and soft, about 5 minutes.

Makes two cakes, one to eat and one to freeze; each Tea Ring furnishes 2,334 calories and 55 grams protein.

NUT STICKS

A yeast cake that rises only 10 minutes.

1 tablespoon dry yeast
⅓ cup warm water
1½ cups whole-wheat flour
¾ to 1 cup unbleached white flour
¼ teaspoon salt
¼ cup oil
2 tablespoons honey
1 teaspoon vanilla
¼ cup yogurt
¾ cup jam
½ cup chopped nuts
¼ cup wheat germ
milk and additional honey for glaze

Sprinkle yeast over warm water and let stand 5 to 10 minutes until dissolved. Combine whole-wheat flour, ¾ cup unbleached flour and salt; blend in oil with fork or pastry cutter until crumbly. Add honey and vanilla to dissolved yeast and add to flour along with yogurt, mixing well to form a smooth dough. Knead, adding additional unbleached flour only if necessary, a full 10 minutes. Roll into a rectangle 12 by 16 inches and cut into 4-inch squares. Flatten each square, spread with 1 tablespoon jam, sprinkle lightly with chopped nuts and 1 teaspoon wheat germ, and roll like a miniature jelly roll. Place on foil-lined baking sheet (to facilitate cleaning) and let rest 10 minutes.

Brush each nut stick with a mixture of equal parts milk and honey, sprinkle with additional nuts, and bake in a 375° oven 20 to 25 minutes, until golden.

Makes 12 nut sticks, each furnishing approximately 220 calories and 3.5 grams protein.

Poppy Sticks: Prepare dough for Nut Sticks; omit jam and nuts and spread with fruit butter. Roll, brush with milk-and-honey glaze, and sprinkle with poppy seeds. Bake as for Nut Sticks.

Poppy Sticks

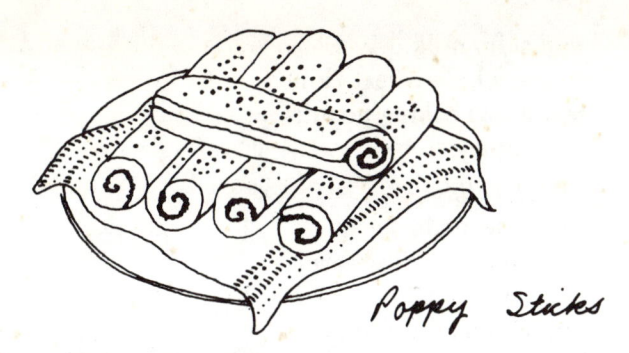

CINNAMON-TOPPED COFFEE CAKE

2 tablespoons dry yeast
1 cup warm water
2½ cups whole-wheat flour, sifted
1 teaspoon salt
½ cup honey
½ cup oil
1 teaspoon vanilla
2 eggs
¼ cup nonfat dry-milk powder

Cinnamon Topping:
½ cup wheat germ
½ cup turbinado sugar
1 teaspoon cinnamon
2 tablespoons oil or melted butter

Dissolve yeast in warm water. Combine flour and salt; then blend in dissolved yeast, honey, and oil. Add vanilla, eggs, and milk powder and beat until smooth, 2 minutes with an electric mixer or 200 strokes by hand. Cover and set to rise in warm place until double, about 30 minutes. Spread into a greased 9-by-13-inch pan or two 9-inch pans and tap sharply on counter to settle batter. Combine ingredients for Cinnamon Topping and sprinkle over batter; press into cake firmly with your fingertips. Let rise 20 to 30 minutes to double, and bake in a 375° oven 20 to 30 minutes, until a toothpick inserted into the center comes out clean.

Extend the life of this coffee cake by toasting the leftovers.

Makes one 9-by-13-inch cake, furnishing 3,600 calories and 84 grams protein; or 300 calories and 7 grams protein per 3-inch square.

APPLE BABKA

A very moist cake that gets even better the second day.

1 tablespoon dry yeast
¼ cup warm apple juice
½ cup honey
¼ cup oil
2 eggs, beaten

¼ teaspoon salt
1 teaspoon vanilla
2 cups whole-wheat flour
2 cups grated apple
¼ cup chopped walnuts
¼ cup raisins or dates
1 tablespoon turbinado sugar
cinnamon

Dissolve yeast in apple juice. Beat together honey, oil, eggs, salt, and vanilla; stir in yeast, then add flour, apples, nuts, and dried fruit and stir into a smooth batter. Turn into an oiled loaf pan, cover, and allow to rise in a warm spot 1 hour. Sprinkle with sugar and cinnamon and bake in a 375° oven 1 hour. Cool completely before cutting.

Makes one loaf, furnishing 2,745 calories and 54 grams protein. A one-inch slice furnishes 305 calories and 6 grams protein.

QUICK COFFEE CAKES
STREUSEL-FILLED COFFEE CAKE

Best the first day.

2 tablespoons oil
2 eggs
¼ cup honey
½ cup skim milk
1¼ cups whole-wheat flour
2 teaspoons baking powder
½ teaspoon salt

Streusel Filling:
⅓ cup turbinado sugar
2 tablespoons wheat germ
2 tablespoons oil
½ cup chopped walnuts
2 teaspoons cinnamon

Combine oil, eggs, honey, and milk. Add dry ingredients and mix into a smooth batter. Pour one-half batter into an oiled 9-inch square baking pan. Combine filling ingredients and sprinkle half over batter, top with remaining batter, and cover with remainder of filling. Bake in a 375° oven 25 minutes.

Makes one cake, furnishing 2,110 calories and 50 grams protein.

ORANGE-OATMEAL COFFEE CAKE

Stays soft and moist long after baking.

1½ cups orange juice
1 cup rolled oats or oatmeal
¼ cup oil
½ cup honey

Orange-Oatmeal Coffee Cake

2 eggs
1½ cups sifted whole-wheat flour
1 teaspoon baking powder
1 teaspoon baking soda
½ cup nonfat dry-milk powder
1 tablespoon chopped orange rind
¼ teaspoon salt
½ teaspoon cinnamon

Coconut Topping:
½ cup chopped walnuts
½ cup shredded unsweetened coconut
¼ cup turbinado sugar

Bring orange juice to boil, pour over oats, and let stand while assembling remaining ingredients. Beat together oil, honey, and egg until light and foamy. Combine flour, baking powder, baking soda, milk powder, orange rind, salt, and cinnamon and add alternately with softened oats to egg mixture, beating gently until smooth. Pour into an oiled 9-by-13-inch baking pan and bake in a 350° oven 20 minutes. Combine topping ingredients, sprinkle over cake and bake 10 minutes longer, until cake tests done.

Makes one cake, furnishing 3,145 calories and 73 grams protein, or 175 calories and 4 grams protein per 2-by-3-inch segment.

HONEY-RYE LOAF

No eggs, no dairy, and no fat. This cake keeps *indefinitely* and is excellent with peanut butter.

1 cup honey
¾ cup water
2 cups rye flour
½ teaspoon baking soda
2 teaspoons baking powder
1 tablespoon cinnamon
½ teaspoon nutmeg
¼ cup chopped or slivered almonds
¼ cup chopped dates
grated rind of 1 orange

Combine honey and water and bring to boil. Beat in flour, baking soda, baking powder, cinnamon, and nutmeg until smooth, at least 5 minutes with an electric mixer. Batter should be thick and gluey. Fold in remaining ingredients and spread batter into an oiled 8-inch loaf pan and bake in a 350° oven 1 hour. Place a pan of water on floor of oven to create steam during baking. Age at least one day before slicing.

One loaf furnishes 1,920 calories and 26 grams protein.

RAISIN TEA CAKES

4 eggs
1 cup whole-wheat flour, sifted
½ cup honey
½ teaspoon baking powder
½ teaspoon vanilla
1 cup raisins
¼ cup finely chopped almonds
¼ cup finely chopped pumpkin seeds

Beat eggs until light. Beat in remaining ingredients in order given, spoon into 12 well-oiled muffin cups, and bake in a 350° oven 20 to 25 minutes. Cool in pan, then loosen carefully around edges with sharp knife to remove. Ice, if desired, with the Honey Frosting below.

Honey Frosting (enough for 12 cupcakes):

3 tablespoons honey
1½ tablespoons milk
½ teaspoon vanilla
¾ cup nonfat dry-milk powder, or more

Beat ingredients until smooth, adding milk powder gradually to thin frosting consistency. Drizzle over cakes. Store leftover iced cakes in refrigerator.

Makes 12 cakes, each furnishing 170 calories and 5 grams protein without icing, 215 calories and 7.5 grams protein with icing.

BREAD AND ROLLS INTO CAKES
SWEET STUFFED ALMOND BUNS

6 small whole-wheat rolls (such as Soft Refrigerator Rolls; see Index)
2 tablespoons milk
¼ cup almonds, ground in blender
2 tablespoons wheat germ
¼ cup honey
cinnamon

Cut lids from rolls and remove as much of the inside as possible. Soak crumbs in milk, then mix well with almonds, wheat germ, and honey. Pack almond mixture into hollowed rolls, replace lids, and sprinkle with cinnamon. Warm in toaster oven or 350° oven about 5 minutes. Rolls can be prepared at any time, stored in refrigerator, and warmed as needed.

Nutritive value depends on the roll but averages 200 calories and 5.5 grams protein per Sweet Stuffed Almond Bun.

HOT FRUIT TURNOVERS

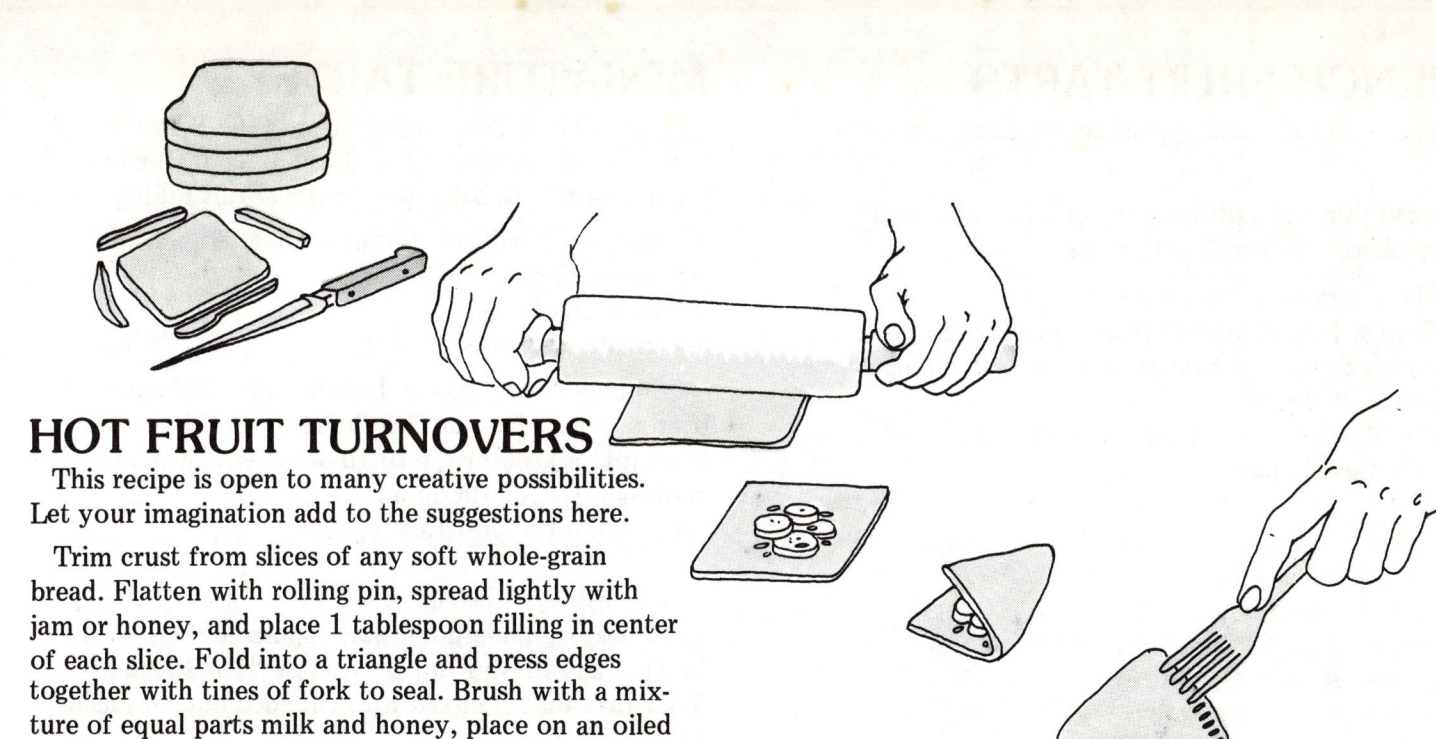

This recipe is open to many creative possibilities. Let your imagination add to the suggestions here.

Trim crust from slices of any soft whole-grain bread. Flatten with rolling pin, spread lightly with jam or honey, and place 1 tablespoon filling in center of each slice. Fold into a triangle and press edges together with tines of fork to seal. Brush with a mixture of equal parts milk and honey, place on an oiled baking sheet, and bake in a 400° oven 15 minutes, until golden.

Fillings:

* Applesauce and chopped walnuts
* Dried fruit butter
* Cottage cheese, cinnamon, and raisins
* Sliced banana and sunflower seeds
* Peanut butter and chopped dates

FRENCH FRUIT TARTS

Prepare with any whole-grain bread, fresh or toasted.

Spread thin slices of bread or toast liberally with cream cheese. Top with any of the following:

* Sliced strawberries and warm honey
* Orange marmalade and fresh tangerine segments
* Apricot halves or banana slices, pistachio nuts, and melted jam
* Sliced peaches, shredded unsweetened coconut, and warm honey

MINIATURE TARTS

Prepare Toast Cups as described in the Toasts section of the chapter "The Bread in Your Breakfast." While Toast Cups bake, prepare this Fruit Filling:

¾ cup diced dried fruit (prunes, dates, figs, raisins in combination)
¼ cup orange juice
¼ cup chopped nuts

Combine dried fruits and orange juice and cook over moderate heat until fruit is soft and almost all the liquid is absorbed, 5 to 10 minutes. Stir in nuts, cool slightly, and spoon into toast cups.

Enough for 6 Miniature Tarts.

More Fillings: Instead of the Fruit Filling you can use 1 heaping tablespoon warm applesauce (fresh is best) or any Fresh Fruit Butter (see "The Bread in Your Breakfast") mixed with chopped nuts or raisins to fill each Toast Cup.

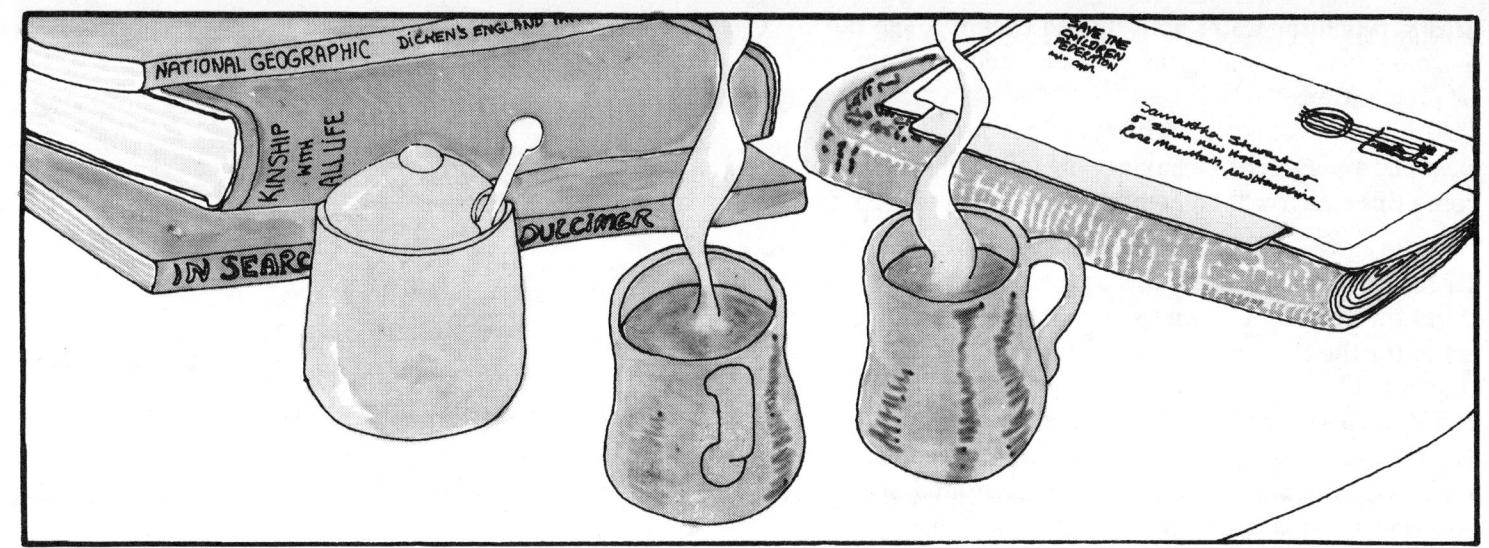

HOT DRINKS

The morning habit of coffee and tea is a worldwide tradition, most probably because of their stimulating qualities. If you're changing your breakfast pattern and energizing with good food you may want to try some of the other hot beverages suggested in this section, particularly the herb teas and the cereal beverages.

COFFEE

Making good coffee depends on the bean, the roast, the grind, the water, the proportion of coffee to water, the method of preparation, and the coffee-maker.

Though opinions differ as to how the best coffee is made, one thing is sure: Coffee should never be boiled, for it is the contact of the boiling water with the coffee that extracts too much caffeine and fatty acids, making coffee irritating to the digestive tract. Most experts agree that the drip method, or filtered coffee, is the best means of extracting the flavorful coffee essence while most of the caffeine and the acids remain in the grounds; percolating, during which the water boils up and back through the ground coffee, is among the least desirable methods of preparation.

Although most coffee drinkers develop their own personal style of coffeemaking, the following are some tips which will be helpful to any method.

1. Buy the grind appropriate to your coffeemaker. Regular or percolator grind is for percolators, drip grind for drip and certain vacuum types, and fine grind for the filter-paper and other vacuum coffeemakers.

2. The best possible coffee is made with beans ground just before preparation, so buy coffee in small quantities unless you use it quickly. Unground beans will remain fresh longer than preground coffee and both are better preserved by cold storage.

3. Experiment to discover the proper measure for the method you use. A good standard to begin with is 2 level tablespoons coffee per 6 ounces (¾ cup) water. You should be able to make about 40 cups from one pound of coffee.

4. Coffee should be made in a glass or ceramic receptacle; contact with metals lowers the quality of coffee.

5. Always use freshly drawn water and heat rapidly to boiling.

6. Do not allow coffee to boil or boiling water to come in contact with coffee (unless otherwise specified).

7. Remove coffee grounds immediately after brewing.

DRIP OR FILTER-PAPER METHOD

Rinse coffee pot with very hot water. Measure coffee into filter, pour measured amount of freshly boiled water into water container (or directly over grounds), cover, and let drip through coffee. A pinch of sugar and a pinch of salt added to the ground coffee is said to help trap the acids. Remove filter section and serve as soon as dripping is ended.

Cup-Size Coffee Filter

VACUUM METHOD

Measure fresh cold water into lower section and heat to boiling. Measure ground coffee into upper bowl and place in position as soon as water boils. When most of the water has risen, stir and let stand over lowered heat about 3 minutes. Remove from heat. When coffee returns to the lower section of the coffeemaker remove the grinds and serve.

PERCOLATED COFFEE

Measure freshly drawn cold water into percolator, making sure the water level is below the bottom of the coffee basket. When water comes to a boil insert basket with coffee, cover, and reduce heat. Let coffee perk *slowly* about 5 minutes (you can determine when it's ready by the color), remove the basket of grounds, and serve.

EGG-CLEARED COFFEE

Bring measured amount of water to boil, using any pot. Combine ground coffee with a crushed egg, shell and all, allowing 1 egg for each 8 tablespoons coffee. (The egg acts as a filter.) When water is boiling, stir in egg-coffee mixture and return to boil. Remove immediately from heat and, when coffee settles, bring back to boil and let settle two more times. Remove from heat, cover, and let grounds sink, about 5 minutes. Strain and serve. This is a good technique to remember when you don't have a coffee pot.

black, regular, or light?

Though many people prefer black coffee, cream and sugar are its traditional accompaniments. For those seeking to avoid refined sugar, molasses and pure maple syrup both make interesting coffee sweeteners; honey tends to leave a bitter aftertaste but is worth a try. Light-coffee drinkers will fare better nutritionally with either of the following Cafe au Laits than they will with fat-rich cream.

CAFÉ AU LAIT

Make extra-strong coffee. Heat an equal volume of whole milk and pour the two liquids simultaneously into cup.

SOLUBLE CAFÉ AU LAIT

The addition of nonfat dry-milk powder makes a creamy beverage that is economical and adds both calcium and protein to your breakfast.

Put 1 tablespoon warm water into coffee cup, add recommended amount of instant coffee, and top with 2 teaspoons nonfat dry-milk powder. Mix to a paste, then stir in boiling water.

instant or soluble coffee

Instant coffee has been perfected to the point where many people can no longer detect the difference. It is neither more nor less harmful than regular coffee. Prepare according to package directions, since brands vary.

cereal grain "coffees"

Various grains and roots like chicory, malt, and barley are commercially processed so they can be used as a hot beverage. Instant Postum and Pero are probably the best known of these drinks. Though most of these "coffee substitutes" bear only a remote resemblance to coffee they are at least harmless and may be quite enjoyable if considered for their own taste.

reheating coffee

Though generally less tasty than freshly brewed coffee, reheated coffee can be quite palatable if the proper steps are taken. Coffee that is more than 24 hours old, however, is hardly worth saving.

If you plan to reheat coffee, transfer it from the pot to a heat-resistant glass jar. Cover and refrigerate. To reheat, place the covered jar in a saucepan, surround with cold water to the depth of the coffee, and heat until the water in the saucepan is boiling. Boil 2 minutes.

TEA

As with coffee, the flavor of tea is enhanced by the use of freshly drawn and freshly boiled water. As soon as the tea has reached the desired strength the leaves (or herbs) should be removed; prolonged steeping brings out a bitter flavor.

leaf tea

Tea can be divided into two general classifications—leaf tea and herb tea. The tea that we are most accustomed to drinking is leaf tea. This tea comes from the East and, in order of strength, may be green (unfermented), oolong (semifermented), or black (fermented). A cup of tea contains approximately half the caffeine of a cup of coffee.

The other titles placed on teas, such as Darjeeling, Earl Grey, Lapsang Souchong, English Breakfast, Constant Comment, and so forth, refer to the particular area in which the leaves were grown, or the blend. Oolong is frequently scented with jasmine petals for a fragrant tea. As with coffee, you must experiment to find the best tea for your taste.

Loose tea turns out to be more economical than tea bags and a pound can be counted on to provide about 200 cups. Loose tea steeped in boiling water also makes a much better-tasting cup than a tea bag, which generally contains lower-quality leaves and siftings.

by the pot

To make tea according to the English experts, rinse the teapot in hot water, measure in tea allowing 1 teaspoon per cup and 1 for the pot, pour in the freshly boiled water, and steep 3 to 5 minutes. Remove tea leaves and serve.

by the cup

Individual tea strainers make it easy to brew loose tea even for individual service. Both metal and bamboo tea strainers are available; since the reaction of the tea leaves with metal may impart a metallic tinge, the latter is preferred.

Measure 1 teaspoon tea leaves into strainer, place in cup, and pour in freshly boiled water. Steep to desired strength, remove tea leaves, and serve.

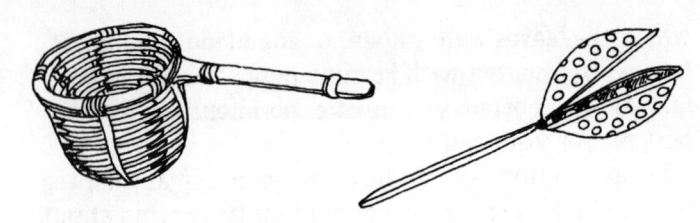

For those who prefer weaker tea, follow the European custom of providing extra hot water for the cup rather than reducing the amount of tea leaves; with too little tea you lose flavor and aroma. If you allow tea leaves to remain in the strainer you can usually use them for a second cup.

People who are really fond of tea drink it plain, without benefit of milk, lemon, or sweetening. It can, however, be nicely flavored with a bit of milk, or a slice of lemon or orange, and honey. In colonial America it was common practice to create "fragrant teas" by adding the petals of roses, gardenias, or violets to the cannister of loose tea leaves. Other variations on this tea party include the addition of a split vanilla bean or a few cloves. Fragrant teas, when brewed, take on the flavor and aroma of the added flowers or spice.

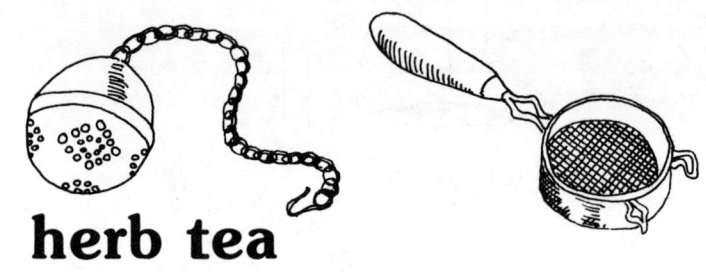

herb tea

Herb teas, unlike traditional leaf teas, contain no tannin or caffeine, and many are endowed with medicinal qualities. Herb teas are good for everyone and are the only teas that should be offered to children.

Herb teas are prepared, for the most part, like leaf teas, and each has its own characteristic flavor. From the long list of selections come such favorites as camomile, mint, lemon verbena or vervain, rose hips and hibiscus, papaya, sassafras, comfrey, and catnip, among others.

Herb teas are preferred plain but may be sweetened with honey.

COCOA AND OTHER HOT MILK DRINKS

The cocoa bean, like the coffee bean, contains a natural stimulant (theobromine); therefore, chocolate-flavored beverages should be limited in their use for children. Another drawback to chocolate is the natural presence of oxalic acid, which inhibits the absorption of calcium, for which milk is so highly praised. If these considerations do not deter you or those you feed, you can cut a few pennies from the food bill by making fresh cocoa or hot chocolate from scratch. An even simpler alternative is to prepare our Homemade Instant Cocoa Mix.

BASIC HOT COCOA

¼ cup cocoa
¼ cup sugar
1 cup water
pinch salt
3 cups milk
¼ teaspoon vanilla

Combine cocoa, sugar, water and salt and bring to boil over moderate heat. Stir in milk and bring to boiling point. Remove from heat, add vanilla and serve.

Makes 4 cups.

BASIC HOT CHOCOLATE

2 ounces (2 squares) baking chocolate
¼ cup sugar
1 cup water
pinch salt
3 cups milk

Combine chocolate, sugar, water and salt and bring to boil over moderate heat. Stir in milk and bring to boiling point. Beat smooth with rotary beater and serve.

Makes 4 cups.

WHIPPED HOT CHOCOLATE

2 ounces (2 squares) baking chocolate
¼ cup sugar
½ cup nonfat dry-milk powder
¼ teaspoon vanilla
2 cups boiling water

Combine all ingredients in blender container and process on low speed until smooth.

Makes 2½ cups.

HOMEMADE INSTANT COCOA MIX

½ cup cocoa
½ cup sugar
½ teaspoon salt
4 cups nonfat dry-milk powder

Mix all ingredients and store in an airtight container or jar. Stir well before using.

To prepare Hot Cocoa: For each serving mix 4 rounded tablespoons with ¼ cup cold water. Stir in ¾ cup boiling water.

In addition to cocoa, other hot milk drinks can be served to sleepy heads to entice them to the table on cold winter mornings.

HOT VANILLA MILK

For 1 large or 2 small servings heat 1 cup milk with 1½ teaspoons honey and 1 teaspoon vanilla.

CAROB COCOA

For 2 6-ounce servings beat together 1½ cups milk, 2 teaspoons carob powder, 1 tablespoon honey and ¼ teaspoon vanilla, with a wire whisk or rotary beater. Heat gently until just below boiling.

HOT PEANUT MILK

For 1 large or 2 small servings beat together 1 cup milk, ½ tablespoon honey and 1½ tablespoons peanut butter with a fork, wire whisk, or rotary beater. Heat gently, stirring occasionally, until just below boiling.

HOT WHEAT DRINK

Add 1 tablespoon wheat germ and a stick of cinnamon to ingredients for Hot Vanilla Milk, heat, and serve. Eat the softened cereal at the bottom of the cup with a spoon.

WHIPPED HOT EGGNOG

2 cups milk
2 tablespoons honey
1 teaspoon vanilla
¼ teaspoon cinnamon
1 egg

Combine all ingredients except egg in saucepan and heat to just below boiling. Beat egg until frothy in a pitcher. Pour in hot milk.

Makes 2½ cups.

MOLASSES POSSET

Serve this hot sweetened whey to comfort those confined to bed with a cold or upset stomach.

1 cup milk
1 tablespoon molasses
1 tablespoon lemon juice

Bring milk to boil. Stir in molasses and lemon juice and let stand until solids and liquid separate. Pour through a strainer and serve the hot liquid. The curd can be chilled and served as a soft cheese.

APPENDIX
BREAKFAST RECOMMENDATIONS FROM INFANCY TO INFINITY

BABY'S BREAKFAST

Babies need not be considered separate from the rest of the family. All the creamed cereals, soft dry cereals (including muesli if the nuts are finely ground), cottage cheese and yogurt dishes, and breakfast breads you serve can be given to the young child. Exclude those foods with chunks of nuts or seeds, whole pieces of fruit, visible fat, or high concentrations of sweetening. Caution must be taken that there are no large pieces of food to get stuck in the windpipe, but any foods can be pulverized in a blender or baby-food grinder.

Cook eggs soft for baby; thin tahini and nut butters until almost saucelike in consistency. Softened raisins and prunes provide valuable iron, and their soaking liquid should be used in pureeing other foods for high mineral content. A little bit of molasses used as sweetening offers mild laxative action.

If juices are taken in a bottle they may require straining to pass through the nipple. Do this for very young children; as they grow make the nipple hole larger instead.

An important thing to remember in feeding infants is they do not consume any solid foods in large enough volume to sustain them and therefore mother's milk or the formula must be recognized as their principal source of nourishment. Make sure infants have enough milk to drink; then introduce other foods to the menu casually.

CHILDREN'S MORNING

At various stages of their growth, children require different amounts of energy; the more active they are, the more calories they burn. But even the most inactive children have a high need for protein, for protein provides the building materials for all bodily tissues, including muscles, bones, and teeth, and the basis for antibodies to fight infection. See that breakfast includes at least 10 grams of protein from ages three to ten, and 15 grams from ten on up. Adjust calories according to weight constancy.

All children experience periods of food despondency; some of the more whimsical recipes in this book will help overcome this, and so will including children in cooking and menu planning. Let youngsters help bake breadstuffs or prepare homemade cereals in the evening and they'll be eager to try them in the morning. Hot cereals that are whipped into puddings, cheese and fruit dishes that allow creativity at the table, and miniature pancakes with a selection of sauces all make breakfast more fun. Milk drinks fortified with fruit and eggs for a meal-in-a-glass pack a lot into a little space. Particularly when children are poor eaters, wheat germ, nonfat dry-milk powder, and brewer's yeast should be added whenever practical (to eggs, spreads, drinks, cereals) for nourishment.

Since food habits are instilled early, make a conscious effort to use skim milk and vegetable oils in place of whole milk and butter in feeding children as well as adults. By adding harmless flavoring ingredients, as we have shown you here, to skim milk it can be made more palatable and is most economical if you use nonfat dry-milk powder. Do not eliminate whole milk or whole milk products altogether, for

Recommended Daily Allowances *

	AGE years	WEIGHT pounds	HEIGHT inches	CALORIES	PROTEIN grams	CALCIUM mg	PHOSPHORUS mg	IODINE mg	MAGNESIUM mg	IRON mg	VITAMIN A iu	VITAMIN D iu	VITAMIN E iu	VITAMIN C mg	NIACIN mg	RIBOFLAVIN mg	THIAMIN mg	VITAMIN B12 mcg	VITAMIN B6 mg	FOLACIN mg	ZINC mg
Infants	0-½	14	24	lb. x 53	lb. x 1.0	360	240	35	60	10	14,400	400	4	35	5	.4	.3	.3	.3	.05	3
	½-1	20	28	lb. x 49	lb. x .9	540	400	45	70	15	2,000	400	5	35	8	.6	.5	.3	.4	.05	5
Children	1-3	28	34	1,300	23	800	800	60	150	15	2,000	400	7	40	9	.8	.7	1.0	.6	.1	10
	4-6	44	44	1,800	30	800	800	80	200	10	2,500	400	9	40	12	1.1	.9	1.5	.9	.2	10
	7-10	66	54	2,400	36	800	800	110	250	10	3,300	400	10	40	16	1.2	1.2	2.0	1.2	.3	10
Males	11-14	97	63	2,800	44	1,200	1,200	130	350	18	5,000	400	12	45	18	1.5	1.4	3.0	1.6	.4	15
	15-18	134	69	3,000	54	1,200	1,200	150	400	18	5,000	400	12	45	20	1.8	1.5	3.0	2.0	.4	15
	19-22	147	69	3,000	54	800	800	140	350	10	5,000	400	15	45	20	1.8	1.5	3.0	2.0	.4	15
	23-50	154	69	2,700	56	800	800	130	350	10	5,000		15	45	18	1.6	1.4	3.0	2.0	.4	15
	51+	154	69	2,400	56	800	800	110	350	10	5,000		15	45	16	1.5	1.2	3.0	2.0	.4	15
Females	11-14	97	62	2,400	44	1,200	1,200	115	300	18	4,000	400	10	45	16	1.3	1.2	3.0	1.6	.4	15
	15-18	119	65	2,100	48	1,200	1,200	115	300	18	4,000	400	11	45	14	1.4	1.1	3.0	2.0	.4	15
	19-22	128	65	2,100	46	800	800	100	300	18	4,000	400	12	45	14	1.4	1.1	3.0	2.0	.4	15
	23-50	128	65	2,000	46	800	800	100	300	18	4,000		12	45	13	1.2	1.0	3.0	2.0	.4	15
	51+	128	65	1,800	46	800	800	80	300	10	4,000		12	45	12	1.1	1.0	3.0	2.0	.4	15
Pregnant				+300	+30	1,200	1,200	125	450	18+	5,000	400	15	60	+2	+.3	+.3	4.0	2.5	.8	20
Lactating				+500	+20	1,200	1,200	150	450	16	6,000	400	15	80	+4	+.5	+.3	4.0	2.5	.6	25

*Revised, 1973. Published by National Academy of Sciences, National Research Council, Food and Nutrition Board.

they are still the best source of vitamin A, and their fat is necessary for the proper absorption of vitamins A and D that are used to fortify most milk. Try to limit egg intake to one per day and extend the nutritive value with milk, wheat germ, whole grains, nuts, and cheeses as exemplified by the recipes in this book.

GROWN-UP BREAKFASTS

Probably the saddest breakfast samples come from the adult breakfast table. The primary excuse for this is lack of time, followed by the desire to lose weight. It's easy enough to sneak in at least five minutes' eating time in the morning, which is more than sufficient to whip up a blender drink, slap together a sandwich, or breakfast on the many suggestions that can be made beforehand and stored for quick starts.

As far as weight control is concerned, one of the worst things you can do in trying to lose pounds is skip breakfast. It is far better to have a really good breakfast and run on this energy until dinnertime than to skip breakfast and push yourself to the point where you can barely fight the hunger pangs. It is then that you give way to the temptation of high-calorie foods or sweets for a quick energy lift.

A breakfast with bulk not only reduces hunger throughout the day but provides roughage that many people require to combat constipation. Fresh fruits, bran, whole-grain cereals and breadstuffs, yogurt, and molasses in the morning will start bowel activity and bring about regulation in a natural manner. What you must remember, however, is that digestion begins in the mouth and unrefined foods must be thoroughly chewed to avoid intestinal abrasions and receive their full nutritional and bulk benefits.

The older we get, the more we begin to consider the effects of our diet on our bodies. Saturated fats become particularly critical in the early adult years and can be controlled through the use of skim milk, non-fat dry-milk powder in cooking, low-fat cheeses like yogurt and cottage cheese, substitution of vegetable oils for butter in cooking, and use of nut butters and unfatty spreads in place of butter on breadstuffs. Cutting egg consumption to seven eggs per week and extending them with other foods to gain their nutritional benefits with less concentration of saturated fat and dietary cholesterol is also a healthy objective.

OCTOGENARIANS, AND THOSE IN THE RUNNING

Though body structure becomes less dependent on building materials in old age, good food is the best preservative for our thought processes. Insufficient diet weakens the ability to concentrate, increases susceptibility to infection, and slows healing.

Vitamin and mineral intake must be exceptionally high to insure good health at this stage of life, and with a decrease in activity it must come with stricter calorie budgeting. Fresh fruits and dried fruits should be the focal point of the breakfast menu and will provide stimulation to both the mind and the digestive tract. As long as your teeth are healthy you can eat anything; nuts and whole grains are no harder to digest as you grow older as long as you chew them properly. Do not crowd out other nutritious foods with an overdependence on breads and other grain foods, but combine them judiciously with cheese, fish, and milk for well-balanced breakfasts.

Eating alone, perhaps after years of company, is apt to decrease enthusiasm for food. For those faced with this problem, informal breakfasts of yogurt and cottage cheese can be depended upon for simple, quick nourishment. But rather than giving in to the boredom, turn cooking into a creative endeavor and invite friends and neighbors who are likely to be facing the same difficulties to join you for breakfast. Use your spare time to bake nutritious breakfast sweets and homemade cereals, and share them with younger people in your family or neighborhood who may not have the chance to prepare these themselves. Remember, even if you've never cooked before, cooking is a craft that can be easily picked up at any age.

THE SELECTION OF INGREDIENTS AND COOKING UTENSILS

NUTRITIONAL BOOSTERS

Each recipe in *The Good Breakfast Book* is carefully balanced with respect to calories, protein, vitamins, and minerals to make it a good nutritional investment. Some of the most effective ingredients for creating good breakfasts, however, have not been fully exploited in our recipes because their overuse tends to smack of "food faddism" and alienate those not acquainted with these less conventional foods. If you do wish an even richer concentration of nutrients on the breakfast menu, the following suggestions will help you add these nutritional boosters on your own.

brewer's yeast

Many people know of brewer's yeast as a diet supplement, a valuable source of high-quality protein, iron, and the B-vitamin complex. In fact, its B-vitamin potency is so great that brewer's yeast is a standard for measuring B-vitamin content, just as orange juice is the standard for vitamin C and eggs for protein. On an ounce-for-ounce basis, brewer's yeast contains almost three times the protein of beef, although we do not consume it in such large quantities.

What few people realize, however, is that brewer's yeast can double as a fine flavoring ingredient as well as an economical source of nutrients.

Available flaked or ground fine, the yeast has a faintly meaty taste and odor. For seasoning, debittered yeast is recommended, as it has been treated to remove the bitter taste characteristic of the hops used in brewing, from which the yeast is a by-product. Since different brands have slightly different flavors, it is important to experiment to find the one that pleases you. It is fairly simple to incorporate the yeast powder into standard recipes. An average of 2 teaspoons yeast added to a pound of cottage cheese, a full recipe for muffins, cake, or a loaf of bread, cereal for four, or one cup of juice exemplifies its versatility. Brewer's yeast can also be added to peanut butter, egg salad, and other sandwich fillings, grated cheese in casseroles and other combination dishes, cheese and other milk-based sauces, meat and fish patties, and soups where you wish to impart a "meaty" flavor. Because some people are not yet in the habit of using brewer's yeast as a seasoning it is not widely included in our recipes. However, we do recommend you try it and enjoy its many benefits.

bran

Both chronic constipation and occasional irregularity are common ailments in this country. One theory for their cause is the lack of bulk in our highly processed diet. Unprocessed bran is an excellent source of dietary bulk and has been successfully used by many to correct constipation and irregularity by natural means. One to three tablespoons bran, taken daily over a continued period of time, will add greater mass and moisture to waste matter causing it to pass smoothly and quickly through the system. Unlike nuts and many coarse-grained foods, bran is not irritating to the digestive tract or the colon.

It is a simple matter to add bran to most breakfast foods. A spoonful of raw bran (which is similar in appearance to wheat germ) can be sprinkled on any cereal, before or after cooking. It can be stirred into fruit juices, applesauce, nut butters, yogurt, cottage cheese, breakfast soups, eggs, the batter for baked goods and milk drinks. It is so mild in flavor that it will go unnoticed in most combination dishes. It should, however, be accompanied by a good supply of liquid since it is almost spongelike in its ability to absorb moisture.

nonfat dry-milk powder

In its powdered state, nonfat dry-milk is a concentrated source of protein, calcium, riboflavin, and other natural milk nutrients. Even though its use in the kitchen is promoted throughout *The Good Breakfast Book*, its possibilities have hardly been exhausted.

Whenever you prepare a milk drink, for example, you can boost the value by adding a tablespoon of nonfat dry-milk powder. When milk is called for in a conventional recipe you can add a tablespoon of milk powder along with each cup of milk without affecting the success of the recipe. A spoonful of the powder can be added to eggs, and it can be combined with cereal grains or flour in baking. It is unexcelled in its ability to enhance food value without excessive calories. Thus, it is particularly valuable to dieters, sedentary folks, and those with small appetites.

nuts and seeds

Nuts and seeds—particularly peanuts, raw cashews, pine nuts, sunflower seeds, pumpkin seeds, and sesame seeds—are good sources of protein, iron, B vitamins, and the trace minerals lacking in refined foods. If unroasted, nuts and seeds have a high enzyme content, but when the enzymes are destroyed, as in boiling, frying, or roasting, they become more difficult to digest. To be well digested, nuts and seeds must also be thoroughly chewed.

Unsalted nuts and seeds, when ground in the blender to a floury consistency, can be used much like flour or wheat germ for thickening soups, sauces, and other liquid combinations. Ground, they can replace bread crumbs as filler and can be used in limited quantity in baked goods and flour coatings. They can be sprinkled on top of fruit salads, cereals, or baked dishes.

Roasted soybeans, often called soy nuts, can be used in the same manner.

oils

In view of the high concentration of saturated fat in butter, it is worthwhile to seek alternatives. For this reason most of the recipes in *The Good Breakfast Book* use oil both as an ingredient and to lubricate the skillet or baking pan.

Liquid vegetable and nut oils are rich in unsaturated fat, an essential dietary factor that enhances absorption of vitamins A, D, E, and K, supplies vital fatty acids, and is believed to help disperse cholesterol throughout the bloodstream so that it does not form deposits in the arteries.

Of the liquid nut and vegetable oils, safflower oil and corn oil are the best sources of polyunsaturated fat. They should be favored in cooking. Since high heat can break down fat, the most heat-resistant oils should be chosen as lubricants; for this job corn and peanut oils are most effective.

Though olive oil is possibly the richest in minerals, vitamin E, and flavor, it is not effective in lowering blood cholesterol, although it does not increase its concentration either; rather, it is neutral in this respect. Coconut oil is high in saturated fat and should be avoided. Blended oils are also less acceptable, since they usually contain large amounts of cottonseed oil. (Because cotton is not recognized as an edible crop, the plants are subject to large doses of chemical spraying that render the by-products potentially hazardous).

soy flour

Soy flour is a high-protein meal made from ground soybeans that can be used to protein-fortify almost any food. In baking, soy flour not only adds protein but tends to keep baked goods moist for a longer time. Since soy flour lacks the elasticity of wheat flour it is best used in combination with other grains or a rather dense product will result.

To use soy flour in baking it is generally recommended you replace 12 percent of the wheat flour with soy flour; or 1½ tablespoons soy flour should substitute for 1½ tablespoons wheat flour out of every cupful. To extend ground meat or fish dishes with soy flour (which is akin to textured vegetable protein), replace ¼ pound ground meat with a mixture of ½ cup soy flour blended with ¾ cup cold water that has been boiled gently until thick and pasty. Or use the residue from making soy milk (see "Milk and Main Dish Beverages").

sprouts

Sprouting is one of the fastest ways to improve the nutritional value of foods. Almost any whole seed can be turned into a sprout, and those that are good to eat raw, like alfalfa sprouts, sunflower-seed sprouts, wheat sprouts, millet sprouts, oat sprouts, and rye sprouts, are favored for breakfast. During the sprouting process the B vitamins, vitamin C, vitamin E, and vitamin A increase from four to ten times.

Once seeds are sprouted they can be blended into drinks (see "Good Beginnings"), ground and added to bread and rolls, used to add crunch to cheese or nut-butter sandwiches, tossed into cereals and fruit salads, or combined with ground meat into burgers, just for starters.

There are many methods for sprouting, but the jar technique is by far the simplest.

JAR SPROUTING

You will need a wide-mouth jar (1 quart or larger), a rust-proof screen or cheesecloth or a nylon stocking, a rubberband or the outer ring from a ball jar (canning jar), and the seeds for sprouting.

Choose a jar large enough to accommodate the growth—four to six times the volume of the sprouting mixture.

soak seeds in water overnight

1. Soak seeds in plenty of water overnight or at least 8 hours. Start with 2 or 3 tablespoons seeds in a quart jar.

2. Drain water from jar through the screen or cheesecloth that has been fastened into place with a rubberband or ball-jar ring. Pour cool tapwater into the jar to rinse and drain once more.

3. Turn jar upside down, laying it at an angle in a bowl to catch the drippings, and put in a dark, warm place like the inside of a kitchen cabinet.

4. Rinse seeds 2 to 3 times a day for 2 to 5 days until sprouts are ¼ to ½ inch long. To increase the vitamin A and chlorophyl content place in sun the *last day* and sprouts will turn green.

After Rinsing in Cool Water Turn Jar Upside Down. Place in a Bowl and Store in a Dark, Warm Place.

The finished sprouts should be stored in the refrigerator and used over the next 5 days in as many ways as you can think of.

sweeteners

The addition of sweetening never benefits anything but the flavor of a food. Sometimes, however, this added flavoring is necessary to make otherwise nutritious dishes palatable. Because some sweetening agents are less harmful than others it is necessary to choose with discretion.

White, refined sugar is the least desirable sweetening agent. All traces of nutriment have been processed out and the remaining sucrose adds empty calories, contributes to tooth decay, and can be irritating to the stomach lining, particularly when taken on an empty stomach.

Honey offers a chance to sweeten foods in a much more subtle manner. The natural sugars in honey are more easily digested than those in cane sugar; therefore, honey is usually recommended for feeding babies. Honey also contains trace minerals and low levels of B vitamins. Unfiltered, raw, or uncooked honey is recommended.

Molasses comes from the residuals of the sugar-making process. Blackstrap molasses contains rich supplies of iron and calcium but is somewhat strong-tasting. Unsulfured molasses is more mellow, contains trace minerals, and has a mild laxative effect on the system.

Pure maple syrup, although costly, is worth every penny in taste. It contains some amounts of iron and calcium and, unlike the maple-flavored syrups, blended syrups, and pancake syrups made in its image, is free of refined sugars, coloring and preservatives.

Turbinado sugar, also known as raw sugar, is one step above white sugar and should be used when none of the other alternatives is appropriate. Although not actually raw, this partially refined sugar does retain some of the molasses, which gives it some nutritional significance.

wheat germ

As with nonfat dry-milk powder, we make liberal use of this commodity in our recipes, but you can give it even greater emphasis in your kitchen if you choose. Sprinkle it on cereals, cottage cheese, yogurt, puddings, eggs or anything with a creamy consistency. Add it to spreads, fish and meat patties, egg and fish salads and blender beverages in any amount that pleases you. In baking replace 1 to 2 tablespoons flour per cup with wheat germ without otherwise changing the recipe.

Wheat germ is one of the few non-animal sources of high-quality protein and has the ability to uplift other grains and vegetable protein. It is richly endowed with B vitamins, vitamin E, and phosphorus and will go a lot further in promoting good health than any vitamin pill.

COOKING UTENSILS

There are certain cooking utensils which also have the ability to add both flavor and food value to the menu.

One invaluable aid to convenience food preparation without the loss of quality is the *electric blender*. With this tool, fresh fruits can be liquified in seconds, nuts can be ground into flour (or nutmeals) and butters, vegetables can be pureed into spreads, soups

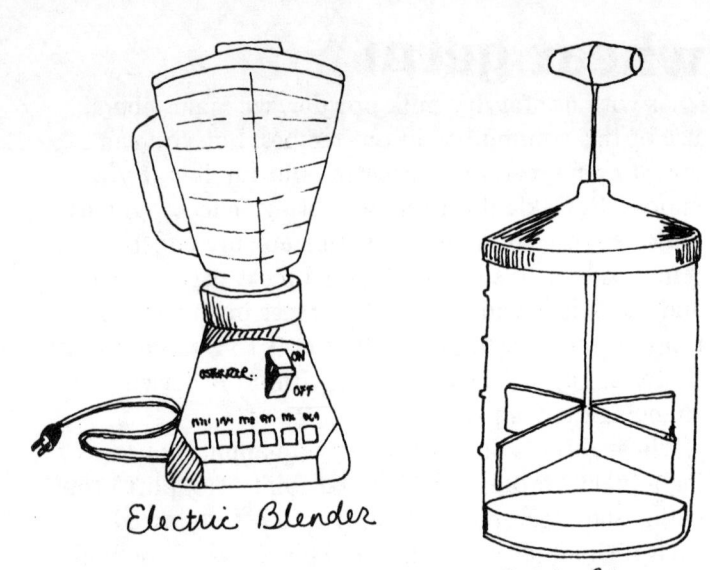

Electric Blender

Nut Chopper

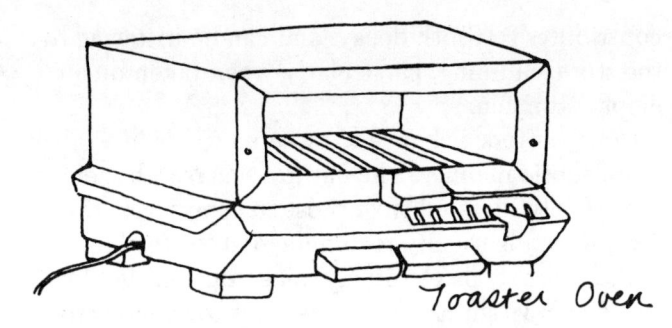

Toaster Oven

can be creamed instantaneously, and leftover grains can be made into quick puddings. Although not an inexpensive item, in the long run it will earn its price.

A *vegetable steamer* or basket can save both fuel and food value. When foods are cooked above rather than in water, water-soluble vitamins are retained. The concentration of heat from the steam can save several minutes of cooking time, and breads, grains, and other cooked foods can be reheated readily in a steamer, so that often you do not have to turn on the oven. Stainless-steel steamers that can be adjusted to fit into a 2-quart or larger pot are inexpensive and available in most gourmet shops, natural-food stores, and large department stores.

For years we resisted buying a *yogurt-maker* under the theory that good yogurt can be incubated in any number of warm spots without wasting electricity. Though this is true, the large appetite for yogurt in our house began to make homemade yogurt-making a time-consuming chore rather than a pleasure. The yogurt-maker has changed all this, and we can now prepare a batch of yogurt in as long as it takes to mix the nonfat dry-milk powder with warm water. We justify the initial investment in the yogurt-maker and the fuel consumption by noting that, with current prices, making yogurt at home is about one-third the cost of store bought yogurt.

A *nut chopper*, though not essential to cooking, is an added convenience that makes granola-making and baking that much simpler. Essentially a jar with a blade and plunger attached to the cap, it makes chopping dried fruits and nuts less messy and cuts down the waste from nuts flying out of the chopping bowl all over the kitchen. Though a blender can be used for the same purpose, coarse chopping is a bit harder to control in the high-powered grinder.

Anyone with a large family or a propensity for pancakes, French toast, grilled sandwiches, or quantity cooking will enjoy having a heavy *cast-iron griddle*, one that fits over two burners and has room for about eight items at a time. With the griddle food preparation is quicker and everyone can eat at once without your having to hold most of the food warm in the oven.

When you need to keep foods warm, or for reheating one or two servings of frozen baked goods at a time, the *toaster oven* is highly recommended. It is particularly useful when everyone eats at a different time and is cheaper to operate for short periods than the oven. It is also excellent for top browning and melted cheese sandwiches.

food values for a balanced breakfast

Protein Foods

Meat
Poultry
Fish
Eggs
Cheese
Milk and milk products
Dried beans
Wheat germ
Nuts and nut butters
Whole grain cereals
Brewer's yeast

Energy Foods

Butter
Vegetable oils
Bread and baked goods
Potatoes
Cereal
Honey, molasses, sugar, and maple syrup
Jam
Dried beans
Cream

Foods that Provide Calcium

Milk, cheese, and yogurt
Sardines
Canned salmon
Egg yolk
Blackstrap molasses
Soy products
Sesame seeds and sesame butter
Almonds
Oats
Dark green, leafy vegetables

Foods that Provide Iron

Meat, particularly organ meat
Egg yolk
Whole-grain and enriched cereals
Whole-grain and enriched breadstuffs
Raisins
Prunes
Dried apricots
Molasses
Dried beans
Dark green, leafy vegetables

Foods that Contain Vitamin A

Butter and fortified margarine
Egg yolk
Cream
Whole and fortified milk
Cheese
Liver
Fish oils
Apricots, peaches (yellow), cantaloupe, nectarines
Corn, sweet potatoes, carrots, tomatoes, pumpkin
Salmon

Foods that Contain B Vitamins

Meat, particularly organ meat
Brewer's yeast
Whole-grain breads and cereals
Wheat germ
Milk and milk products
Nuts and seeds
Dried beans
Avocado
Bananas
Mushrooms

Foods that Contain Vitamin C

Oranges, grapefruit, and lemons
Berries
Rosehips
Guavas, mangos
Cantaloupe
Tomatoes
Sprouts

Foods that Furnish Potassium

Bananas
Avocado
Dried fruits
Nuts
Dried beans
Cocoa
Tomatoes
Buckwheat

Foods that Furnish Vitamin D

Fortified milk
Egg yolk
Fish oils

Foods that Contain Vitamin E
Unrefined vegetable oils
Whole grains
Wheat germ
Unroasted nuts and seeds

Foods High in Saturated Fat
Meat
Egg yolk
Butter
Cream
Whole milk and whole-milk cheese
Hydrogenated shortening
Coconut and coconut oil
Chocolate

Foods High in Unsaturated Fat
Liquid oils, especially corn, safflower, and soy
Fish
Mayonnaise
Nuts and nut butters

Foods High in Cholesterol
Organ meats
Meat
Egg yolk
Cream
Whole milk and whole-milk cheese
Butter

OUT TO BREAKFAST

If you've ever had the chance to look through any restaurant-trade or food-merchandising magazines you are probably aware of the changes that have taken place in mass food preparation. Every day more and more of the meals that are served come in pre-packaged, frozen, individual portions that are merely defrosted in the restaurant kitchen. Eggs today come powdered in cans; potatoes are distributed as flakes or dehydrated lumps in hermetically sealed packets; meats and fish are bought pre-seasoned, pre-breaded, pre-weighed, in packets of foil; and muffins, danish, doughnuts and other baked favorites arrive in their own cellophane wrappers. Despite this, if you're willing to be both persistent and intuitive you can still get a good breakfast outside your own home.

To begin with, you should make it a point to patronize and to publicize those restaurants that do take pride in their cooking and fulfill their responsibility of feeding the public by preparing foods from fresh ingredients, squeezing fresh juices and perhaps doing some of their own baking. In addition, here are some general suggestions that will help you to get the most out of restaurant breakfasts.

When it comes to fruit or juice you will probably have a good variety to select from. Most restaurants stock canned, unsweetened grapefruit juice, orange juice, pineapple juice and tomato juice. Naturally, if you happen on a restaurant that squeezes fresh O.J. you won't have to look any further. You may also often have the chance to order a half-grapefruit or melon in season.

Most cold breakfast cereals are a poor choice unless you happen to be carrying some wheat germ with you. However, consult the table A Comparison of Packaged Dry Cereals in the chapter "Hot and Cold Cereal," so that if you do include cereal in your breakfast you'll know which ones are the most nutritious. As an alternative to cold cereals, many breakfast haunts cook up a pot of hot porridge, particularly in the colder sections of the country. Cream of wheat and oatmeal are the most common offerings. Skip the cream of (refined) wheat, but feel free to order the oatmeal and add lots of milk to it.

Pancakes are almost always the standard white-flour-from-a-mix kind. Occasionally you'll find buckwheat cakes on the menu—a more rewarding choice. French toast, too, is made with white bread, but if it is prepared fresh and to order (rather than arriving frozen from the central warehouse) you may convince them to substitute whole-wheat bread for your order. The next problem you'll encounter is the syrup. Pure maple syrup is a rarity in commercial eating places. So ask for honey, since many restaurants do keep it in stock. It will come in handy for sweetening cereals and beverages, too.

Eggs, of course, are found everywhere. If you have cause to wonder whether they are fresh or powdered (dried eggs are often used in chain restaurants, cafeterias, and, we're sorry to say, are also becoming more popular in neighborhood establishments), order yours poached, fried or in the shell. There's no way to dehydrate these as yet. If you're a fried-egg fancier give poached eggs a chance. They're far less greasy (and that grease could be anything from bacon fat, to butter, to margarine, to oil) and much easier to digest.

Try for whole-wheat bread. If this fails, remember most brands of English muffins are made with unbleached flour, and rye bread is at least 2 percent rye flour. Many coffee shops, diners and other places that cater to a breakfast crowd offer fresh-baked muffins. Bran muffins are top choice since they add valuable roughage to the diet (along with the white flour and sugar). Corn bread and muffins are generally made with degerminated meal, but particularly in the South, you may be rewarded with a praiseworthy bread. Depending on what part of the country you're in, corn bread may be sweet or savory.

If you like potatoes, eat them at home. French fries

are cooked in superheated fat that has been used over and over again. Home fries and hash browns sit on the stove so long that all the food value has been cooked away. In addition, very few restaurants want to go to the trouble of peeling and cooking fresh potatoes so they usually purchase them already prepared—and prepared with chemicals to keep them from browning and spoiling. Your only hope is to try to secure one of the potatoes they are baking for lunch. Grits, like cornmeal, are also degerminated but they are usually enriched, which means they do offer some B-vitamin value and interesting variety to the menu.

Other good breakfasts you can usually obtain include:

* Cottage cheese with fresh fruit (or banana, at least)
* Grilled cheese. Ask for Swiss rather than American since it is less likely to be processed, or Cheddar if it's on the menu. Always specify whole-wheat bread.
* A sliced-egg sandwich
* Yogurt
* Sardines, tuna fish or canned salmon

Beverage choices will be quite conventional: coffee, tea, hot chocolate or milk. If you're a light-coffee or tea-with-milk drinker, be sure to ask if the "cream" really is. In most places non-dairy creamer (which is chock full of chemicals and, if made with a coconut oil base, still highly saturated) has replaced the real thing. If this is the case it is worth it to ask for and, if necessary, to buy milk to lighten your beverage. Perhaps then you'll even feel compelled to drink the extra milk rather than waste it. If you drink your coffee or tea sweet, again, ask for honey.

One last tip! When you breakfast out, don't be shy. If you object to cream substitutes; if you would like to see hot cereals, honey and whole-wheat bread become standard restaurant fare; or if you, perchance, do not want to see prepared foods totally replace fresh eggs, real potatoes, homemade griddle-cakes and similar baked goods, you'd better make it known now.

Index

Almond
    baked apples with, 10-11
    buns, sweet stuffed, 174
    milk, 122
Apples, 9-11
    -and-cheese squares, 136
    babka, 171-172
    baked, 10
    baked with almond, 10-11
    -buttermilk soup, 118
    grist cereal, 30
    honey, 10
    juices, 7
    pancake, baked, 109
    sautéed ham and, 79
    snacks, 10
Applesauce, 10
Applewiches, 10
Apricot
    milk, 125
    -orange nectar, 4
    pancake topping, 112
Apricots à la Little Ms. Muffet, 42-43
Arab cheese (Labani), 51
Avocado
    baked with cheese, 43
    cubes, 12
    in juices, 7
    -pineapple butter, 101

Babies, breakfasts for, 185
Bacon, 74-75
    Canadian, 75

Bagels, 144-145
Baking fish, 73
Banana
    baked, 11
    cookies, 132
    fruit butter, 100
    milk, 124
    pops, frozen, 11
    rolls, 11
    toast, 97
Bauernfrühstuck, 64
Beans
    and cheese rarebit, 91
    frijoles colades, 116
    Mexican, 91
Beef
    chopped, extended, 78
    chopped on toast, 77
    roast, overnight, 78-79
    steak, Dutch, 78
Biscuits
    drop, 154
    flavored, 155
    hot sunshine, 145-146
    jelly-rolled, 156-157
    rolled, 154-155
    scones, 157
Blenders, electric, 193-194
Blini, potato, 108-109
Blintzes, 41
    baked matzoh, 46
Blueberry muffins, 154
Brains
    scrambled eggs and, 63
    sweetbreads and, 75
Bran
    biscuits, 155
    flakes, 28
    hot raisin cereal, 22-23
    muffins, 153
    as nutritional booster, 189

Bread (see also Breads, homemade; Griddlecakes; Waffles)
    cakes, 89
    crumb cereal, 32
    diced as cereal, 23
    French toast, 86-88
    hot egg rolls, 96
    Japanese toast, 92
    matzoh brie, sweet, 90-91
    nut butters, 100-101
    pudding, baked, 89-90
    pudding, skillet, 90
    raisin scramble, 89
    and sauce, 92-93
    spreads, savory, 101-102
    spreads, sweet, 98-100
Breads, homemade (see also Griddlecakes; Waffles)
    quick breads
        about, 150-151
        biscuits, 154-157
        buttermilk brown bread, 158-159
        corn bread, 158
        leftovers, 159-160
        muffins, 152-154
        Norwegian cereal bread, 158
        peanut butter bread, 159
        rye rolls, 157
        scones, 157
        sweet Indian meal bread, 159
    with yeast
        bagels, 144-145
        biscuits, 145-146
        cheese bread, 147-148
        cinnamon loaf, 146-147
        English muffins, 142-143
        flat onion breads, 143-144
        no-kneading, 148
        raisin pumpernickel, 149-150
        rolls, 145
        rye bread, 149
        storing, 150
Brewer's yeast, 188-189
Brown bread, buttermilk, 158-159

Buckwheat griddlecakes, 106-107
Buttermilk, 121
    brown bread, 158-159
    homemade, 121-122
    shake, 125
    soup, 117-118

Café au lait, 180
Cakes, 129-131. *See also* Coffee cakes
Canadian bacon, 75
Cantaloupe
    cubes, 12
    cups, 13
    and ham salad, 80
    in juices, 6, 7
Carob
    cocoa, 184
    milk, 125
Carrot
    butter, 102
    cakes, 165-166
    cream soup, 117
    cupcakes, 131
    in juice, 7
    -pineapple juice, 6
Cashew
    cookies, 132
    milk, 123
Casings, sausage, 82
Cereal
    bread, Norwegian, 158
    crunchy crumb, 32
    scones, 26
Cereals
    cold, 27-33
    dry, 34-35
    hot, 18-27
        to cook, 18-20
        leftover, 24-27
        souped-up, 24
    milks for, 36-37
    molded, 25
    store-bought, 34-35
    toppings, table of, 36

Cheese, 38-53 (*see also* Cottage cheese; Yogurt)
    -and-apple squares, 136
    baked avocado and, 43
    baked eggs with, 60
    and bean rarebit, 91
    biscuits, 155
    blintzes, 41
    bread, 147-148
    broiled peaches and, 43
    broiled tomatoes and, 43
    butter, 102
    fried, 44
    homemade soft, 47-53
    kochkaese, 52
    main dishes, 39-46
    Melt, 97
    Mexican beans and, 164
    muffins, 152
    nests, hot-egg-and, 96
    noodles and, 41
    Pudding, 45-46
    rolled, 42
    -rolled biscuits, 157
    rolls, ham-and-, 80
    Russian, 53
    sandwiches, 93-95
    soy, 51
    sticks, 134
Cheesecake cookies, 131
Chicken
    patties, 77
    slices, deviled, 79
    spread, deviled, 80
Children, breakfasts for, 185-186
Choate wheat flakes, 28
Chocolate
    hot, 183
    -pudding cereal, 21

Cinnamon
    loaf, 146-147
    toast, 97
    -topped coffee cake, 171
Cocoa, 182-184
    bran muffins, 153
    carob, 184
    homemade instant mix, 183-184
Coconut oil, about, 191
Coffee, 177-180
    café au lait, 180
Coffee cakes, 168-176
    breads and rolls into, 174-176
    quick, 172-174
    with yeast, 169-172
Coney Island Cookies, 132
Cookies, 131-134
    banana, 132
    cashew, 132
    cheesecake, 131
    peanut-butter shortbread, 133-134
    peanut clusters, 134
    peanut snaps, 133
Corn
    bread, 158
    cream porridge, 116
    muffins, 154
    oil, about, 190
Corncakes, 107
Cornmeal
    cereals
        chocolate-pudding, 21
        fried mush, 27
        Indian pudding, 21
        Mammaliga, 21
        polenta, 27
    sweet Indian bread, 129
Cottage Cheese
    and baked avocado, 43
    baked custard, 45
    and broiled peaches, 43
    and broiled tomatoes, 43
    cakes, 43
    fondue, 46

Cottage Cheese, cont.
   and fruit platter, 42
   homemade, 49-50
   scrambled eggs and, 62
   topping, 14
   and vegetables, 41-42
Couscous, 22
Cracked rice cereal, 21
Crackers 'n milk cereal, 33
Cranberry
   juice, fresh, 5
   -orange jam, 100
   syrup, 113
Cream cheese, 50-51
Cream of brown rice cereal, 20
Cream of fruit cereal, 25
Cream of whole wheat cereal, 20
Cream sauce for fruit, 14
Crumb cereal, crunchy, 32
Cupcakes, carrot, 131
Custard, baked, 44-45

Danish potatoes, 168
Date-nut spread, 99
Deviled
   meat spread, 80
   poultry slices, 79
Dried fruit. *See* Fruit, dried

Egg
   biscuits, fried, 155
   -and-cheese nests, hot, 96
   -cleared coffee, 179
   rolls, hot, 96
   sandwiches, 95
Eggs
   baked, 59-60
   baked with cheese, 60
   Bauernfrühstuck, 64
   boiled, 55-57
   French toast, 86-88, 97
   fried, 60-61
   in fruit juice nogs, 4-5
   Golden, 57
   Mary Janes, 61
   omelets, 64-66
   poached, 58-59
   raisin scramble, 89
   salad, 57
   scrambled, 61-63
   soft-cooked, 56-57
   Spanish, 58-59
Eggnog, 127
   orange-pineapple, 4-5
   whipped hot, 184
English muffins, 142-143
Extractors, juice, 8

Farmer cheese, fried, 44
Farmer's Breakfast (Bauernfrühstuck), 64
Fava beans, 165
Fig Miltons, 136-137
Finnan Haddie, 69
Fish, 67-73
   cakes, 70
   to cook, 72-73
   Finnan Haddie, 69
   "Gothic" brunch, 71
   hash, 71
   kippers, 68-69
   pancakes, 70
   pickled, 69-70
   salmon cakes, 70
   sandwiches, cold, 95-96
   sardine spread, 71
   table of values, 83-84
Fondue
   cottage cheese, 46
   French-toast, 88
40-Second Cashew Cookies, 132
French fruit tarts, 175
French toast, 86-88
   sandwiches, 97
Fritters, brain and sweetbread, 75

Fruit, 2-15
   baked custard with, 45
   butter, 100
   cereal, cream of, 25
   cranberry-orange jam, 100
   cream topping for cereal, 36, 37
   dressings, 14
   dried, 11-12
      compote, 11
      juices, 5, 6
      milk, 125
   French tarts, 175-176
   in griddlecakes, 105
   juices, 2-9
      in cereal, 22
   shake, creamy, 128
   shake, yogurt, 126
   soup, 118
   spread, creamy, 99
   strips, 135
   table of values, 15
   toppings, pancakes, 112-114
   turnovers, 175
Fruitanas, refrigerator, 12
Frying pans, to season, 64
Fuul Mudammas, 165

Golden eggs, 57
Golden milk, 36
"Gothic" brunch, 71
Grains. *See* Cereals
Granola, 28-29
Grapefruit, broiled, 12
Greek tahini soup, 116
Griddlecakes, 103-109 (*see also* Pancakes)
   baked-apple, 109
   basic wholewheat, 105
   buckwheat, 106-107
   corncakes, 107
   leftovers, 111-112
   potato blini, 108-109
   rice, 108
   seed, 108
   sour-dough, 106

soy, 107
    toppings, 112-114
Griddles, cast-iron, 195
Grits, 166
Guavas, 13

Halvah spread, 99
Ham
    and apples, sautéed, 79
    -and-cheese rolls, 80
    deviled spread, 80
    -and-melon salad, 80
    and pineapple, sautéed, 79
Hash
    browned potatoes, 162
    diner style, 81
    fish, 71
Herb tea, 182
Hoe cakes, 107
Honey, 193
    -bun filled biscuits, 156
    -rye loaf, 173-174
Honeydew melon
    cubes, 12
    and ham salad, 80
    juice, 6

Indian meal bread, sweet, 159
Indian pudding, 21
Irish potatoes, 163-164
Italian style fried cheese, 44

Jam. *See* Spreads, sweet
Jam muffins, 152
Japanese toast, 92
Jelly-rolled biscuits, 156-157
Johnny cakes, 107
Juice extractors, 8
Juicers, 2-3
Juices, fruit, 2-9
    in cereal, 22

Kasha, 166
    country-style cereal, 23
Kibbutz Breakfast, 40

Kidney beans, 164
Kidneys, grilled, 76
Kippers, 68-69
Kochkaese, quick, 52

Labani (Arab cheese), 51
Lamb roast, overnight, 78-79
Lemonade, 5
Lemon-molasses syrup, 113
Liver
    pancakes, 76
    patties, 77
    sautéed, 76

Mammaliga, 21
Mangoes, 13
Maple
    cream topping, pancakes, 112
    syrup, about, 193
Mary Janes, 61
Matzoh
    blintzes, 46
    brie, sweet, 90-91
    scrambled eggs, 62
Meat, 74-84 (*see also* individual listings)
    cooking times, 79
    food values table, 83-84
    ground, extended, 78
    hash, 81
    muffins, 152-153
    patties, 77
    porridge, 80
    rolled biscuits, 157
    sandwiches, 95-96
    spread, deviled, 80
    variety, 75-76
Melba toast, 97
Melon
    cubed, 12
    juice, 6
    salad, ham-and-, 80

Milk
    almond, 122
    banana, 124
    carob, 125, 184
    cashew, 123
    for cereals, 36-37
    cocoa, 182-184
    dried fruit, 125
    eggnog, 127, 184
    flavored, 124
    handling, 123
    molasses posset, 184
    nonfat powdered, 189-190
    peanut, 123, 184
    rich skim, 121
    seed, 123
    sesame, 123
    shakes, 126-128
    souring, 124
    soy, 122
    soybean, 122
    soy-flour, 122
    sprout, 123
    table of values, 120
    taffy, 125
    -toast cereal, 23
    vanilla, 125, 184
    wheat drink, hot, 184
Miso butter, 102
Molasses, 193
    -lemon syrup, 113
    -orange syrup, 113
    posset, 184
    taffy, 138
Mozzarella, fried, 44
Muesli, 31
Muffin cereal, 32-33
Muffins, 150-154
    blueberry, 154
    bran, 153
    eggless, 153
    whole wheat, 152
Mush, fried, 27

Nonfat-dry-milk
    as nutritional booster, 189-190
    yogurt, 47-48
Noodles and cheese, 41
Norwegian cereal bread, 158
Nut
    butters, 100-101
        dressing for fruit, 14
    choppers, 194-195
    cream for cereal, 37
    -date spread, 99
    milks, 122-123
    sticks (coffee cake), 170
    waffles, crunchy, 111
Nuts
    and berries cereal, 33
    in griddlecakes, 105
    as nutritional boosters, 190

Oatmeal
    -orange coffee cake, 172-173
    pudding, 26
Oils, about, 190-191
Old age, breakfast and, 187-188
Omelets, 64-66
    basic, 64-65
    fillings for, 66
    French, 65
Onion
    breads, flat, 143-144
    corn bread, 158
Orange
    -apricot nectar, 4
    biscuits, 155
    -cranberry jam, 100
    juice, 2-5, 7, 8
        frozen treats, 4
    milk shakes, 127-128
    -molasses syrup, 113
    -oatmeal coffee cake, 172-173
    peeling an, 12
    -pineapple juice nog, 4-5
    -pomegranate juice, 4

syrup for pancakes, 112
yogurt drink, 126
Oriental style fried cheese, 44

Pancakes (*see also* Griddlecakes; Waffles)
    fish, 70
    liver, 76
Papayas, 13
Peaches
    baked, 13
    broiled with cheese, 43
    in juices, 7
    poached, 13
    salads, 13
Pears
    baked, 13
    in juices, 7
    poached, 13
Peanut (*see also* Peanut butter)
    clusters, 134
    croquetten, 135
    milk, 123
    snaps, 133
Peanut butter, 100-101
    balls, 137
    biscuits, 155
    bread, 159
    custard, baked, 45
    griddlecakes, 105
    homemade, 101
    milk, hot, 184
    shortbread, 133-134
    types of sandwiches, 95
Pecan toast, 97
Pero, 180
Pineapple
    -avocado butter, 101
    -buttermilk soup, 118
    juice, fresh, 6

and orange juice nog, 4-5
sautéed ham and, 79
Pinto beans, 164
Plantains, fried, 165
Polenta, 27
Pomegranate and orange juice nog, 4
Poppy seed coffee cakes, 170
Pork (*see also* Ham)
    bacon, 74-75
    roast, overnight, 78-79
    sausage, 81-83
Postum, 180
Potato
    blini, 108-109
    sauce (Sauce Kartoffle), 116-117
Potatoes
    cakes, 163
    Danish, 163
    hash browns, 162
    home fries, 162
    Irish, 163-164
    sweet, fried, 162
Pot cheese (*see also* Cottage cheese)
    topping, 14
Poultry. *See* Chicken; Turkey
Prune
    -filled tea ring, 169-170
    flip, 128
    milk, 125
Prunes, spiced, 11
Pumpernickel, raisin, 149-150

Raisin
    bran cereal, hot, 22-23
    milk, 125
    muffins, 152
    pumpernickel, 149-150
    scramble, 89
    tea cakes, 174
Rarebit, cheese and bean, 91
Recommended daily allowances, 186
Rice
    cereal, cold, 32

cereal, hot
    cracked-rice, 21
    cream of brown, 20
    pudding, 25
    pancakes, 108
    quick-cooked, 166-167
    sweet scrambled, 63
Rich skim milk, 121
Roast, overnight, 78-79
Rolled cheese, 42
Rolls
    hot egg, 96
    quick rye, 157
    soft refrigerator, 145
Russian cheese, 53
Rye
    bread, 149
    -honey loaf, 173-174
    quick rolls, 157
    waffles, 110

Salmon
    cakes, 70
    "Gothic" brunch, 71
Sandwiches
    cheese, 93-95
    egg, cold, 95
    fish, cold, 95-96
    French-toasted, 97
    meat, cold, 95-96
    peanut butter "and", 95
Sardine spread, 71
Sauce Kartoffle, 116-117
Sausage, 81-83
Scones, 157
    cereal, 26
Seed
    milk, 123
    pancakes, 108
    spread, 99
Seeds, as nutritional boosters, 190
Sesame seed
    cereal, 30
    milk, 123

rolls, 137
Shortcakes, 155
Simon bread cereal, 32
Skim milk, rich, 121. *See also* Nonfat-dry-milk
Soups
    buttermilk, 117
    carrot cream, 117
    frijoles colades, 116
    fruit, 118
    garnishes, 118
    Greek tahini, 116
    Sauce Kartoffle, 116-117
Sour cream, 50-51
Sour-dough griddlecakes, 106
Sour milk, 124
    griddlecakes, 105-106
Soy
    cheese, 51
    flour
        in baking, 191
        milk, 122
    milk, 122
    pancakes, 107
    spice cakes, 130
Soybean milk, 122
Spanish eggs, 58-59
Spice
    cakes, soy, 130
    muffins, 152-153
Spreads
    nut butters, 100-101
    savory, 101-102
    sweet, 98-100
Sprout milk, 123
Sprouts
    home-grown, 191-192
    in juices, 6-7
Squash cakes, 165-166
Steak
    Dutch, 78
    ham, 78

Steamers, vegetable, 194
    to cook fish, 72
Strawberry
    drink, 5
    whip topping, 14
Streusel-filled coffee cake, 172
Sugar
    turbinado, about, 193
    white, about, 192-193
Sundaes, breakfast, 39-40
Sweetbreads, brains and, 75
Sweeteners, about, 192-193
Sweet potatoes, home-fried, 162-163
Sweets, table of breakfast, 130. *See also* Cakes; Cookies
Sweet stuffed almond buns, 174
Syrups
    maple, 193
    for waffles, 112-114

Taffy
    milk, 125
    molasses, 138
Tahini soup, Greek, 116
Tarts
    French fruit, 175
    miniature, 176
Teas, 181-182
Toast (*see also* French toast)
    cheese melt, 97
    cups, 98
    Japanese, 92
    types of, 97
Toaster ovens, 194-195
Tofu, fired, 44
Tomato
    juice, 7
    Breakfast, 128
Tomatoes, broiled with cheese, 43
Toppings
    for griddlecakes and waffles, 112-114
    pot cheese, for fruit, 14
Turbinado sugar, 193

Turkey
    roasted overnight, 79
    slices, deviled, 79
    spread, deviled, 80
Turnovers, fruit, 175

Ukrainian style fried cheese, 44

Vanilla
    extract as sweetener, 37
    milk, cold, 125
    milk, hot, 184
Variety meats, 75-76
Veal
    patties, 77
    roast, overnight, 78-79
    salad, fruited, 81
Vegetables, cottage cheese and, 41-42
Vegetable steamers, 194

Waffles, 109-111
    leftovers, 111-112
    nut, 111
    rye, 110
    toppings, 112-114
    whole wheat with yogurt, 110
Watermelon
    cubes, 12
    in juices, 6, 7
Wheat
    drink, hot, 184
    flakes, choate, 28
    germ, as nutritional booster, 193
    sprouts in juices, 6-7
Whip and Chill Cereal, 22
Whole wheat
    brand cereal, 23
    cereal, cream of, 20
    muffins, 152
    toast cereal, 23

Yeast, making bread with, 140-142. *See also*
        Breads, homemade

Yogurt
    Continental, 40-41
    drinks, 125-127
    homemade, 47-49
    -maker, 194
    whole-wheat waffles, 110